4-5 art vs. Life
religious / Holly Allerheiligste → clothes
(//pornography)

6 → marriage vs writing
6 history
7 aestheticism + asceticism (supplementary)
9-10 approaches to Kafka
10-11 Lukács on Kafka-Mann
12 Modernism = universalization of symptoms of decadence Gersonsky
(+ critique)

217 show-off / impress + disappear
219 Verkehr, 14.
151 on Lombroso's theory → arbitrariness

Kafka's Clothes

Kafka's Clothes

Ornament and Aestheticism in the Habsburg Fin de Siècle

MARK M. ANDERSON

CLARENDON PRESS · OXFORD

1992

Oxford University Press, Walton Street, Oxford OX2 6DP
Oxford New York Toronto
Delhi Bombay Calcutta Madras Karachi
Petaling Jaya Singapore Hong Kong Tokyo
Nairobi Dar es Salaam Cape Town
Melbourne Auckland
and associated companies in
Berlin Ibadan

Oxford is a trade mark of Oxford University Press

Published in the United States
by Oxford University Press, New York

British Library Cataloguing in Publication Data
Data available

Library of Congress Cataloging in Publication Data
Anderson, Mark, 1955–
Kafka's clothes: ornament and aestheticism in the Habsburg fin de siècle / Mark Anderson.
Includes bibliographical references and index.
1. Kafka, Franz, 1883–1924—Criticism and interpretation.
2. Kafka, Franz, 1883–1924—Contemporary Austria. 3. Austria—Intellectual life. 4. Decadence (Literary movement)
5. Aestheticism (Literature) 6. Dandies. 7. Decoration and ornament—Art nouveau. I. Title.
PT2621.A26Z5734 1992
833'.912—dc20 91–30590
ISBN 0–19–815162–4

Typeset by Hope Services (Abingdon) Ltd.
Printed and bound in
Great Britain by Bookcraft Ltd.
Midsomer Norton, Bath

To my father and mother

Acknowledgements

The present study is a strongly reworked version of my doctoral thesis, which was completed in 1985 at the Johns Hopkins University. Although the basic idea behind the thesis has not changed, its historical component has been greatly expanded—a change I recognized as necessary at the time but was incapable of making. The intervening years have allowed me to read widely in the fields of aesthetics, architecture, legal anthropology, and cultural history. Along the way I have incurred many intellectual debts to individuals and institutions which I am happy to acknowledge here. My thanks go first to Rainer Nägele and Neil Hertz, my thesis advisers, as well as to the members of the Humanities Center at Johns Hopkins, all of whom provided the intellectual stimulation and independence for the original study. Since then Marthe Robert, Giuliano Baioni, Malcolm Pasley, Sander Gilman, and Stanley Corngold have read drafts of my work at various stages, generously offering advice and much-needed criticism. Laura De Angelis, Andreas Huyssen, Antoine Compagnon, Sara Bershtel, Philip Boehm, Alessandro Fambrini, Miriam Hansen, Chantal Thomas, André Guyaux, and Jacques Le Rider have given me unflagging intellectual encouragement and, most importantly, the gift of their friendship. Arnold Browne provided expert assistance in preparing the illustrations. Finally, I would like to thank Ritchie Robertson, without whose help I would never have reached the end of this project.

The Columbia University Council for Research in the Humanities supported work in New York and West Germany during the summers of 1986 and 1987. Earlier versions of Chapters 4 and 7 originally appeared in, respectively, *Modernity and the Text: Revisions of German Modernism* (Columbia University Press, 1989) and *New German Critique*, 43 (winter 1988); permission to reprint is here gratefully acknowledged.

Contents

List of Illustrations

Note on Citations and Abbreviations

The present state of Kafka's works is greatly complicated by discrepancies between English and American editions, as well as by the recent but still incomplete critical edition in German. Wherever possible, quotations from the diaries and letters have been indicated by date and correspondent; all other quotations will be noted in the text with page number and initials listed below. Unless otherwise indicated, all citations from Kafka's work are from the following widely available editions (all published by Schocken Books, New York), which on occasion have been silently emended.

A	*Amerika*, trans. Willa and Edwin Muir, 1962.
C	*The Castle*, trans. Willa and Edwin Muir, 1974.
CS	*Complete Stories*, ed. Nahum Glatzer, 1976.
D1	*Diaries 1910–1913*, ed. Max Brod, trans. Joseph Kresh, 1965.
D2	*Diaries 1914–1923*, ed. Max Brod, trans. Martin Greenberg and Hannah Arendt, 1965.
DF	*Dearest Father*, trans. Ernst Kaiser and Eithne Wilkins, 1954.
F	*Letters to Felice*, ed. Erich Heller and Jürgen Born, trans. James Stern and Elisabeth Duckworth, 1973
L	*Letters to Friends, Family, and Editors*, trans. Richard and Clara Winston, 1977.
M	*Letters to Milena*, expanded and revised edition, trans. Philip Boehm, 1990.
T	*The Trial*, trans. Willa and Edwin Muir, 1968

Und die Menschen gehn in Kleidern.

(*Description of a Struggle*)

Introduction: Decadence and the Crisis of Ornament

> One should either be a work of art, or wear one.
>
> (Oscar Wilde)

> I am made of literature, I am nothing else, and cannot be anything else.
>
> (Kafka)

THE idea for the present book arose nearly a decade ago when I first read Kafka's *Letters to Milena* and discovered that the author of perhaps the most horrific literary presentations of the modern world, the author of *The Trial* and 'In the Penal Colony', was also an avid observer of women's fashion. At the time of their correspondence Milena Jesenská was living in Vienna and wrote fashion articles for Czech newspapers in her native Prague. Kafka would read her descriptions of hats and summer dresses with great pleasure and expertise, overlooking no detail in what he understood to be secret letters written for him alone and then weaving these sartorial references back into the text of their correspondence. 'No, you're wrong to underrate your fashion articles,' he admonished her in a letter of 7 August. 'I'm really grateful to you that I can read them in the open (since like a scoundrel I've been reading them in secret often).'[1] I realized then, with that odd sense of elation provoked by seeing a canonical figure dislodged from the grip of stereotype, that Kafka's own writings, with their repeated references to fashion, elegant clothing, uniforms, and fur, revealed a surprisingly acute sense for the 'superficial' spectacle of urban life; and that in his writings he invariably presented the world as a shining and deceptive surface, presented it as *clothing*.

Kafka's interest in Milena Jesenská's fashion articles, as I learned later, was not merely the result of their brief erotic relation but stemmed from his earliest childhood experiences. His father ran a

[1] See the expanded version of the *Letters to Milena*, recently published in English, trans. P. Boehm (New York: Schocken Books, 1990), which includes a selection of Milena's newspaper articles.

clothing accessories store in Prague that carried fancy goods (*Galanteriewaren*) such as silk handkerchiefs, lace, buttons, slippers, parasols, and the like; in the 'Letter to His Father' Kafka calls the shop his first 'school'. Not surprisingly, clothes were an important part of his developing identity. In a diary entry for 31 December 1911 he reflects back on his 'miserable' adolescent appearance: 'I naturally noticed—it was obvious—that I was unusually badly dressed, and even had an eye for others who were well dressed, but for years on end my mind did not succeed in recognizing in my clothes the cause of my miserable appearance.' He therefore set out to change this appearance, his 'identity in the world', by adopting the clothes and personal mannerisms of the literary aesthete. The photographs from 1900 to 1910—the years of his studies at the Charles University and his first forays into Prague's cafés, brothels, and cabarets—show him wearing wide English neckties, upturned collars, and bowlers with a rather stiff flamboyance. One celebrated image, although often cropped to display him alone, is of Kafka sitting in formal dress next to a jauntily smiling prostitute (Hansi the 'Trocadéro Valkyrie') and her dog; another reveals him in a tan summer suit, leaning almost coquettishly against a wrought-iron fence covered with swirling vines. The Austrian writer Felix Stössinger, long before he was formally introduced to Kafka, remembers being fascinated by a tall, elegant *habitué* of Prague's literary cafés, the 'best-dressed man' he had ever seen.[2]

Although it jars the stereotypical image of him as the otherworldly, anonymous poet of modern alienation, acquaintances from this period all concur in this image of the young Kafka as an aesthete. In addition to his elegant clothing, he struck observers by his withdrawn and mysterious personal manner, speaking rarely and in paradoxical aphorisms, in a hushed voice.[3] He also enjoyed giving his friends rare and beautiful books (such as first editions of Stefan George's poetry), writing rather precious verse that he included in long, self-consciously literary letters to his schoolfriend Oskar Pollak. And although Max Brod later portrayed

[2] Written communication from Marthe Robert.

[3] Cf. Willy Haas's reminiscences of Kafka, 'Um 1910 in Prag', *Forum*, 4 (1957), 221–6.

his friend in quite different terms, he too first saw Kafka as an aesthete. In his 1907 story 'The Carina Island' he used him as the model for Carus, who speaks of his refined aestheticized existence far from 'Life' and its true emotion in the following artfully chosen terms:

We live out our lives, far away from Life, in our villas at the edge of the world that is called the city. We look into this valley as if into a beckoning wine glass, but we drink only a few drops that have wandered up to the glass's edge. And we pay each other visits at this edge, like two pious monks in the *Thebaid*, and we show each other vases we have collected and strange portraits and books and hard jewels, all the showpieces of a rich life that others have led. How strange, how strange that you have never felt the longing to bow your head and drink from the glass whose drops, lost at the edge, are so sweet.[4]

Kafka's early aestheticism would mean nothing if it had no importance for his writing. But it does. One need only look at the repeated references to fashion and clothing in crucial passages in his texts, references that the literary critic Wilhelm Emrich has described as highly symbolic but that he and all other commentators have neglected to explore in any systematic way.[5] To cite only one prominent example, Joseph K. at the beginning of *The Trial* is forced to put on clothing approved by the men who arrest him, and his execution takes place only when he has been undressed. As we shall see, clothing is not merely one motif or literary figure among many others in his work, but a matrix for reading the work as a whole. One might call it the 'master trope' in so far as it both informs and symbolizes the very act of covering blank sheets of paper with linguistic signs: for a writer's style *is* his

[4] 'Die Insel Carina', in *Experimente* (Berlin: Axel Juncker, 1907), 35–6, my translation. In his biography of Kafka's youth, Klaus Wagenbach atempts to distinguish Kafka's writing from the 'experimental', overwrought works of Brod, Leppin, Meyrink, and other Prague writers, referring to the title of Brod's early stories as proof (*Franz Kafka: Eine Biographie seiner Jugend* (Berne: Francke, 1958), 94–7). The irony is that Brod apparently took this title from Kafka, giving Carus the following words: 'I believe you won't contradict me, when I say that we are free, *that we can conduct experiments with our lives*, that we don't need to live out our lives so joylessly' ('Die Insel Carina', 37, Brod's emphasis). On the joint reading of Huysmans's novel, see Wagenbach, *Biographie seiner Jugend*, 159.

[5] *Franz Kafka* (Wiesbaden: Athenäum, 1981), 296. Scattered remarks on the subject of clothing can of course be found throughout the secondary literature and will be dealt with at the appropriate moments.

clothing, his appearance in the world. To anticipate the argument presented in the following chapters, clothing is for Kafka the hieroglyph of material existence, the mysteriously ineradicable sign of the human world, mortality, and history. The verse epigraph of his earliest extant text, *Description of a Struggle*, begins with the seemingly self-evident observation that people wear clothes when they go for a walk in a public park: 'And people stroll about in clothes, | Swaying over the gravel pathways.' This equation between clothing and people *in the world* illuminates all of Kafka's subsequent writing like a metaphysical beacon. Human history begins with clothing, begins when 'the Lord God made for Adam and for his wife garments of skins, and clothed them', as Kafka noted when he copied this sentence from Genesis into his diary.[6] In this sense fashionable clothing, inevitably linked to the realm of his father, serves him as the exemplary figure for human existence in history, that is, in a world of impermanence, false appearances, error, and guilt. And therefore as a figure for what the writer must give up in his quest for the absolute.

In a meditation in the third octavo notebook, written in January 1918, Kafka offers a parable that may stand as an epigraph to the present work:

> Before setting foot in the Holy of Holies you must take off your shoes, yet not only your shoes, but everything; you must take off your traveling garment and lay down your luggage; and under that you must shed your nakedness and everything that is under the nakedness and everything that hides beneath that, and then the core and the core of the core, then the remainder and then the residue and then even the glimmer of the undying fire. Only the fire itself is absorbed by the Holy of Holies and lets itself be absorbed by it; neither can resist the other. (DF 87)

Here Kafka characteristically uses the figure of clothing to depict the metaphysical relation between truth and appearance, the situation of being in the human world and struggling to reach a sacred realm beyond it. But like most of his autobiographical texts, this one speaks from his perspective as a writer. The *writer* must strip off all his 'clothing', all the false coverings of the empirical self, in his search for the 'undying fire' of aesthetic

[6] Diary entry for 19 June 1916.

truth, the 'Holy of Holies'. Art and Life are thus irresolvably opposed, as the commitment to writing takes Kafka away from the world's 'clothing' toward the sacred realm of *das Allerheiligste*.[7] Indeed, the self is undressed in order to be sacrificed at the altar of art: 'Not shaking off the self,' he concludes, 'but consuming the self.'

This radical commitment to writing 'even unto death' has been taken as the sign of Kafka's modernity, as the guarantor of a distinctly new form of writing.[8] Two important qualifications to this view should however be registered. The first is that the process of 'undressing' the self, according to the logic of infinite deferral familiar to us from Kafka's other works, is an endless task. As readers of *The Trial* know, there is always one more doorkeeper to be confronted, one more flight of stairs to be climbed, one last item of clothing to be removed before the protagonist can gain access to the realm of true knowledge and transcendence. He never does: though undressed, Joseph K. dies without ever glimpsing the supreme judge who has sentenced him. Properly speaking, then, Kafka's writings take place in the realm of 'clothing', that is, in the very temporal order of the body, material existence, suffering, and death that they strive to overcome. Indeed, Kafka's status as a modern *depends* on the failure of his effort to reach *das Allerheiligste*. If he is the Dante of the modern age (as Auden called him), it is because the way out of Hell is forever barred to him; there is sin but no redemption. The frequent references to clothing in his writings result from this fact and serve to mark the ceaseless and invariably negative conflict between self and world, human and sacred.

Second, although this passage describes the ascetic movement away from the order of clothing and the body privileged by aestheticism, the very notion of writing as a religious quest stems from the various aestheticizing movements of the European *fin de siècle* such as decadence, Symbolism, 'l'art pour l'art' or the *Jugendstil*.[9] Art is opposed to life because it alone can take the place

[7] As Kafka had noted in the octavo notebooks on 22 Jan. 1918, 'The point of view of art and that of life are different even in the artist himself.'

[8] See for instance Maurice Blanchot's 1947 essay 'La Littérature et le droit à la mort', in *De Kafka à Kafka* (Paris: Gallimard, 1981), 11–61.

[9] In the following pages I use the terms 'decadence', 'aestheticism', and '*Jugendstil*'

of a discredited religion.[10] Numerous comments attest to Kafka's conception of a religious dedication to writing *in place of* organized belief. In an early letter to Oskar Pollak he speaks of the necessity of his writing even when God is against him; in letters to Felice Bauer and diary entries of 1913–16, marriage and sexuality are opposed to the 'purity' of his literary vocation; a famous fragment from the same period defines writing as a *Form des Gebetes*, a 'form of prayer'; and in January 1922 'this whole literature' is described as potentially a 'new secret teaching, a Kabbalah'. Throughout his life Kafka always saw in literature—and only in literature—the means for personal salvation and transcendence, even or perhaps especially when his own work fell short of this goal. The realm of unadorned, sacred truth designated by the term *Allerheiligste* is accessible only through the writer's private struggle with the word, not through any mediated, institutionalized forms of belief. In this sense Kafka maintains the aestheticist opposition between life and art in which art has access to the sacred, though admittedly both these terms remain essentially private and unspecific.

Taken together, then, these two qualifications serve to locate Kafka's conception of writing in terms of an ambivalent relation toward history, and particularly toward his own historical origins in the *fin de siècle*. The writer must take off his shoes and travelling garment, detach himself from the material world: this injunction corresponds closely to Kafka's actual literary texts which, purged of the conventional references to time, place, and proper names in nineteenth-century realist narratives, seek to deny their relation to history in an increasingly abstract, anonymous, and modern literary form. And yet the conception of the self as layers of clothing, the irresolvable opposition between Art and Life, and

as rough equivalents of one another, although in specific contexts they can take on an oppositional character; '*fin de siècle*' and 'turn of the century' designate competing conservative and modern aspects of the period. Needless to say, 'decadence' is meant as a descriptive, not a normative, term. For a useful overview of the problem in German literature, see J. M. Fischer, *Fin de siècle: Kommentar zu einer Epoche* (Munich: Winkler, 1978).

[10] For the entire generation of *fin-de-siècle* writers and artists, including Kafka, Nietzsche's influence here is decisive not only through his much-hailed announcement of the death of God but also through his early claim in *The Birth of Tragedy* (1870) that life could only be justified on aesthetic, not ethical, grounds.

the notion of writing as a religious quest for (private) redemption tie Kafka to the very historical period in which he began writing and whose outward features he sought, after a brief interlude, to discard. To put it somewhat differently, the urge to escape history is a function of his particular place in an age of transition between the centuries. In a passage that has often been quoted as an indication of his ambivalence toward religion but that refers equally to the question of aestheticism in an age without faith, Kafka claimed he was 'an end or a beginning' (*DF* 99–100). A modern, yes, but also a child of the *fin de siècle*.

Consider, for instance, the letter Kafka wrote to Oskar Pollak in 1903 in which his ambivalence toward his writing has the specific origin of *fin-de-siècle* literary stylization and bombast: 'Of the few thousand lines I'm sending you there might be perhaps ten that I could listen to patiently . . . The greatest part of it, I openly say, I find repulsive . . . But you must remember I began at a time when one "created masterworks" when one wrote high-flown stuff [*Schwulst*]; there is no worse time to begin. And I was so enthralled by grand phrases.'[11] Or again, in the same letter, his critical reference to the aestheticizing arts and crafts movement and his need for artistic 'discipline': 'There is one thing that is entirely missing in [my] copy-books, that is hard work, perseverance, and whatever all these strange things are called. . . . Above all, I know this now: Art needs hard work more than hard work needs art.' This ambivalence is not only Kafka's; indeed, decadence and aestheticism are remarkable as cultural movements in part because of their own ambivalent espousal of what was commonly viewed as an ethical anathema. It none the less serves to locate the origin of his own peculiarly modern writing. Kafka's 'purity', the 'stripped-down', 'anonymous', 'existential' quality of his texts, is a function of the repression of his own aestheticist origins, his negative relation to *fin-de-siècle* ornament.

Despite his early dissatisfaction with the 'grand phrases' of the late nineteenth century, Kafka made his first literary attempts under the sign of European decadence and aestheticism. Max Brod's literary model was the Prague writer Gustav Meyrink,

[11] Unpublished letter, partially quoted by Brod in his biography of Kafka (New York: Schocken Books, 1947, enlarged edn. 1960), 58, translation slightly altered.

author of 'The Violet Death'. Brod's own early work—such as the collections of stories *Experiments* and *Excursions into Darkness*—is written in the purple hues of Meyrink's decadent exoticism and deals explicitly with the problem of aestheticism; the protagonist of his novel *Nornepygge Castle* is an aesthete bachelor aristocrat, the last of his 'race', who commits suicide because of the ethical dilemma posed by aestheticism. Kafka's literary model was more refined but equally implicated in aestheticism: the young Viennese poet Hugo von Hofmannsthal, whose poems and stories in the 1890s were based on decadent models furnished by Huysmans, d'Annunzio, Verlaine, and Maeterlinck. Brod recalls: 'As an example [of what he himself liked] Kafka quoted a passage from Hofmannsthal, "the smell of damp flagstones in a hall." And he kept silent for a long while, said no more, as if this hidden, improbable thing must speak for itself.'[12] Together they read Schopenhauer, the 'philosopher of decadence' (as Nietzsche calls him), as well as such 'classics' of French decadence as J.-K. Huysmans's *A rebours*, H. F. Amiel's *Fragments d'un journal intime*, and, most probably, Octave Mirbeau's *Le Jardin des supplices* (*Torture Garden*). An important literary figure for both of them at this time was Franz Blei, the editor of erotic bibliophile journals like *Amethyst* and *Opale* (to which Brod and Kafka subscribed), as well as of the elegant but short-lived journal *Hyperion*, in which Kafka's first literary publications appeared. Blei was the author of *The Powder Puff*, a collection of essays on clothing, make-up, jewellery, masks, and other decadent topics which Kafka reviewed in 1909 in a mannered prose style mirroring Blei's own.

Anyone familiar with Kafka's early writings (chiefly, *Description of a Struggle*, *Meditation*, and the letters to Oskar Pollak of 1902–4) will recognize the importance of aestheticist and decadent paradigms in his development as a writer. For the most part these writings are stylistically ornate, even precious, and adopt bizarre, far-flung metaphors and word constructions. But around 1907–10, a period which witnessed a similar 'crisis of ornament' in European painting, music and architecture, Kafka consciously

[12] *Biography*, 44.

sought to transform this idiom into a dramatic, unadorned prose style that would be at once classical and modern. The diary he began keeping on a regular basis in 1910, although it displays traces of his earlier aestheticist themes and style, basically employs the laconic, transparent writing familiar from his later works. So does the 1910 text 'The Aeroplanes in Brescia', a journalistic account of an aeroplane competition he witnessed while on vacation in Italy. But it was not until September 1912 that this stylistic change would bring forth the successful literary narratives that he had long been striving for and that are now synonymous with his name. As he noted in the oft-quoted diary passage of 23 September 1912 after finishing his 'breakthrough' story 'The Judgment': '*Only in this way* can writing be done . . . only with such a complete opening of the body and soul.' Thanks to this miraculous event, which seemed to answer his longing for transcendence through art, Kafka absorbed himself almost entirely in the writing process during the following months. In this period he wrote the bulk of his first novel and what is perhaps his best, and certainly his most famous, story, *The Metamorphosis*. Here, in Kafka's view, was his birth as a mature writer, the beginning of his 'true' work.[13]

In the following pages I have sought to describe and analyse the crisis of ornament that led up to this breakthrough into Kafka's recognizable modern idiom. This approach breaks with previous criticism in several important ways and deserves a brief word of explanation. The overwhelming majority of critics have followed Kafka's lead in taking 1912 as the beginning of his work; with few exceptions critical studies have not been concerned with the 'young Kafka'.[14] And for the most part they have insisted on formal rather than historical methodologies.[15] Whether Freudian,

[13] See the diary entry for 11 Feb. 1913.

[14] An early exception is Klaus Wagenbach's 1958 biography of Kafka's youth, which however is only marginally concerned with the literary work. See also the recent anthology of essays edited by G. Kurz, *Der junge Kafka* (Frankfurt: Suhrkamp, 1984).

[15] The ahistorical tendency of Kafka secondary literature has been more pronounced in the United States than in Europe, where traditional literary history has never lost its place in the university. Wagenbach's biography offers an invaluable source of information about Prague, Zionism, anti-Semitism, as well as contemporary philosophical and literary issues important for Kafka's development. Since then Hartmut

existentialist, New Critical, structuralist, or poststructuralist, these interpretations have offered readings of individual texts in terms of a critical methodology that tended to eclipse the historical dimensions of Kafka's texts. Rooted in no particular culture or period, so ran the implicit assumption, his writings seemed to be meant for all cultures, thus providing an example of the hermetic, autonomous, *sui generis* modern artwork that apparently validated these very formalist, ahistorical methodologies. The few critics who sought to locate his work in a literary context generally invoked classical sources (the Bible, Goethe, Kleist, Flaubert), or his immediate Expressionist contemporaries (Brod, Werfel, Hasenclever), or a European *Zeitgeist* linking him to Proust, Joyce, Beckett, and other canonical twentieth-century writers; connections with decadent precursors were explicitly ruled out. For all critics, however, especially for the generation of Jewish–German exiles like Walter Benjamin, Theodor Adorno, Hannah Arendt, and Günther Anders who first mediated his work in France and the United States, Kafka represented the quintessentially modern writer who had no literary predecessors, who had broken with tradition, who stood outside history and the canon. As Walter Benjamin remarked in a letter to Gershom Scholem of 12 June 1938, Kafka's work was 'essentially *isolated* in literature'.[16]

Historically, the only major critic to treat Kafka in terms of his relation to *fin-de-siècle* aestheticism and decadence was Georg Lukács. In his essay 'Franz Kafka or Thomas Mann?' he developed a definition of stylistic decadence originally proposed by the French critic Paul Bourget as the breakdown of a work's narrative unity

Binder and Christoph Stölzl have added important historical contributions, Stölzl's study of anti-Semitism in 19th-century Bohemia providing an invaluable link between contemporary politics and Kafka's 'negative' relationship to history. Subsequent studies in various languages—notably Marthe Robert's *Seul, comme Franz Kafka* (Paris: Calmann-Lévy, 1979), Giuliano Baioni's *Kafka: Letteratura ed ebraismo* (Turin: Einaudi, 1984), Ritchie Robertson's *Kafka: Judaism, Literature and Politics* (Oxford: Oxford University Press, 1985), and, in the United States, Sander Gilman's wide-ranging study *Jewish Self-Hatred: Anti-Semitism and the Hidden Language of the Jews* (Baltimore: Johns Hopkins University Press, 1986)—have all added immeasurably to our understanding of the political and social dimensions of Kafka's writing.

[16] For a fuller account of this development, see my introduction to *Reading Kafka: Prague, Politics, and the Fin de Siècle* (New York: Schocken Books, 1989).

into unrelated, descriptive details.[17] For Lukács Thomas Mann represented the 'healthy' continuation of Balzacian realism in which description is subordinate to narration; Kafka represented instead an 'alienated' exacerbation of the Naturalist or Symbolist preoccupation with detail and the corresponding loss of global narrative perspective and unity. His protagonists were themselves the prisoners of this breakdown of the narrative whole: confronted always by the detail, the fragment of reality, they had no true knowledge of their circumstances in the world and hence no basis for effective action. A symptom of capitalist alienation, Kafka's work thus offered an irrational (bourgeois) mystification of reality that Lukács branded as 'decadent modernism', opposing it to Mann's 'fruitful critical realism'.[18]

This is not the place to deal with Lukács's dismissal of Kafka other than to note that it failed to appreciate features of his work that would become constitutive of modern European art and literature generally. Despite its aesthetic and ethical misconceptions, however, Lukács's description of the 'decadent' features of Kafka's work is basically accurate, as Peter Cersowsky's recent study of Kafka 'in the context of literary decadence' suggests.[19] Pointing to a number of decadent writers important for the young Kafka, Cersowsky focuses on such decadent stylistic features as fragmentation, perspectivism, and loss of totality in the early text *Description of a Struggle*.[20] He also locates what he calls a decadent 'type' in Kafka's fictions generally: the isolated, melancholy bachelor who is cut off from nature and prone to highly aestheticized, subjective visions of reality. Rooted in decadent literature,

[17] In his well-known essay on Baudelaire (1883), Bourget advances a 'theory of decadence' based on the stylistic decomposition of a book's unity into disparate particles. See the related discussion in Ch. 1 below.

[18] Published in English translation in *The Meaning of Contemporary Realism*, trans. J. and N. Mander (London: Merlin Press, 1979), 92.

[19] Peter Cersowsky, *'Mein ganzes Wesen ist auf Literatur gerichtet': Franz Kafka im Kontext der literarischen Dekadenz* (Würzburg: Königshausen & Neumann, 1983).

[20] Fragmentation is of course characteristic of all Kafka's later writing and can be seen especially in his treatment of clothing details. See the insightful article by David Miles, '"Pleats, Pockets, Buckles and Buttons": Kafka's New Literalism and the Poetics of the Fragment', in B. Bennett, A. Kaes, and W. J. Lillyman (eds.), *Probleme der Moderne: Studien zur deutschen Literatur von Nietzsche bis Brecht* (Tübingen: Max Niemeyer verlag, 1983), 331–42.

Kafka's texts 'radicalize and universalize the symptoms of decadence', thereby producing a characteristically modern form of writing. 'Both its radicalization of and historical relation to [decadent] literature', Cersowsky concludes, 'constitutes the specificity of Kafka's mode of representation' (86).

Cersowky's essay raises the important question of Kafka's relation to the *fin de siècle*, but it has serious limitations. Apart from a few passing remarks on the persistence of decadence in Kafka's later works, it offers no sustained readings of the novels and stories most responsible for his literary reputation. It also uses the term 'decadent' uncritically, at times adopting the rhetoric of disease, symptoms, and typology that characterized hostile accounts of decadence at the turn of the century. Most importantly, however, it neglects those sources and manifestations of decadence in Kafka that lie outside literature. In doing so it excludes the social and cultural aspects of a movement whose major programmatic aim, after all, was precisely the transformation of life into art. Important historical aspects of Kafka's relation to aestheticism such as Hermann Kafka's fancy-goods business, his interest in fashion, the clothing-reform movement, *Jugendstil* design, or nudism thus simply drop out of the picture. Further, if aestheticism is responsible for the collapse in Kafka of the distinction between 'fictional subjectivity and autobiographical reality', as Cersowsky maintains, we need some account of his life as the self-consciously constructed vehicle of art, of life *as* literature (rather than its origin and empirical source). As Kafka himself remarked in a letter to Felice Bauer of 14 August 1913, 'I have no literary interests, but am made of literature, I am nothing else, and cannot be anything else.'

Accordingly, the following essays all seek to open up the question of Kafka's relation to the *fin de siècle* along historical and social lines and in terms of the aestheticist project to reverse the traditional relationship between Life and Art. The notion of 'clothing' has a dual function in this account. On a simple textual level it means the clothes that appear in Kafka's literary works as figural elements in a structure of symbolic meaning. In each of his major texts clothing provides an 'internal' or phenomenological means of describing the relation between self and world; and because of its status as a 'master trope', clothing also serves as a heuristic tool for interpreting the text's larger meanings in specifically literary terms. But in a historical sense 'clothing' refers to the manifold, complex, and largely uncharted relations linking this work to the *fin-de-siècle* society in which it originated. It concerns first of all Kafka's own dandyism and aestheticism, his significant debt to decadent authors like Huysmans, Strindberg, Leopold von Sacher-Masoch, and Octave Mirbeau. It also connects to broad aesthetic, philosophical, and social issues of the period: German cultural nationalism; the youth and clothing-reform movements; the 'anthropological' legal theories he encountered at the University of Prague; and the misogyny, anti-Semitism, and 'Jewish self-hatred' so prevalent in Austro-Hungarian society at that time. Finally, as the subtitle of this study suggests, I seek to establish a link between Kafka and *fin-de-siècle* Vienna, between Kafka's 'clothing' and the aestheticism of the 'Jung Wien' group of poets (Hofmannsthal, Schnitzler, Altenberg) during the 1890s; and between his rejection of aestheticism and the modernist battle against ornament waged by Karl Kraus and Adolf Loos in the first decade of the twentieth century.[21] In sum, it implies a historical reading of Kafka in terms of those contemporary problems and questions he sought to escape and whose influence, at least superficially, does not appear evident in his major writings.

The first three chapters of this book provide a historical portrait of the young Kafka against the backdrop of late nineteenth- and early twentieth-century European culture. 'The Traffic of Clothes' begins with Kafka's relations to his father's fancy-goods business, his aestheticism, and the themes of clothing, fashion, and an aestheticized urban world in his only two extant major works of this period, *Description of a Struggle* and *Meditation*. Clothing functions here as a metaphor for the instability and contingency of modern life, which has migrated to the surface of things. But it

[21] In this respect the present study is indebted to the admirably interdisciplinary and cross-cultural studies of turn-of-the-century Vienna, especially C. Schorske's *Fin-de-Siècle Vienna* (New York: Vintage Books, 1981), W. Johnston's *The Austrian Mind: An Intellectual and Social History, 1848–1938* (Berkeley, Calif.: University of California Press, 1972), A. Janik and S. Toulmin's *Wittgenstein's Vienna* (New York: Simon & Schuster, 1973). Not surprisingly, Kafka does not figure prominently in any of these studies.

also serves as a self-referential metaphor for the linguistic signs, the 'clothes' of language, which circulate on a horizontal plane in the text like fashion commodities in society. The key term is *Verkehr* or 'traffic', which Kafka introduces as a richly ambiguous term for the movement of the modern world as well as his own writing, and which he will continue to use in all his later work. In 'The *Jugendstil* Body' the focus is on Kafka's participation in the clothing-reform movement and the cultural politics of the *Kunstwart* (*Art Guard*), a conservative journal that influenced him in an early phase with its championing of Germanic artistic traditions as well as its populist, *Jugendstil* aestheticization of everyday life. Chapter 3 traces Kafka's long-standing practice of 'body culture', gymnastic exercises, the youth movement, nudism, and various other activities related to *Naturheilkunde*, singling out the motif of the gymnast or 'body artist' as the privileged emblem of the ascetic writer. A central figure in Kafka's literary texts, the disciplined body of the writer-gymnast represents the culmination as well as the overcoming of his early aestheticism.

Loosely organized around his biography and stylistic development from 1900 to 1912, these three chapters document Kafka's aestheticist and *Jugendstil* personae as well as the ascetic purge of ornament. The diary entry for 3 January 1912, in which Kafka speaks of 'dieting' from the pleasures of life for the sake of his writing 'organism', represents a crucial moment at the end of this phase.[22] But this chronology should not be taken too strictly. 'Aestheticism', '*Jugendstil*', and 'body culture' are interrelated features of German society at the turn of the century and, in Kafka's case, are perhaps best seen not as successive phases but as simultaneous impulses which appear in differing proportions according to context. The entire period between 1900 and 1912 is one of experimentation, eclecticism, discontinuity, anachronism. For example, the 'prose poems' in the collection *Meditation*, although first published in 1913, stem from an aestheticist con-

[22] 'When it became clear in my organism that writing was the most productive direction for my being to take, everything rushed in that direction and left empty all those abilities which were directed toward the joys of sex, eating, drinking, philosophical reflection and above all music. I dieted in all these directions. . . . 'My development is now complete and, so far as I can see, there is nothing left to sacrifice.'

ception of literature privileging the short form, fragmentation, and musicality; as such they belong with texts like *Description of a Struggle* or the letters written to Oskar Pollak from 1902 to 1904, not with the 'breakthrough' texts of 1912. Another example is Kafka's joint subscription with Max Brod to Blei's decadent journals *Amethyst* and *Opale* in the very years in which they took naturalist swimming excursions in the Prague countryside and Kafka attended lectures on clothing reform. Thus, while one can note an increasing asceticism in Kafka's life and writing in this early period, the aestheticist impulse never entirely disappears. Indeed, one begins to understand asceticism as the continuation of aestheticism, both attitudes being linked in a complex economy of artistic desire oscillating between self-denial and self-display.[23] For as Baudelaire had pointed out half a century earlier in his essay 'The Painter of Modern Life', dandyism requires a moral rigour comparable to that of monastic orders.[24] And even in Kafka's most ascetic moments, late in his life when he wrote without thought of publication, he saw himself and his writing as being *on display*, constantly observed by an invisible spectator and judge.

This historical contextualization of the young Kafka only acquires its full significance when the traces of *fin-de-siècle* ornament have been revealed in his 'mature' work. For this reason I have sought to fuse historical analysis with sustained, formal *readings* of five major literary texts. Mindful of the aesthetic autonomy and coherence Kafka strove to impart to these texts, I have developed a form of interpretation that, while drawing on diverse historical sources, responds to the specific aesthetic problems posed by individual works. Although interrelated, these chapters all have a degree of interpretative autonomy. Thus in

[23] See G. G. Harpham's *The Ascetic Imperative in Culture and Criticism* (Chicago: University of Chicago Press, 1987).

[24] 'In truth I was not altogether wrong to consider dandyism as a kind of religion. The strictest monastic rule [was] no more despotic, and no more obeyed, than this doctrine of elegance and originality, which also imposes upon its humble and ambitious disciplines . . . the terrible formula: *Perinde ac cadaver!*' Cf. 'The Painter of Modern Life', in *The Painter of Modern Life and Other Essays*, trans. and ed. J. Mayne (London: Phaidon Press, 1964), 28.

Chapter 4 I interpret *Amerika*[25] through Kafka's early conception of the big city, using the notion of *Verkehr* to account for his elaboration of what I call a 'travelling narrative', opposed to the nineteenth-century historical novel and akin to early cinematic techniques. In my analysis of *The Metamorphosis*, Gregor Samsa's transformation is seen as an instance of a 'will to art' and aesthetic autonomy that can be compared to Ernst Haeckel's monistic conception of an originary *Kunsttrieb* in all plant and animal species. The world of the Samsa family and of Gregor's past life is marked by clothing, his new-found animal condition by a radical aesthetic freedom reminiscent of that of the aesthete. *The Trial*, in my view, incorporates aspects of *fin-de-siècle* legal anthropology that Kafka undoubtedly came into contact with through Hans Gross, his law professor at the University of Prague (and the father of Otto Gross, the Nietzschean psychoanalyst with whom Kafka was later to plan an anti-patriarchal journal). Cesare Lombroso's concept of the 'born criminal'—supposedly identifiable through a 'physiognomy of guilt', physical anomalies, and clothing—provides the basis for the odd legal mechanism behind Joseph K.'s trial as well as for the nineteenth-century mode of literary characterization (Balzac, Dickens) that Kafka explicitly opposed.

'In the Penal Colony', which Kafka wrote during his work on *The Trial*, continues his confrontation with Lombroso's and Gross's typological categorizations, specifically, with their belief that a criminal nature always 'expressed itself' in tattoos on the criminal body. But, as Wayne Burns noted as early as 1957 in a brief note that has gone largely unheeded,[26] Kafka's tale is also the re-elaboration of a *fin-de-siècle* classic of decadence, Octave Mirbeau's *Torture Garden* (1899), and as such represents Kafka's reflection on his past as a 'decadent aesthete', the writer who has turned his own body into an embellished text. The final chapter deals with Kafka's last story, 'Josephine the Singer or the Mice Folk', connecting its ambiguous references to mice, femininity,

[25] The German title of Kafka's first novel is actually *Der Verschollene* (*The Man who Disappeared*), although Max Brod originally published it as *Amerika*, which was also used for the American edition. Given the lack of an alternative English-language edition, this title will be used here.

[26] '"In the Penal Colony": Variations on a Theme by Octave Mirbeau', *Accent*, 17 (1957), 45–51.

music, and the Jewish people with the anti-Semitic tradition in German culture that denied Jews an innate capacity for music and related them to animals and women. This chapter raises the sensitive and, among Kafka scholars, generally taboo issue of Kafka's 'Jewish self-hatred', which informs his early aestheticist idealization of Germanic art, accounts in part for his stylistic purism, and, in my view, is finally taken back in 'Josephine'.

It is my hope that the historical material introduced here, almost all of which is new to Kafka criticism, will provide the basis for original readings of his texts and a basic change in the way we understand his relation to tradition. In its use of contemporary sources, it should offer an alternative to the plethora of formalist criticism that has now reached Byzantine proportions and is obscuring the literary texts it originally meant to elucidate. I have tried to assemble what Walter Benjamin called 'constellations', clusters of related historical materials which are interesting in their own right and which paralleled, if not always actually influenced, Kafka's own situation. This study is therefore as much about contemporary cultural issues as it is about Kafka.

If the essays in this book are successful, it should become possible to understand Kafka's relation to clothing, aestheticism, and decadence as the key to his paradigmatic status as a modern writer and therefore to his place in literary tradition. We often forget that virtually all of the constitutive figures of literary modernism—Poe, Baudelaire, Flaubert, Mallarmé, Proust, Dostoevsky, Strindberg, Svevo, Hofmannsthal, Musil, Thomas Mann, Wilde, Joyce—were also directly implicated in the decadent movement. Often explicitly reactionary or conservative in political terms, decadence was always an aesthetic avant-garde.[27] This discontinuity between politics and art may help to explain the ambivalence of self-proclaimed decadents toward their own decadence, as something simultaneously desired and repudiated, as the 'sickness' of modernity that had to be overcome by an ascetic self-denial. As Nietzsche wrote in 'The Case of Wagner', 'I am, no less than Wagner, a child of this time; that is, a decadent:

[27] See A. Compagnon's recent study *Les Cinq Paradoxes de la modernité* (Paris: Seuil, 1990), 7–13, and A. Huyssen's *After the Great Divide: Modernism, Mass Culture, Postmodernism* (Bloomington, Ind.: Indiana University Press, 1986), 3–15.

but I comprehended this, I resisted it. The philosopher in me resisted.' Kafka was also a decadent, but like Nietzsche resisted it, establishing through ascetic self-denial an essentially negative relation to his own time and culture. 'I have vigorously absorbed the negative element of the age in which I live', he wrote in 1917, 'an age that is of course very close to me, which I have no right ever to fight against, but as it were a right to represent' (*DF* 99). It is in this sense that the following pages address the decadence and modernity of 'Kafka's clothes'.

I

The Traffic of Clothes: Meditation *and* Description of a Struggle

I

> She probably put on some specially chosen blouse, the thing these Prague Jewesses are good at, and straightaway, of course, you made up your mind to marry her.
>
> (Hermann Kafka to his son, *DF* 187)

THE story of Kafka's clothes begins with Kafka's father, whose shop in Prague specialized in fashion accessories or what in German are called *Galanteriewaren*, 'fancy goods'. Like many Jews of the Bohemian provinces, Hermann Kafka had decided to leave his native village to seek his fortune in the city. After a brief stint in the Austro-Hungarian army as a drill sergeant, he set up a retail store in Prague dealing in 'haberdashery, fashion articles, fancy goods, parasols, umbrellas, walking sticks, cotton',[1] and gradually expanded it through hard work and an advantageous marriage into one of the major wholesale businesses in the city and the surrounding provinces. His first shop was in the Zeltnergasse; later he moved it to the Kinsky Palace, an elegant building on the Old Town Square which was also the site of Kafka's *Gymnasium*.

That Hermann Kafka did not take up his father's trade—Jakob Kafka was a kosher butcher in the small village of Wossek—is indicative of the shift in economic and social conditions in central Europe during the nineteenth century. With the official emancipation of Bohemian Jews in 1848 (Hermann Kafka was born in 1852), residency requirements and restrictions on marriage and professional occupations were lifted, thus favouring the move of

[1] As Hermann Kafka noted in a Prague address book of 1907.

many Jews from the *shtetl* to the city and the development of a politically liberal and increasingly wealthy Jewish bourgeoisie.[2] The Bohemian textile industry was then in the process of rapid expansion and by the end of the century it constituted one of the region's major sources of income. The fathers of Sigmund Freud and Franz Werfel, to cite only two famous examples, were both manufacturers in the clothing industry, which in Vienna, Prague, and the Moravian hinterlands depended heavily on the participation of Jewish manufacturers and merchants.[3]

In his 'Letter to His Father', Kafka gives us a vivid portrait of his father's fancy-goods shop. He calls it his first 'school', the first stage on which he watched the spectacle of his father in the world:

> First, the business. In itself, particularly in my childhood, so long as it was a shop, I ought to have liked it very much, it was so animated, the lights lit at evening, so much to see and hear, being able to help now and then and to distinguish oneself, but above all to admire you for your magnificent commercial talents, the way you sold things, managed people, made jokes . . . even the way you wrapped up a parcel or opened a crate was a spectacle worth watching, and all in all certainly not the worst school for a child. (*DF* 160)

But this favourable image of his father's shop quickly changes. Fearing his father, Kafka comes to fear his shop as well, which becomes a locus of conflict between them: 'But since you gradually began to terrify me on all sides and the business and you became one for me, the business too made me feel uneasy.' Hermann Kafka's aggressive handling of his Czech (and mostly Gentile) employees, whom he calls 'mangy dogs' or 'paid enemies', especially shames his son:

[2] See C. Stölzl, *Kafkas böses Böhmen: Zur Sozialgeschichte eines Prager Juden* (rev. edn. Frankfurt: Ullstein, 1989), ch. 2. Kafka himself characterizes his father's itinerary (and consequent loss of religion) as being 'much the same [as] a large section of this transitional generation of Jews, which had migrated from the still comparatively devout countryside to the towns' (*DF* 174).

[3] 'Jewish traders, generally from Poland-Lithuania, played a considerable role both as buyers and sellers of fabrics and clothes on market days and at the fairs in central Europe. . . . After the official abolition of all restrictions on Jewish trade (1859; 1867) the participation of Jews in the Viennese textile trade became virtually a monopoly. [In Bohemia and Moravia] Jews not only supplied the raw material but sold off the finished goods, primarily in Prague, where almost all the textile merchants were Jews.' 'Textiles', *Encyclopedia Judaica* (Jerusalem: Keter, 1972), 1040–1.

Things that had at first been a matter of course for me there now began to torment and shame me, particularly the way you treated the staff . . . For instance, the way you would push goods you did not want to have mixed up with others, knocking them off the counter . . . and the assistant had to pick them up. . . . There I learned the great lesson that you could be unjust. (*DF* 161)

Thus the business serves Kafka as the first point outside the home where he can judge the father in his dealings with strangers. He comes to hate the shop, the *Geschäft*, which is part of a massive rejection of his father's world and his turn to law and the 'higher ideas' of literature.

It is a measure of Kafka's hatred and ambivalence for this shop that he avoids all explicit reference to its contents in his 'Letter': the 'fancy-goods shop' has become simply a 'shop' or 'business', the *Galanteriewaren* simply 'merchandise' (*Waren*). As in his literary writings, Kafka here 'dematerializes' the empirical, referential world he is describing. Yet these fancy goods need to be spelled out, for, as we shall see, they serve to evoke the father's presence metonymically in his writings. Nothing from his father's world was a matter of indifference to him, least of all these tangible signs of paternal talent, wealth, and power. When he names them in his writings (and he does so, repeatedly, in crucial passages), we need to be able to recognize them to determine the particular form of struggle and ambivalence they embody.

At the end of the nineteenth century, the term *Galanteriewaren* included a broad range of personal and domestic decorative objects. A contemporary encyclopedia defines them as 'luxury items pertaining to personal adornment and grooming, with the exception of clothing: silk ribbons, small kerchiefs, scarves, gloves, fans, jewellery, small boxes; elegant decorative objects made of cast-iron, bronze, zinc, silver, leather, wood, ivory, glass, lead, etc.'.[4] Two aspects of Hermann Kafka's business are of importance for a consideration of his son's writing. The first is that this merchandise had a primarily decorative, aesthetic function. Hermann Kafka did not sell clothing to protect the body, but clothing accessories; he did not sell furniture, but decorative furnishings, bibelots, and knick-knacks. He dealt, in other words,

[4] *Meyers Konversationslexikon* (Leipzig: Bibliographisches Institut, 1896).

in fashionable 'inessentials', luxury items and 'gallant' wares that could be used to impress, entice, seduce, or otherwise gain power in personal and social relationships. These fancy goods are part of a developing urban, modern landscape: commodity goods that adorn the personal wardrobes and rental apartments of an increasingly affluent bourgeoisie. Second, Hermann Kafka was a wholesale distributor, not the producer of fancy goods. His business was like the hub of a giant wheel, serving the outlying provinces from the urban centre. As we shall see, Kafka's understanding of 'business', of *Geschäft*, is closely related to the notion of a large network of trade in which goods circulate in a constant, complex flow. Generalizing from this example, he comes to define the world's 'traffic' in similar terms of circulation, exchange, flow—what he will later call *Verkehr*. And in reaction to this model, he idealizes rural and semi-rural activities such as farming, hand crafts, building—anything that is stable and tied to the land.

Through the window of his father's shop, Kafka thus had a privileged view of the developing industries of fashion, clothing accessories, and domestic adornment at the turn of the century. And because his father's business serves him as his first contact with the world outside the family, because the shop and his father merge into one figure ('the business and you became one for me'), Kafka comes to perceive social reality *per se* in these terms, that is, as the circulation or 'traffic' of 'fancy goods'. The paternal world is comprised of shiny, elegant, perhaps beautiful, but inevitably deceptive surfaces—'gallant wares' which circle in an unstable, never-ending process of change and movement. The world is not fixed, is not 'grounded' in property or land, is never without some covering, concealing surface. Although he avoids labelling it as 'capitalist', 'urban', 'modern', or even 'Jewish', Kafka nonetheless puts forward a vision of the world that derives from these historical categories and that he first learned in Prague in his father's 'school'.

It is in this sense that Kafka uses the term *Verkehr*, a complex notion that explains much in his work and that has largely determined the analyses in this book. Etymologically related to 'turning', a 'turning around', or a 'false turn', *Verkehr* means in German the movement of people, goods, money, or information.

Its primary meanings are thus traffic, trade, commerce, exchange, social and sexual intercourse. But in composite form it includes epistolary correspondence (*Briefverkehr*), tourism (*Fremdenverkehr*), the circulation of bureaucratic documents (*Aktenverkehr*) or legal clients (*Parteienverkehr*) or merchandise (*Warenverkehr*). For Kafka it functions as a kind of code word for the realm of the father: commerce, sexuality, power in the world; but also (through the fancy-goods business) elegant clothes and clothing accessories, fashion, capitalism, and the modern circulation of money, commodity goods, and information. It is for this reason that Kafka frequently designates clothing as 'traveling' or 'tourist' clothing (*Reisekleider*), for it functions as a private cipher in his writing for the realm of both father and fancy-goods business, for the *movement* of elegant surfaces in an unstable urban world.

In the following pages I shall explore the relation between the 'traffic of clothes' and paternal authority, developing the thesis that Hermann Kafka's fancy-goods business serves as the implicit model for Kafka's notion of *Verkehr* in his early writings. In part this model operates on a literal, mimetic level: texts such as 'The Tradesman', 'On the Tram' in *Meditation*, and portions of *Description of a Struggle* clearly draw on Kafka's experience of business and fashion as it was filtered through the prism of his father's shop. But this experience is quickly related to other phenomena of the city that Kafka, like other writers of the *fin de siècle*, not only depicts but attempts to imitate through specific literary forms like the prose poem and the Impressionist sketch: the crowd, the randomness of urban life, fleeting surfaces like clothing, gestures, fragments of conversation—the instability of a world in movement. The point of view for these early pieces, although it shifts ground and is itself caught up in the movement of urban life, is that of the observing poet, dandy, *flâneur*, or dilettante—all terms from the vocabulary of the European *fin de siècle*—who find themselves located somewhere at the margin of this spectacle. Kafka is not usually situated on the Franco-German cultural axis linking Baudelaire, Huysmans, and Mallarmé to Rilke, Simmel, Hofmannsthal, and Benjamin—the axis that celebrates and critiques the experience of modernity in terms of fashion and urban 'traffic'. But he should be. His early texts in particular offer an archaeology of the modern European city that is informed by his intense, ambivalent relation to the paternal 'traffic of clothes'. A close reading of the two major extant works from his early period, *Meditation* and *Description of a Struggle*, will clarify his position along this axis as well as give more detailed substance to his early definition of *Verkehr*.

II

> His passion and his profession are to become one flesh with the crowd. For the perfect *flâneur*, for the passionate spectator, it is an immense joy to set up house in the heart of the multitude, amid the ebb and flow of movement, in the midst of the fugitive and the infinite
>
> (Baudelaire, 'The Painter of Modern Life')

The publication date of 1913 for the seventeen individual prose pieces Kafka gathered together under the title *Meditation* is misleading, for most of the texts were written much earlier, some corresponding almost word for word to passages in the then unpublished *Description of a Struggle* (1904–6), which in turn derived from letters, diary entries, and literary sketches from his first years at the university. None the less, Kafka still felt strongly enough about these texts in 1912—the year of 'The Judgment', *Amerika*, and *The Metamorphosis*—to publish them. As such *Meditation* represents a kind of balance sheet for his literary production until this point, the few scant texts salvaged from more than a decade of writing. The book appeared in an elegant, unusual format, Kafka having asked Ernst Rowohlt for 'the largest possible typeface' and 'a dark cardboard binding with tinted paper' (*L* 85).

To the book's first readers, *Meditation* seemed to belong to the genre of Impressionist literary sketches popularized by Peter Altenberg, Robert Walser, and Jules Laforgue (the latter in German translations by Franz Blei and Max Brod)—whimsical, gracefully fragmented presentations of the surfaces of everyday life. The stylistic resemblance between Walser and the young Kafka was so strong that Franz Blei had to reassure a friend that

'Kafka isn't Walser but really a young man in Prague with that name'.[5] Tucholsky, Musil, and other contemporaries also drew the analogy with the Swiss author, whose writings Kafka in fact admired.[6] The short, highly polished form of the texts in *Meditation*—one can truly speak of 'prose poems'—was extremely popular at the time. In his prose collection *Wie ich es sehe* (*How I See It*, 1896), Altenberg prefaced his own 'telegrams of the soul' with the following programmatic quotation from Huysmans's novel *A Rebours*: 'En un mot, le poème en prose représentait, ainsi composé, pour le duc, le suc concret, l'osmazome de la littérature, l'huile essentielle de l'art, l'art bavard réduit en sobre silence, la mer de la prose réduite en une goutte de poésie!'[7] Like the aphorism (another popular *fin-de-siècle* genre that Kafka would employ), the prose poem offers a 'condensation' of art, 'the sea of prose reduced to a drop of poetry'.

Subsequent generations of critics have tended to avoid *Meditation*, preferring to it the longer, more sustained narrative of *Description* or rejecting both works as 'juvenilia' to focus on the 'mature' texts written after the so-called breakthrough of autumn 1912, when Kafka wrote 'The Judgment', *The Metamorphosis*, and the first five chapters of *Amerika* in a few short months.[8] Recently however an interest in 'the young Kafka' has resulted in a more serious attempt to come to terms with the elusive, fleeting quality of Kafka's first published work.[9] James Rolleston notes the

[5] J. Born (ed.), *Kafka-Symposion* (Berlin: Wagenbach, 1965), 8.

[6] See Bernhard Böschenstein, 'Nah und fern zugleich: Franz Kafka's *Betrachtung* und Robert Walsers Berliner Skizzen', in G. Kurz (ed.), *Der junge Kafka* (Frankfurt: Suhrkamp, 1984), 200–12.

[7] Kafka possessed the 5th, expanded edition of Altenberg's book (published in 1910), as well as the 3rd edition of his *Märchen des Lebens* (1911), but undoubtedly was familiar with his work before then through literary journals (K. Wagenbach, *Franz Kafka: eine Biographie seiner Jugend* (Berne: Francke, 1958), 251). With his interests in reform clothing, vegetarianism, and physical culture, together with his cult of 'pure poetry', Altenberg provides an intriguing parallel to the '*Jugendstil*' Kafka. For a discussion of Altenberg, see the excellent but brief remarks by J. M. Fischer, *Fin-de-siècle: Kommentar zu einer Epoche* (Munich: Winkler, 1978), 157–68.

[8] Heinz Politzer's description of *Meditation* as 'a hodgepodge of reminiscences and promises, an odd assortment of paragraphs, gleaned from a poet's imaginary diary' (*Franz Kafka: Parable and Paradox* (Ithaca, NY: Cornell University Press, 1962; rev. edn. 1966), 29) is typical.

[9] See the essays collected in Kurz (ed.), *Der junge Kafka*. The following references are to this work.

unstable quality of narration in *Meditation*, which he attributes to the 'imaginary doubles of a Kafkan self' that will emerge in true literary form in 'The Judgment' (185). Taking up the connection with Robert Walser (Kafka admired the latter's literary sketches and his novel *Jakob von Gunten*), Bernhard Böschenstein notes the theatricality of *Meditation*, which foregrounds its own 'playful, theatrical character in the self's ironic, self-effacing perception of its own emptiness' (203). Significantly, Böschenstein stresses that the global narrative perspective in these texts repeatedly gives way to the tentative, fragmenting gaze of Kafka's narrators, who seize on a 'random, concretely evoked detail' of the outside world in order to assure themselves of their own reality (210).

Such assessments, while helpful, still tend to consider *Meditation* the 'five-finger exercises, models of the *kleine Form*' derided by previous critics,[10] thus obscuring the formal perfection of these prose poems (which so appealed to Kafka's first publishers, Franz Blei and Kurt Wolff) as well as the seriousness of Kafka's reflection on problems of contemporary society. In the period of the first automobiles, aeroplanes, and cinema, the author of *Meditation* was acutely interested in the problem of movement, especially in the big city: traffic patterns, the motion of the crowd, the proliferation of visual images, the circulation of commodities, telephone and telegraph messages, signs—*Verkehr*. Clothing, especially elegant and fashionable clothing, occupies a prominent position in these pieces as both a metaphor for and embodiment of this modern 'traffic', which contains the movement of modern capitalist life itself. As Georg Simmel (whose essays on the city and the 'psychology of ornament' can be read in tandem with Kafka's early texts) noted in 'The Psychology of Fashion', the 'essence of fashion' is a perpetual movement of modern social forces:

Thus we understand how fashion, the changing and contradictory form of life itself has come to occupy so many new territories since the domination of the bourgeoisie, resounding in so many quicker and more colorful rhythms, acquiring ever greater currency. . . . Classes and individuals who

[10] Politzer, *Parable and Paradox*, 29.

demand constant change . . . find in fashion something that keeps pace with their own soul-movements.[11]

III

In 'The Tradesman', the seventh story in *Meditation*, we find an accurate if complex portrait of Hermann Kafka's fancy-goods business, characterized by the 'changing and contradictory form' of fashion and commerce.[12] 'My small business fills me with worries', exclaims the unnamed narrator:

I have to spend hours . . . puzzling out in one season of the year what the next season's fashions are to be, not such as are followed by the people I know but those that will appeal to inaccessible populations in the depths of the country.

My money is in the hands of strangers; the state of their affairs must be a mystery to me; the ill luck that might overwhelm them I cannot foresee. (*CS* 385)

The first seven paragraphs describe the tradesman in his shop, the centre of a wholesale fashion business that serves surrounding villages and towns, the centre therefore of commercial traffic, the *Verkehr* of clothing. His anxiety stems from the uncertainty of his position—the fluctuations in the market, the perpetually shifting nature of fashion, the 'epistemological' difficulty of dealing with clients one never sees and cannot understand ('I cannot know the state of their affairs', the tradesman laments, his clients are 'inaccessible'), finally the unstable nature of capital 'in the hands of strangers' (or 'foreigners', *fremde Leute*). The shop also requires physical labour: at the end of the day the tradesman's hands and face are sweaty and dirty, his coat dusty and his boots scratched by crate nails.

[11] 'Fashion', in *On Individuality and Social Forms*, ed. D. Levine (Chicago: University of Chicago Press, 1971), 318.

[12] Max Brod writes: 'In Kafka's *Meditation* and other works of his early period, and of course in the diary, you can see the manifold impressions left by the sights and situations of [Hermann Kafka's] warehouse. Who are these "inaccessible populations in the depths of the country", whose fashions the "tradesmen" must puzzle out in advance, "not such as are followed by people of my own circles"? Hermann Kafka's wholesale shop stocked fancy goods for sale to retailers in villages and country towns.' (*Franz Kafka: A Biography*, (New York: Schocken Books, 1947; enlarged edn. 1960), 8, translation slightly altered.)

The tradesman's entrance into the lift, halfway through the text, effects an abrupt change: 'I see now that I'm suddenly alone'. Bending down to look at himself in the mirror, he begins an ornate rhetorical address to imaginary spirits, using the antiquated 'Ihr' form and the stylized 'e' in the commands ('Flieget weg', 'genießet', 'Winket', etc.): 'Fly then, let your wings, which I have never seen, carry you into the village hollow or as far as Paris, if that's where you want to go'. The text is thus organized according to a series of oppositions: the horizontal traffic of the tradesman's business transactions against his solitary vertical rise in the 'Lift' (Kafka uses the English term, a recent and fashionable import into German); the manual, dirtying labour of the shop against the elegance of the lift with its 'milky glass panes' and mirror; mundane business preoccupations expressed in unadorned prose against the precious, thoroughly untradesman-like images and language of his final speech.

Kafka's carefully polished prose poem, then, is organized around an antinomy, two opposing figures and associative realms that have been collapsed into the single 'tradesman'. In this sense it offers a condensed version of 'The Judgment', where the tradesman is split into two protagonists, father and son, the latter maintaining an epistolary relation to his 'Russian friend' in opposition to the paternal 'business'. On a biographical and historical level, this antinomy corresponds to the division between fathers and sons that marked Kafka's entire generation, the division between assimilated Jewish businessmen and their educated, solidly middle-class sons who eschewed the world of commerce for the 'higher' activities of law, medicine, and above all literature.[13] Although the text never explicitly mentions the tradesman's origin, the nature of his trade and the anxiety of having his money loaned out to 'strangers'—'Mein Geld haben fremde Leute'—

[13] *Mutatis mutandis*, this generalization is valid for the entire Prague circle around Kafka and Brod, as well as for the generation of German Expressionist poets, Freud; Zweig, Herzl, Buber, Schnitzler, Benjamin, Scholem, and countless other German Jews who came of age in the last decades of the 19th century. See Stölzl, *Kafkas böses Böhmen*, and for a larger perspective, S. Gilman, *Jewish Self-Hatred: Anti-Semitism and the Hidden Language of the Jews* (Baltimore: Johns Hopkins University Press, 1985) and S. Aschheim, *Brothers and Strangers: The East European Jew in German and German Jewish Consciousness, 1800–1923* (Madison, Wis.: University of Wisconsin Press, 1982).

give a social and ethnic resonance to the notion of commercial *Verkehr* and its precarious status.[14] For a Jewish shopowner in the Habsburg Empire had much to fear: in the last decades of the nineteenth century Czech nationalists boycotted Jewish shopkeepers and repeatedly vandalized their shops. During one such incident Hermann Kafka's shop was spared only because the vandals thought he was Czech.[15]

In the lift, however, the tradesman leaves this world below him, assuming the stylized, precious gestures of the *fin-de-siècle* dandy, enclosed in the elegant space of an English 'lift', perorating fantastically into the mirror about 'Paris', the capital of fashion and aestheticism.[16] As he leaves the lift he is greeted by an unnamed and featureless *Mädchen*—on one level no doubt merely a servant, but on a literary plane perhaps also the muse of his imagination, much like the *Mädchen* figures in René Rilke's early poems or Peter Altenberg's 'telegrams of the soul'. The two modes of *Verkehr* are simultaneously opposed and intertwined, the lift working as a literal 'vehicle' of the imagination, raising the anxious tradesman from the ground of commercial exchanges into the space of language, poetic fantasy, metaphor.

The fashion 'business' thus serves Kafka as an image for an aestheticized relation to the urban world. Central to this image is his conviction that the substance of modern urban life has migrated to the surface of things. Life is to be described not in terms of essences but phenomenologically, in terms of brief encounters, fleeting moments, unstable, shifting impressions. The Kafkan narrator in *Meditation* is never strong enough to 'marry the crowd', to merge with it like Baudelaire's *flâneur* in a process of shifting sensual pleasure. Rather, he insists on a certain aesthetic

[14] This notion of the 'rootless' nature of Jewish life in the city was a commonplace in contemporary writings, Zionist as well as anti-Semitic. As late as 1940, Max Horkheimer defined European Jews as 'agents of circulation' in their respective national cultures; see 'Die Juden und Europa', *Zeitschrift für Sozialforschung* (1940), 131.

[15] See Wagenbach, *Biographie seiner Jugend*, 19, and Stölzl, *Kafkas böses Böhmen*.

[16] Compare the similar passages from *Description of a Struggle*: '"Good evening, gentle nobleman . . . you, no doubt, hail from the great city of Paris—bearing extraordinary, well-nigh singable names"; "Are there people in Paris who consist only of sumptuous dresses . . . "; "Eight elegant Siberian wolfhounds come prancing out and jump barking across the boulevard. And it's said that they are young Parisian dandies in disguise' (*CS* 41–3).

distance, a window or some other vantage point that both frames the observed object and holds it at bay. Thus the spirits that fly toward Paris in 'The Tradesman' are advised to enjoy the aesthetic spectacle of urban movement from a window above the street: 'But enjoy yourselves there looking out of the window, watch the processions converging out of three streets at once. . . . Wave your handkerchiefs, be indignant, be moved, acclaim the beautiful lady who drives past' (*CS* 386). Similarly, in the text entitled 'The Street Window', a solitary observer 'clings' for support to this window, which simultaneously reveals and checks the *Verkehr* in the street below, the 'train of vehicles and tumult' (*CS* 384).[17] In 'Absent-Minded Window-Gazing' the unidentified observer sees a setting sun 'lighting up the face of the little girl who strolls along' (*CS* 387)—a framed, illuminated, moving image that is nearly cinematic and anticipates Kafka's later efforts in this vein.[18]

At the same time as he celebrates this spectacle of modern urban life, Kafka's fascination with fashion is marked by an undercurrent of distrust, uneasiness, even disgust. We sense his ambivalence in the twelfth text of *Meditation*, also a rhythmically cadenced prose poem modelled after Walser and Altenberg, which Kafka entitled 'Clothes':

> Often when I see clothes with manifold pleats, frills, and appendages which fit so smoothly onto lovely bodies I think they won't keep that smoothness long, but will get creases that can't be ironed out, dust lying so thick in the embroidery that it can't be brushed away, and that no one would want to be so unhappy and so foolish as to wear the same valuable gown every day from early morning till night. (*CS* 382)

The clothes described here are not the everyday clothes of a merchant or shopgirl but festive, ornamental garments emblem-

[17] As critics have noted, 'The Street Window' is a reformulation of a letter Kafka wrote to Oskar Pollak on 9 Nov. 1903 explaining that his friend was 'something like a window through which I could see the streets' (*L*9). Less frequently noted is Kafka's proximity to the contemporary problematic of *Lebensferne*, of the solitary artist cut off from 'life'. The 'Young Vienna' poets all used the window motif in this sense, from Hofmannsthal's *Der Tor und der Tod* (1893), Schnitzler's *Sterben* (1892) and Richard Beer-Hofmann's *Der Tod Georgs* (1900). See J. Le Rider's illuminating discussion in *Modernité viennoise et crises de l'identité* (Paris: Presses Universitaires de France, 1990), 44.

[18] See the discussion of Kafka's 'cinematic' narrative in *Amerika* in Ch. 4.

atic of the multilayered, constricting clothing of the *fin de siècle*. Heavy, burdened by pleats and other appendages, the clothes are also dirty, old, and worn; they cry out for an aesthetic of simpler, more hygienic forms that, as we shall see, Kafka will also subscribe to. The text however is not realistic, but based on a narrative *trompe-l'œil* that is abruptly presented by the second, and concluding sentence: the 'clothes' turn out to be the faces of young women, their muscles, and small bones, and masses of delicate hair serving as a 'natural fancy dress', a 'natürliche Maskenanzug'. We are suddenly in the world of baroque allegory, confronting now a beautiful woman's face, now her old, and decaying clothing. Not surprisingly, Kafka again introduces the aestheticizing trope of the mirror, which here serves to disfigure the face, to distort it into a 'living mask': 'Only sometimes at night, on coming home late from a party, it seems in the looking glass to be worn out, puffy, dusty, already seen by too many people, and hardly wearable any longer.'

The negative motif of feminine *vanitas* in this text betrays an uneasiness toward female figures that lies just below the surface of *Meditation*, and emerges in positive but equally reductive idealizations (the 'beautiful lady' in 'The Tradesman', and 'Reflections of Gentlemen Jockeys', or the numerous *Mädchen* figures). Indeed, in the passage in *Description of a Struggle* from which 'Clothes' was taken, the Companion attributes to his girlfriend the sinister traits of the *femme fatale* of the turn of the century, a vampire-like siren.[19]

Although marked by the precious language of his early years, the conceit of the body as clothing in 'Clothes' anticipates Kafka's frequent depiction of the body as an opaque surface, a mask that blocks the observing protagonist's access into the interior, psychological space of other characters. Metamorphosed into clothes,

[19] 'Yes, she is beautiful. . . . But when she laughs she doesn't show her teeth as one would expect; instead, all one sees is the dark, narrow, curved opening of the mouth. Now this looks sly and senile, even though she throws back her head while laughing' (*CS* 48). The narrator then responds in agreement that 'it's the beauty of girls altogether', continuing with the text later published as 'Clothes'. For a discussion of Kafka's female characters in terms of *fin de siècle* stereotypes, see Rainer Stach's *Kafkas erotischer Mythos: Eine ästhetische Konstruktion des Weiblichen* (Frankfurt: Fischer Taschenbuch, 1987).

the faces of these girls appear grotesque, alien, opaque. What was 'natural' has suddenly become cultural and social (the *Verkehr* of clothing, parties, courtship), distancing the human subjects of the text from the reader, making them into aesthetic but lifeless and repulsive objects. The body is only its 'clothing', only a dirty, ornamental surface; and the feminine psyche is vacant.

The social moment of *Verkehr*, which introduces the gaze of a second person, is crucial to this grotesque, distorting metamorphosis of the body. The execution of polite, conventional formalities has alienated the body from its pre-social identity and shaped it into a mask. Here we encounter a crucial element in Kafka's early thinking about society. Clothes insert the individual into a social context of set values, beliefs, activities. But unlike realist and naturalist authors of the nineteenth century, Kafka sees this insertion as a disfiguring, distorting process. Clothes no longer serve as legible signs of a protagonist's social standing and historical background, but as an impenetrable, opaque, 'unreadable' surface—as a visual stimulus for the observer's imagination but one which is not grounded in an external, social reality. We never see anything but the girls' 'clothes', although paradoxically there is no actual clothing to be found.

Situated immediately after 'Clothes', the prose text entitled 'Rejection' also addresses the possibility of seeing through clothes, of reading the history, character, and intentions of a 'pretty girl' through her appearance. But the reading is purely imaginary. The narrator meets the girl on the street, and she walks by without a word, her silence allowing the narrator to construct the possible train of her thoughts as: 'You are no Duke with a famous name, no broad American with a Red Indian figure . . .' (383). He responds with similarly negative, imaginary affirmations:

> You forget that no automobile swings you through the street in long thrusts; I see no gentlemen escorting you in a close half-circle, pressing on your skirts from behind, and murmuring blessings on your head; your breasts are well laced into your bodice, but your thighs and hips make up for that restraint; you are wearing a taffeta dress with a pleated skirt such as delighted all of us last autumn.

Here again we meet the practised eye of the fashion connoisseur, trained in his father's 'school', who notes an outmoded dress, savours its aesthetic details, and 'reads' the wearer's inner thoughts through her visible appearance. *Verkehr* here displays its sexual connotations, evident in the narrator's desiring gaze which focuses on the girl's breasts and thighs underneath their clothing, but also evident metaphorically in the 'long thrusts' of the automobile in the street—'traffic' in Kafka's texts is always also sexual motion.[20] Yet their erotic 'encounter' remains within the narrator's head, insubstantial, a negative version of the encounter in Baudelaire's famous poem 'A une passante' in which the poet addresses to a passing woman his silent declaration of love: 'Ô toi que j'eusse aimée, ô toi qui le savais!'

'On the Tram' also stages a silent encounter in the *Verkehr* of urban desire. The text's opening sentence declares the instability and tenuousness of the protagonist's situation: 'I stand on the end platform of the tram and am completely unsure of my footing in this world, in this town, in my family.' The movement of the tram, the randomness with which the people on it have been assembled, the lack of relations between people—these are the existential parameters of 'traffic'. The second paragraph introduces an unnamed 'girl' who stands close to the narrator and is ready to get off, her clothing and fashion accessories (all fancy goods from Hermann Kafka's shop) attracting his desiring gaze: 'She is as distinct to me as if I had run my hands over her. She is dressed in black, the pleats of her skirt hang almost still, her blouse is tight and has a collar of white fine-meshed lace . . . the umbrella in her right hand rests on the second top step' (389).

In the realist novels of, say, Balzac or Fontane, such detailed description would lead to a comprehensive, global view of the protagonist; description has the specific narrative function of situating a character in a web of social relations. But like much 'decadent' literature of the period (as Paul Bourget and Nietzsche

[20] We should not forget that this is the period in which Kafka and Brod subscribed and contributed to the erotic journals *Amethyst* and *Opale*; as George Mosse has argued, bold depictions of sexuality constituted one of the 'modern' forms of assaulting 'bourgeois sexuality' (cf. his 'The rediscovery of the Human Body', in *Nationalism and Sexuality: Respectability and Abnormal Sexuality in Modern Europe* (New York: Howard Fertig, 1985) and the related discussion in Ch. 3 below). The graphic nature of Kafka's depictions increased over time, as in Karl Rossmann's seduction in *Amerika*, the primal coupling of the Samsas in *The Metamorphosis*, of Frieda and K. in *The Castle*, etc.

noted[21]), Kafka's text privileges the detail over the whole, the narrator losing himself in a vertiginously fetishistic, fragmenting gaze: 'Her face is brown, her nose, slightly pinched at the sides, has a broad round tip. . . . Her small ear is close-set, but since I am near her I can see the whole ridge of the whorl of her right ear and the shadow at the root of it.' Here too the body appears as clothing, as a distorting, impenetrable mask provoking the narrator's amazement. 'How is it that she is not amazed at herself?' the narrator wonders, when it is in fact *his* gaze, in the setting of urban *Verkehr*, that has produced her 'astonishing' appearance. No voice issues from the girl's interior ('she keeps her lips closed and makes no such remark'); she remains an empty cipher, a silent vision immobilized and fragmented by the narrator's gaze, a projection of his imagination. She is, to quote Kafka's contemporary Otto Weininger, the 'egoless woman', a purely material appearance with no deeper, substantive identity.[22]

This is obviously the point where the notion of ornamental clothing as figures of speech, as figures for Kafka's own textual metaphors, can be brought to bear on the self-reflexive tendencies in *Meditation*. In this early aestheticizing period, Kafka is extremely self-conscious about fashioning an authorial identity for himself, about 'experimenting' with a new, decorative language as a mask for the self. In a letter to Oskar Pollak of 10 January 1904, a period in which many of the pieces in *Meditation* were first conceived, he notes: 'It's fine if we can use words to cover ourselves up from ourselves, but even better if we can adorn and drape ourselves with words until we have become the kind of person that in our hearts we wish to be.' This wish to fashion one's own identity

[21] In his well-known essay on Baudelaire (1883), Paul Bourget advances a 'theory of decadence' whose style he describes thus: 'Un style de décadence est celui où l'unité du livre se décompose pour laisser la place à l'indépendance de la page, où la page se décompose pour laisser la place à l'indépendance de la phrase, et la phrase pour laisser la place à l'indépendance du mot' (*Essais de psychologie contemporaine* (Paris: Lemerre, 1883), 25). This definition was later used almost word for word by Nietzsche in his attack on Wagner as a 'decadent' in 'The Case of Wagner', and by Hofmannsthal in his famous Lord Chandos 'Letter'.

[22] Weininger's phrase is of course the mysogynist adaptation of Ernst Mach's 'egoless' individual. For a discussion of Kafka's characterization of women and its relation to Otto Weininger's notion of the 'egoless' woman, see Rainer Stach's recent study *Kafkas erotischer Mythos*.

recalls the words that Max Brod lent to Kafka as the aesthete Carus in the 'Carina Island', who wants to 'conduct experiments' with his life. Here however it is through *language* that these experiments with life are carried out; words are the ornaments and decorative clothing that cover the writer's body until he becomes the person—the persona—in his 'heart'. Not simply emblems of a decorative, shifting reality, the use of elegant clothing in the early texts also has a self-referential function for Kafka's attempt to forge his own ornamental literary identity, to merge with his writing.

This is apparently the sense of the 'pack of nobodies' in 'dress suits' in 'Excursion into the Mountains', an obscure text that punningly refers to the appearance of printed letters on the page. 'I'd love to go on an excursion', exclaims an unnamed narrator, 'with a pack of nobodies. Into the mountains, of course, where else? How these nobodies jostle each other, all these lifted arms linked together, these numberless feet treading so close! Of course they are all in dress suits' (*Versteht sich, daß alle im Frack sind*, *CS* 383). As Hans-Thies Lehmann has recently argued, these 'nobodies' that stand next to each other, arms linked, dressed in black formal wear, resemble the characters with which the text is written on the page, the *Frack* recalling the *Frakturschrift* or Gothic script of Kafka's own hand.[23] The movement from the city into the mountains, the *Verkehr* of an 'excursion', brings these bizarre characters (in both senses of the word) to the point of language, of song; but it characteristically stops short, leaving them silent: 'We go so gaily, the wind blows through us and the gaps in our company. Our throats swell and are free in the mountains! It's a wonder that we don't burst into song.' They embody language as written, visual text, not as voice.

Before turning to *Description of a Struggle*, it is worth re-emphasizing that the narrator's fascination with fashion and ornament in *Meditation* is tempered by a deep ambivalence. The world of clothes and urban traffic is predominantly a paternal realm in which he has no fixed place. As the German title of 'On

[23] Hence also the importance of silence in this text, which begins: '"I don't know," I cried soundlessly [*rief ich ohne Klang*].' See 'Der buchstäbliche Körper: Zur selbstinszenierung der Literatur bei Franz Kafka', in Kurz (ed.), *Der junge Kafka*, 216.

the Tram' ('Der Fahrgast') suggests, the narrator is only a 'guest' in the world's traffic. Dressed in black, the woman appears to him (again like Baudelaire's widow in 'A une passante') as an omen of death and mourning. Even the leather strap supporting the narrator in the flux of urban movement is termed a 'Schlinge', a noose. The traffic of clothes is thus presented to us from the passive point of view of one who feels himself superfluous, marginal, defensively indifferent: 'I have not even any defense to offer for standing on this platform, holding on to this strap, letting myself be carried along by this tram . . . Nobody asks me to put up a defense, indeed, but that is irrelevant' (388). In this world of flux the only support for the indifferent narrator may be the *Schlinge*, an instrument of suicide. Death will put an end to this movement, will lift him from the paternal traffic of clothes. Death, or writing, or perhaps both.

IV

> The almanacs, the elegant older fashion journals, the calendars—that is where the wishes for modern intercourse are expressed.
>
> (Oskar Bie, *Der gesellschaftliche Verkehr*)

In *Description of a Struggle*, a complex, shifting narrative that Kafka wrote and re-wrote from 1904 to 1908 and that was first published in its full (though still unfinished) form after his death, one finds the same fascination with clothing and ornamental surfaces that informs *Meditation*. Festive clothing, theatrical façades, stylized gesture and speech define a narrative space largely contiguous with the Impressionist and *Jugendstil* prose of German and Austrian literature at the *fin de siècle*. Although its length of some fifty pages may seem to distance it from the prose poems of *Meditation*, in fact *Description of a Struggle* is composed of a series of shorter, interlocking segments, some of which repeat word for word the texts of *Meditation* and which all have a lyrical, highly polished aspect. With its stylized, musical language, the text differs sharply from Kafka's later works, as is immediately clear from the unusual verse epigraph with which it begins:

Und die Menschen gehn in Kleidern
Schwankend auf dem Kies spazieren
Unter diesem großen Himmel,
Der von Hügeln in der Ferne
Sich zu fernen Hügeln breitet.[24]

The lilting cadence of these lines evokes the poetry of Hugo von Hofmannsthal, the young Viennese poet that Kafka literally idolized in this period. One thinks for example of the rhythm in his poem 'Ballad of the Outer Life', which begins: 'And children grow with deeply wondering eyes | That know of nothing, grow a while and die, | And every one of us goes his own way'.[25] But the subject of Kafka's verse presents several oddities. The very first line is surprising in its affirmation of the fact that people wear clothes when they go for a walk in the park.[26] What is so significant about these clothes that they deserve to be pointed out? And why are the people described as 'swaying' (*schwankend*)? Is there a relationship, one is tempted to ask, between their instability and their clothing? Or perhaps with the 'immense sky' (or 'heaven' (*Himmel*)), that stretches into an infinite distance? And if so, is it because the 'sky' is immense or because it is empty, that is, lacking a divine presence that would give these people metaphysical stability?[27] In any case these lines establish the central motif of clothed, that is, *social* beings, against the background of an infinitely receding Nature. Later in the text we will encounter figures who are dizzy, drunk, 'seasick on land', without a stable 'ground' beneath them; figures who unaccountably 'fall in the street and lie there dead' (*CS* 35). The metaphysical resonance of the opening epigraph anticipates these figures and suggests a

[24] 'And people stroll about in clothes | Swaying on the gravel pathways | Under this enormous sky | Stretching out from hills to hills | Far in the distance.'

[25] Translation by M. Hamburger, *Hugo von Hofmannsthal: Poems and verse Plays* (New York: Pantheon, 1961), 33. The German text reads: 'Und Kinder wachsen auf mit tiefen Augen, | Die von nichts wissen, wachsen auf und sterben, | und alle Menschen gehen ihre Wege.'

[26] The English translation of 'wearing their Sunday best' destroys the oddity of Kafka's text, which reads simply: 'Und die Menschen gehn in Kleidern.'

[27] Already in high school Kafka was a devoted reader of Nietzsche, whom he defended strenuously when Max Brod attacked him in a lecture on Schopenhauer at the Prague Redehalle (university reading club) in 1903. See Brod's account of their discussion in *Streitbares Leben* (Frankfurt: Insel, 1979), 159.

biblical reference, the 'clothing' and the 'immense heaven' serving as signs of human fallenness and mortality.

By insisting on the fact that people wear clothes, Kafka's verse inserts them into a worldly sphere—the world of 'traffic'. The parade of clothing in a public park ('auf dem Kies spazieren') constitutes an exemplary moment of modern *Verkehr*, the moment in which clothing becomes the stylized, ritual vehicle of social intercourse and aesthetic spectacle. The first paragraph of the text re-formulates these questions in the context of conventional language, social relations, and clothing:

At about midnight a few people rose, bowed, shook hands, said it had been a pleasant evening, and then passed through the wide doorway into the vestibule, to put on their coats. The hostess stood in the middle of the room and made agile bowing movements, while the ornate folds of her skirt swung back and forth.[28]

Somewhere in a city (Prague, we learn later), near midnight, people are leaving a party. The hostess is in motion, the automaton-like motion of repeated bowing, while her ornate dress swings 'back and forth'. Just as the people are 'swaying' in the verse epigraph, the folds in the dress are swinging or spinning (*schaukelnd*) in a dizzying motion. Like the parade of fashion in an urban park at the turn of the century, this scene constitutes a moment of stylized performance and observation—a moment of theatre. At the same time the actors execute their gestures automatically, as if without interior reflection. The hostess's decorative clothing and 'agile bowing movements' are all we see of her. Impressionistic description of surface has supplanted psychological detail.

The sexual connotations of this social *Verkehr* are made explicit in the following paragraphs. An unnamed narrator is sitting alone, drinking schnapps and eating pastry, when an 'acquaintance'—

[28] There are two versions for *Description of a Struggle*, an early version written in Kafka's Gothic handwriting (and thus composed before 1907) and a second unfinished rewriting of 1908 or 1909. Ludwig Dietz published the two versions in a parallel edition in 1969. The English translation is of the text established by Max Brod, who collated the two versions. In my citations I generally follow the English translation, occasionally modifying it to pick up elements of the first version, whose deliberately antiquated, stylized character is quite pronounced. Notice for instance Kafka's spelling (then already antiquated) of words like 'Thürrahmen'.

the two have met that evening—importunes him with a report of his amorous adventures in the adjoining room. This report so disturbs the narrator that he proposes they leave the party—the world of *Verkehr*—to climb the Laurenziberg outside. Before their escape into Nature, however, they encounter a servant in a brief scene that embodies the interplay of clothing, fetishistic detail, and sexual desire that is typical of Kafka's understanding of 'traffic':

> In the vestibule stood a housemaid, whom we hadn't seen before. She helped us into our coats and then took a small lantern to light us down the stairs. Her neck was bare save for a black velvet ribbon around her throat; her loosely clothed body was stooped and kept stretching as she went down the stairs before us, holding the lantern low. Her cheeks were flushed, for she had drunk some wine. (*CS* 10)

This description leads to a moment of commerce that is both sexual and financial: 'At the foot of the stairs she put down the lantern, took a step toward my acquaintance, embraced him, kissed him, and remained in the embrace'. Only when the narrator 'presses a coin' into her hand does she release him and let the two male companions go out into the night.

With this opening scene Kafka establishes the principal thematic structures of his narrative: on the one hand the world of aestheticized social (and implicitly sexual and economic) *Verkehr*; on the other a more natural, private, but equally aestheticized world—the Laurenziberg, the empty nocturnal streets of Prague, and a series of fantastic, imaginary nature landscapes. Between these two worlds stand the narrator and his acquaintance (as well as fictional doubles like the Supplicant and the Fat Man), the former unsure of his social position as well as the reality of his own self. As the text later reveals, he is in the same situation as Eduard Raban in the novel fragment of 1907, *Wedding Preparations in the Country*, or Georg Bendemann in 'The Judgment': engaged to be married, that is poised to enter the world of sexual and social 'traffic'. But the bulk of the text consists in a series of whimsical fictional interludes to this narrative frame, the 'traffic of clothes' serving as the matrix for the conflict between self and world.

A self-consciously experimental text, *Description of a Struggle* bears the influence of various contemporary sources, including Hugo von Hofmannsthal's well-known Lord Chandos 'Letter' and his essay on Stefan George's poetry, 'Über Gedichte'.[29] In the following pages I will examine two other contemporary texts that have escaped critical attention and that seem to have shaped Kafka's depiction of the world of social 'traffic' in this early narrative: Oskar Bie's essay *Social Intercourse* (*Der gesellschaftliche Verkehr*), first published in Cornelius Gurlitt's bibliophile series *Die Kultur* in 1905 when Kafka was busy writing *Description of a Struggle*; and August Strindberg's autobiographical novella 'Alone', which appeared in German translation a year earlier.[30]

A leading *Jugendstil* essayist, Oskar Bie also served as editor and contributor to the *Neue Rundschau*, a journal that Kafka subscribed to and read regularly after 1904. Though by training a music and dance critic, Bie was fascinated by fashion and all aesthetic moments of modern life, writing on such topics as 'Bicycle Aesthetics' (1897), 'Modern Graphic Design' (1905), and 'The Psychology of Fashion' (1908).[31] His elegantly printed, bibliophile texts espoused a philosophy of life characteristic of the *fin-de-siècle* period, which sought to transform the events of everyday life into an aesthetic spectacle. His essay on *Social Intercourse* is decidedly not the German equivalent of Emily Post that Kafka's biographers, Wagenbach and Ernst Pawel among them, have claimed it to be.[32] Rather, it is a cultural, philosophical

[29] See Wagenbach, *Biographie seiner Jugend*, 121–3.

[30] O. Bie, *Der gesellschaftliche Verkehr* (Berlin: Gurlitt, 1905). Kafka owned the 1st edition and presumably read it when it was first published (Wagenbach, *Biographie seiner Jugend*, 252). He probably read Strindberg's novella in the *Neue Rundschau* (Berlin: Fischer) in 1904, as it appeared in the same issue as Hofmannsthal's essay 'Über Gedichte', which Kafka greatly admired. On 9 Dec. 1912, two days after finishing *The Metamorphosis*, he recalled the novella's impact on him in a postcard depicting Strindberg to Felice Bauer: 'Do you know his story *Alone*. I was overwhelmed by it once, a long time ago' (*F* 96).

[31] In the *Kunstwart* and the *Neue Rundschau*, respectively. See also Bie's essay 'Maskenzüge' (in the same 1904 issue of the *Neue Rundschau* as Strindberg's 'Einsam' and Hofmannsthal's 'Über Gedichte'), which begins: 'Clothes make characters.' Years later, on 16 Feb. 1912, Kafka heard Bie lecture on dance and Hofmannsthal read from his works at the Herder Association in Prague.

[32] Wagenbach mentions Kafka's acquisition of Bie's work in connection with his frequenting of Prague's upper classes (*Biographie seiner Jugend*, 134). Ernst Pawel reproduces and amplifies Wagenbach's mistake, describing Bie's essay as 'the standard work on proper manners . . . the Emily Post of his day' (*The Nightmare of Reason: A Life of Franz Kafka*, (New York: Farrar, Straus & Giroux, 1984), 135).

essay in the spirit of Georg Simmel's *Lebensphilosophie* that relates the aesthetic qualities of modern urban existence to the Italian Renaissance, the court of Louis XIV, and the paintings of Watteau. Elegantly printed in Latin type and abundantly illustrated with *Jugendstil* marginalia, Bie's essay was itself an elegant example of the aestheticism that it preached. With shifting, Impressionistic details, Bie develops the notion that *Verkehr*, especially but not only in the sense of traffic, is the characteristic form of modern Western culture. It fulfils the function that dance served in antiquity, and court ritual served in Renaissance society. 'The free rhythmic arts of society, the high organization of the dance of society has developed in the modern world through the culture of traffic [*Verkehr*]. That is its difference from the old world, with everything that was called dance and society in the pre-Germanic era' (3).

Rather than reject modern industrial and mass society, Bie sees in it the elements of a modern aesthetics. Like many subsequent experiments in cinema, his essay portrays the mechanical rhythms of trains, factories, machines, and commuting masses as an artistic spectacle, as a symphony or an abstract painting in motion.[33] The similarities to *Description of a Struggle* are striking and deserve to be quoted at length.

> The spectacle of human traffic . . . is an artwork endowed with such strong and various charms that it can never be fully grasped. Each second on city streets and in apartments, the rhythmic movements of people in social motion [*verkehrende Menschen*] are carried out according to fixed laws . . . The noise that rises up from the street, the symphony of the first alarm clocks in the morning . . . the hundred variations of people entering and leaving an apartment building, the confusing *tempi* of life . . . these phenomena are all part of the infinite poem in which the world seems to carry out its business. . . . Even here the masses stylize life. (3–4)

Bie centres on the modern means of transport as the principal agents of this urban artwork: 'Trains go over the countryside, ships over the oceans, streetcars through the city—they all represent the summation of individual rhythms, and their timetable is the

[33] See for instance Walter Ruttman's depiction of Berlin as 'optical music' in his 1927 film *Symphony of a Big City*.

book of their artfully stylized motion, the product of an infinitely complex codification of mass traffic' (4).

The individual who steps into the fabric of this traffic is himself immediately stylized, absorbed into the immense 'spectacle' of modern life: 'The individual enters into this firm network of uniform traffic rhythms, constituting the multicoloured variety of individual traffic. Every pedestrian . . . unites with this indescribable concert' (5). Drawing on the distinction between *Gesellschaft* and *Gemeinschaft*, Bie opposes city to country, claiming that the latter is characterized by sharp contrasts, the former by gradations of 'traffic elements'. But city life, though abstract, is not alienating. He evokes briefly the carnival of Venice as a precursor of modern street theatre, and eighteenth-century Paris as the 'burgeoning order of metropolitan traffic' (7). However, the direction of his argument leads him inevitably to North America. Even more than Paris and Berlin, the model for this modern art of *Verkehr* is, must be, New York, 'the world city of American life itself' (7).

Much later Kafka will devote an entire novel to the description of modern *Verkehr* in America—its ocean liners, automobiles, elevators, street traffic, and political demonstrations. But already his early writing is dominated by the notion of *Verkehr* in the literal sense of urban traffic. As we have seen, even the titles of the individual pieces in *Meditation*—'Passers-By', 'On the Tram', 'Street Window', 'The Sudden Walk'—reveal the centrality of this movement. Similarly, *Description of a Struggle* presents a vision of street 'traffic' whose aestheticization recalls Bie's essay: 'It might happen that two carriages stop on a crowded boulevard of a distinguished neighborhood. Serious-looking menservants open the doors. Eight elegant Siberian wolfhounds come prancing out and jump barking across the boulevard. And it's said that they are young Parisian dandies in disguise' (*CS* 43).

The above vision is related by the Supplicant and takes place in Paris, a city which serves (as it does in 'The Tradesman') as the paradigm for artifice and ornament. In the imagination of the naïve Supplicant, the Parisians are made of 'sumptuous clothing'; society ladies stand on high, illuminated terraces while their liveried servants lift giant painted canvases to create the illusion of a foggy morning. As he remarks to a 'geschmuckter Herr', a 'bespangled nobleman':

Good evening, gentle nobleman. . . . You, no doubt, hail from the great city of Paris [and] are surrounded by the quite unnatural odor of the dissolute Court of France. No doubt your tinted eyes have beheld those great ladies standing on the high shining terrace, ironically twisting their narrow waists while the ends of their decorated trains, spread over the steps, are still lying on the sand. (*CS* 41)

This portrait of French 'dissoluteness' and ornamental 'decadence' is given an ironic twist by the nobleman's drunken condition, which makes him incapable of responding to the Supplicant other than by a decidedly unaesthetic belching. Undeterred, the Supplicant pursues his imaginative evocation:

I ask you, much-bespangled sir, is it true what I have been told? Are there people in Paris who consist only of sumptuous dresses, and are there houses that are only portals, and is it true that on summer days the sky over the city is a fleeting blue embellished only by little white clouds glued onto it, all in the shape of hearts? (*CS* 42)

As in *Meditation*, the urban world appears as mere surface—without any deeper foundation, without any (metaphysical) truth that would ground it as a permanent reality. Hence the Supplicant's anxiety that this Paris of theatrical façades, pink clouds, and playful illusion will dissolve into a labyrinth of accident, disorder, uncertainty, rootlessness, and death—the underside of urban *Verkehr*. The Supplicant, who is yet without a name, without his own stable identity, asks the Frenchman:

Isn't it true that these Paris streets suddenly fork out in different directions? They're turbulent [*unruhig*], aren't they? Not everything is in order there—how could it be? Sometimes there's an accident, people gather together from side streets with that big city stride that hardly touches the pavement . . . they breathe fast and crane their tiny heads forward. (*CS* 43)

Confronted with this accidental victim of *Verkehr*, the Parisian crowd reacts with conventional, lightly grotesque excuses: '"I'm so sorry . . . it wasn't intentional, it's so crowded, please excuse me." That's the way they talk', comments the narrator, 'while the street lies numb and chimney smoke falls between the buildings.'

In contrast, Bie's account is resolutely affirmative. Consider for instance his account of fashion and gesture. In pages that directly recall scenes from both *Description of a Struggle* and *Meditation*, he depicts the art of *Verkehr* inside the home, in literary salons and cafés, formal parties, and small, informal gatherings. In the Berlin of 1900 he would like to see the same stylization of everyday life that characterized aristocratic comportment in the Italian Renaissance and the court spectacles of Louis XIV at Versailles. Invoking, as had Jacob Burckhardt a generation earlier, Castiglione's *Il Cortegiano* and Della Casa's *Galateo*, Bie emphasizes the movement of clothing and the body:

> Count Castiglione in *The Courtier* understands not only the individuality of clothing but of clothing in movement. The movement of clothing, the way it hangs, differentiates it from the masculine body; it dances with the rocking motion of *dolcezza femminile*. The Renaissance creates a wonderfully harmonious social artwork out of man and woman . . . the inner, elegant artwork of the sexes, of the vibrations of their souls, is brought into a public, stylized form. (11–12)

In Bie's aesthetic Utopia, 'superficial' moments of life take on the importance they have in theatre. Costume, posture, gait, gesture, voice—all are potential characteristics of a lived work of art that unites the various participants in a harmonious whole. His ideal is a modern classicism. Thus one of Bie's illustrations represents five sequential moments of a woman in neo-classical garb executing a curtsy. The classical work of art is posited as the model for everyday modern life. The deepest aspirations of modern society, he claims, reside at the elegant surface of life: 'The almanacs, the elegant older fashion journals, the calendars—that is where the wishes for modern intercourse are expressed' (61).

Bie's harmonious vision of social 'traffic' informs *Description of a Struggle*, but it does so ironically, as the Supplicant's imaginary visions of Paris or as the model of a social order in which he and the narrator are too awkward and self-conscious to participate with the necessary grace. Kafka's protagonists are never in control of their bodies or their clothing, which, rather than insert them into the 'fabric' and 'dance' of society, keep them isolated from this world, a prisoner of its forms. In 'The Supplicant's Story', perhaps the key interlude in the entire text, the thin, elegantly dressed Supplicant experiences a physical inability to merge with the 'traffic' of polite, conventional discourse: 'I was just bowing to a young lady in the gaslight and saying: "I'm so glad winter's approaching"—I was just bowing with these words when to my annoyance I noticed that my right thigh had slipped out of joint' (*CS* 36). In a hilarious sequence worthy of a Chaplin movie, the Supplicant describes his attempt to continue his polite conversation while squeezing and pushing his fractious leg back into order. Here too the reader is confronted with an aestheticized social world of artifice and ornate decoration, which the Supplicant vainly tries to mimic: 'And stretching out my arm I took a large bunch of grapes hanging heavily from a bowl held up by a bronze winged cupid . . . then laid it on a small blue plate which I handed to the girl, not without a certain elegance' (*CS* 37). He would like to participate in the party's musical performance and insists on playing the piano. Unlike Bie's modern city-dweller, however, who effortlessly merges with his aesthetic environment, the Supplicant is a passive, childlike clown performing in a dream world:

> At that moment two gentlemen seized the [piano] bench and, whistling a song and rocking me to and fro, carried me far away from the piano to the dining table.
>
> Everyone watched with approval and the girl said: 'You see, madame, he played quite well. I knew he would. And you were so worried'.
>
> I understood and thanked her with a bow, which I carried out well'. (*CS* 39)

The Supplicant thus remains an ironic prisoner of Bie's *gesellschaftliche Verkehr*, a predicament which Kafka characteristically literalizes through clothing:

> [The host] went out and promptly returned with an enormous top hat and a copper-brown overcoat with a flowery design. 'Here are your things'.
>
> They weren't my things, of course, but I didn't want to put him to the trouble of looking again. The host helped me into the overcoat which fitted beautifully, clinging tightly to my thin body. Bending over slowly, a lady with a kind face buttoned the coat all the way down.
>
> 'Goodbye', said the hostess, 'and come back soon. You know you're always welcome'. Whereupon everyone bowed as though they thought it

necessary. I tried to do likewise, but my coat was too tight. So I took my hat and, no doubt too awkwardly, walked out of the room. (*CS* 40)

This mismatch between clothing and body, between signifying surface and inner self, points to a general disruption of the symbol in *Description of a Struggle*, one that, as Adorno has noted, will become one of the constitutive features of Kafka's writing.[34] Here it is a sign of the problematic relationship between reality and appearance, which Kafka formulates in one of the most successful passages of his text, the almost biblical parable that he later entitled 'The Trees' and included in *Meditation*: 'For we are like tree trunks in the snow. In appearance they lie sleekly and a little push should be enough to set them rolling. No, it can't be done, for they are firmly wedded to the ground. But see, even that is only appearance' (*CS* 382).

That Kafka's deeper interest in *Description of a Struggle* is indeed metaphysical, that the motif of clothing embodies the problematic relationship between reality and appearance in the ungrounded world of *Verkehr* beneath an 'immense sky', can also be seen from the following exchange between the Supplicant and an unnamed *Mädchen* at a party: 'There's no doubt, sir, that for you the truth is too tiring. Just look at yourself! The entire length of you is cut out of silk paper [*Seidenpapier*], yellow silk paper, like a silhouette, and when you walk one ought to hear you rustle' (*CS* 37).

Although suspicious of the 'traffic of clothes', Kafka's protagonist is not yet sure enough of his identity to affirm the reality of a self outside this clothing. His own body appears as unreal to him as Nature and the realm of social intercourse. He fears that his own corporeality, his *Körperlichkeit*, will disappear, that he will be only an ornamental surface on a non-existent, theatrical stage. And yet he insists that ornament is the basis for 'true' existence. To the girl who accuses him of being too 'weak' to withstand truth, he can only respond that 'one day everyone

[34] A disruption, we might add, that Kafka never tires of depicting in terms of clothing, be it the ill-fitting uniform Karl Rossmann is given to wear in the Hotel Occidental or Gregor Samsa's grotesque beetle shell. Adorno writes: 'Each sentence is literal and each signifies. The two moments are not merged, as the symbol would have it, but yawn apart.' Cf. his 'Notes on Kafka', in *Prisms*, trans. S. and S. Weber (Cambridge, Mass.: MIT Press, 1983), 246.

wanting to live will look like me—cut out of silk paper, like silhouettes, as you pointed out—and when they walk they will be heard to rustle' (*CS* 38). No image better captures the aestheticist impulse than this one: the body reduced to the silhouette of yellow silk paper, as clothing or as the silk-like pages of beautiful books. The world is reduced to mere appearance, elegant surface, *Schein*—to a beautiful but vacant sign.[35]

V

As an alternative to Bie's celebration of *Verkehr* and a measure of Kafka's own ambivalence toward it, it is worth looking at August Strindberg's novella 'Alone', which appeared in the *Neue Rundschau* in German translation in 1904 and which, as Kafka himself later remarked, 'overwhelmed' him when he first read it (*F* 96). A denunciation of the world's 'traffic' in the name of personal and artistic freedom, Strindberg's autobiographical portrait begins with a description of a bachelor-artist who has progressively cut himself off from society for the sake of his art: 'Gradually I had become solitary, occupied only with the external communication [*Verkehr*] necessary for my work, which was carried out mostly by telephone' (361). This lonely waiting has a positive function, however. Strindberg describes it as the necessary preparation for a 'metamorphosis', for the magical transformation effected by art: 'That is finally what it means to be alone: to spin oneself into the silk of one's own soul, mask oneself in one's own cocoon, and wait for the metamorphosis, which never fails to occur' (366). The metamorphosis Strindberg is alluding to here is the same one that takes place in Kafka's story of the same name: the transformation through writing of the empirical body into a work of art. A fierce critic of bourgeois marriage, Strindberg understood the bachelor's solitude as the enabling condition for his creative work. Like Kleist, Grillparzer, and Flaubert (whom Kafka called his 'blood relatives'), and like many decadent authors of the

[35] Nietzsche, with his claim in *The Birth of Tragedy* that life is justified only as an aesthetic phenomenon, is again the crucial philosophical figure here, as well as for the Young Vienna group of aesthete poets that included Hofmannsthal. It is also possible that Kafka knew Nietzsche's posthumous essay 'On truth and Falsehood in an Extra-Moral Sense', which supports a similar position and was first published in 1904.

period with their notion of a 'fin de race' (Huysmans, Hofmannsthal, the young Thomas Mann, and Max Brod), he saw life and art as incompatible; the writer must remain 'pure', must sacrifice biological continuity for artistic creation. To spin the silk of one's own soul in writing, to mask oneself in the 'cocoon' of a self-created identity, to remove oneself from society's 'traffic'—these are the necessary preparations for the redemptive metamorphosis of the self into the literary text. Bachelorhood is the result of an extreme literary vocation, the necessary price of a radicalized aestheticism.[36]

Strindberg regards clothing—the analogy is a common one at the turn of the century—as material fetters on his individual artistic freedom. In a tone of Schopenhauerian resignation recalling Kafka's own later writings, he concludes his narrative with an evocation of the nightly removal of these fetters, the last traces of society's *Verkehr*:

> When I free my body from its clothes, from all their buttons, belts, and laces, it seems to me that my soul takes a deeper, freer breath. And when I get into bed after my Eastern ablutions, my entire being begins to expand. The will to life, struggle, and conflict fades away, and the longing for sleep resembles the yearning for death.

Nothing could be further from Bie's praise of fashion. Buttons, belts, straps, and ribbons—these accoutrements of *fin-de-siècle* European dress (all of them fancy goods sold in Hermann Kafka's shop) are presented as the chains with which the individual is bound to society. Undressing the body liberates the soul, gives the artistic self room to breathe. Death appears as a form of spiritual renewal, of life, as suggested by the baptismal reference to 'Eastern' ablutions. The bachelor-artist's solitude, his naked death in life, is the guarantor of the soul's freedom.

The notion of the bachelor-artist will emerge forcefully in Kafka's subsequent writings; in *Wedding Preparations in the Country* (1907) and especially the 'breakthrough' stories of 1912. In *Description of a Struggle* it lies just beneath the surface, appearing in the

[36] See Cersowsky's discussion of the bachelor 'type' in Kafka and its relation to literary decadence, '*Mein ganzes Wesen ist auf Literatur gerichtet*': *Franz Kafka im Kontext der literarischen Dekadenz* (Würzburg: Königshausen & Neumann, 1983).

story's tentative concluding pages in a curious scene between the narrator and his acquaintance that takes place on the wintry Laurenziberg high above Prague. Here, finally, we find an attempt to get beyond the surface of clothing to the 'reality' of the body, pain and blood. Claiming that the narrator is 'incapable of loving', the acquaintance opens his overcoat, vest, and shirt to reveal a 'broad and beautiful' chest. The narrator responds by claiming that he is engaged to be married, a claim that, though perhaps untruthful, reverses the power relations between them and seems to trigger the latent homoerotic element in their association. The acquaintance looks 'quite exhausted', asks the narrator to put his hand on his forehead, and then without warning plunges a knife into his arm: 'Blood promptly began to flow. His round cheeks grew pale. I pulled out the knife, cut up the sleeve of his overcoat and jacket, tore his shirt sleeve open. . . . I sucked a little at the deep wound' (*CS* 50). Although the narrator tries to comfort his acquaintance by referring to the world of *Verkehr*, of walks with 'carefully dressed people' or horse-rides in the country with his girlfriend, the acquaintance is despondent. His babbling response reveals an unmistakably metaphysical anxiety: '"Oh God," he said, stood up, leaned on me and we went on, '"oh God, that won't help. That won't make me happy. Excuse me. Is it late? . . . Oh God."' The text's final image is of broken shadows, the play of insubstantial surfaces on white snow that harks back to the metaphysical parable of appearance and reality in 'The Trees':

> A lantern was burning close to the wall above; it threw the shadows of the tree trunks across the road and the white snow, while on the slope the shadows of all the branches lay bent, as though broken.

2

The Jugendstil *Body: Reform Clothing and the Cultural Politics of the* Kunstwart

> One cannot deny you a certain talent, but it lies in a much different area than you think. You have the imagination of a clothing designer. Make women's clothing.
>
> (Adolf Loos to *Jugendstil* artists and architects)

I

'WHEN I free my body from its clothes, from all their buttons, belts, and laces, it seems to me that my soul takes a deeper, freer breath. And when I get into bed after my Eastern ablutions, my entire being begins to expand. The will to life, struggle, and conflict fades away, and the longing for sleep resembles the yearning for death'. As witnessed in the previous chapter, Strindberg's metaphysical lament in 'Alone' depicts clothing as the tangible incursion on the freedom of body and spirit. Clothes are fetters on the soul. The metaphor is a common one for the European *fin de siècle* with its overdressed bodies and stuffed interiors. Strindberg responds with a mystical turn to Oriental philosophies of abnegation of the will, to the melancholy resignation of Schopenhauer. Others, younger than Strindberg, turn to a socially enlightened hedonism that frees the body from its material fetters and exposes it to the restorative elements of light, air, water, and earth. Clothing reforms, especially for women, are proposed; nudist colonies and natural health centres are set up in isolated rural landscapes; the enervated, consumptive *Stadtmensch* yearns for the invigorating freedom of the country in which body and soul, unencumbered by the 'clothes' of city life, may at last thrive like innocent children or healthy plants.[1]

[1] The secondary literature on the *Jugendstil* as an artistic and cultural movement is immense and cannot be dealt with adequately here. On the question of a literary

In the visual and literary arts, contemporary social movements to liberate the *fin-de-siècle* body from its overdressed condition find their equivalent in *Jugendstil* representations of the human form. Here the body is often clothed in loose-fitting garments or depicted in a state of adolescent, chaste undress. In place of the constricting forms of *fin-de-siècle* clothing—laced corsets, high buttoned shoes, layers of tight petticoats—the *Jugendstil* proposes an aesthetics of flowing movement, of free play between garment and body. The body itself becomes a kind of plant: supple, vigorous, and capable of winding itself into a decorative series of vegetal arabesques that would seem to participate in a natural cycle of the elements.

In his early years as a student, as we have seen, Kafka consciously played the role of dandy and *littérateur*, dressing with the refined elegance that was then common for an aspiring writer, and frequenting the popular literary clubs, cafés, and cabarets of Prague. The photographs from this period show him almost foppishly elegant, sporting broad, upturned collars, fancy silk neckties, even a top hat, tuxedo, and gloves. In a flirtatious letter of November 1907 to Hedwig Weiler, who had complimented him on his elegant appearance, Kafka admitted that 'I merely try casually and in a hit-and-miss way to dress well', drawing the line between himself and writers who 'paint their fingernails'. At the same time, in uneasy company with this socially codified elegance, Kafka participated in various movements of the *Jahrhundertwende* that sought to liberate the individual from the tyranny of fashion, urban stylization, and 'decadence'. He idealizes the simplicity of country life, attends lectures on clothing reform for women, and develops a lifelong commitment to *Nacktkultur*,[2] visiting rural

Jugendstil see the anthologies edited by Jürg Mathes, *Prosa des Jugenstils* (Stuttgart: Reclam, 1982) and *Theorie des literarischen Jugenstils* (Stuttgart: Reclam, 1984; Hartmut Scheible's *Literarischer Jugenstil in Wien* (Munich: Artemis, 1984); the section devoted to literature in the excellent anthology *Jugendstil*, ed. Jost Hermand (Darmstadt: Wissenschaftliche Buchgesellschaft, 1971); and finally Gert Mattenklott's *Bilderdienst: Aesthetische Opposition bei Beardsley und George* (expanded edn., Berlin: Syndikat, 1985), especially the last chapter on 'Der ästhetische Mensch'. Needless to say, Kafka appears nowhere in these volumes.

[2] The term nudism hardly does justice to the German phenomenon, which has all the weight of a *Weltanschauung*, cultural programme, and political rallying cry at the turn of the century.

nudist retreats like Jungborn to purge himself of the physical and moral toxins of urban life.[3] His objection is not to clothing *per se* but to the 'unnatural' and disfiguring relationship to one's body that fashion and urban life promote. Thus he depicts the 'ladies of fashion' in his early description of an aviation contest in Italy as 'degrading everything', intimidated by a tight-fitting corset that slims their waist and broadens their hips to an unnatural degree.[4] Working women are also exposed, disfigured, and alienated by the conditions of urban labour, as Kafka notes after a visit to his family's asbestos factory:

> Yesterday in the factory. The girls, in their unbearably dirty and untidy clothes, their hair disheveled . . . the expressions on their faces fixed by the incessant noise . . . they aren't people, you don't greet them, you don't apologize when you bump into them . . . they stand there in petticoats, they are at the mercy of the pettiest power. (Diary entry for 5 February 1912)

Kafka's aversion to the city and his commitment to what he saw as the simplicity and naturalness of rural life never wavered. In August 1922 he wrote to Max Brod: 'I have spent almost four days in Prague and have returned to the relative peace here [in Planá, a village in Bohemia]. This pattern, a few days in the city, a few months in the country, might be the right one for me'. Complaining of the 'half-naked' women in Prague, especially of a woman on vacation from the city who was dressed like a 'fine poisonous toadstool', he praises the dress of the village women:

> Here in the village women are altogether different . . . They are never half-naked, and even though they own little more than one dress, they are always completely clothed. They do not get fat until deepest old age, and only an occasional young girl is buxom. . . . [T]he women are dry . . . It is a special kind of dryness, produced by wind, weather, work, cares, and childbearing, but there is nothing of urban misery about it, rather a tranquil, upright cheerfulness.

Again, the opposition here is not between urban clothing and rural nudity but between 'unnatural' and 'natural' relations to the

[3] Jungborn, a retreat near Weimar that Kafka visited in the summer of 1912, was founded by Adolf Just along principles that mixed a Rousseauian belief in Nature with an overtly Christian programme of spiritual renewal. See the related discussion in Ch. 3.

[4] 'Die Aeroplane in Brescia', in *Die Aeroplane in Brescia und andere Texte* (Frankfurt: Fischer, 1977), 20–1.

body, whereby 'natural' for Kafka seems to imply an unsensual ('dry') obliviousness to the body.

This ambivalence toward the clothing (or semi-nudity) of the city forms an unmistakable if generally unnoticed aspect of Kafka's literary writings. On the one hand, clothing provides protection, identity, a secure place in the world's traffic. Disaster often befalls Kafka's protagonists when they are in bed, undressed and vulnerable. Thus Joseph K. is arrested in bed in his nightshirt by a man wearing a 'travelling suit'; at the end of the novel two men dressed in formal evening attire remove his coat, waistcoat, 'and finally his shirt' before putting the butcher's knife in his heart. At the end of 'A Country Doctor', the protagonist is forced to wander naked through a winter landscape, his fur coat dangling behind him, 'exposed to the frost of this most unhappy of ages'. In 'In the Penal Colony' the officer wears a full-dress uniform that signifies his belonging to a distant colonial power: 'These uniforms are too heavy for the tropics, surely . . . but they mean home to us; we don't want to lose our homeland' (*CS* 140–1).

Yet clothing also figures as material fetters on an essential, pre-social self, as an incursion on the body's freedom, natural expressivity, and identity. Karl Rossmann's uniform gives him a ready-made identity in the Hotel Occidental, but it is so tight that he must first do breathing exercises 'to see if it was still possible to breathe at all' (*A* 143). Gregor Samsa's metamorphosis frees him from the 'traffic of clothes' he participated in literally as a travelling cloth salesman, restoring him to the 'natural' state of a 'naked' animal form. All of Kafka's human protagonists long for the undressed freedom of the animal. Edward Raban, Gregor Samsa's precursor in *Wedding Preparations in the Country*, dreams of sending his 'clothed body' into the world while he remains in bed as a big beetle, 'naked' and protected (*CS* 55–6). Red Peter in 'A Report to an Academy' evokes nostalgically his Utopian animal existence on the 'Gold Coast' before his capture and socialization, before he was made to dress and talk like an adult human in the realm of *Verkehr*.

Women are often the victims of fashion in Kafka's texts, their bodies literally imprisoned, dirtied, or trivialized by their clothing. Brunelda's elegant attire in *Amerika* is also repulsively dirty and disordered. The mistress of a prosecuting attorney in *The Trial* wears a dress which 'she doubtless thought becoming and stylish [but was] actually an old ball-dress bedizened with trimmings and draped with several rows of conspicuously unsightly fringes' (*T* 243). Women in *The Castle* are dependent on their elegant dresses and silk underwear to receive the favours of the castle lords and advance in the social hierarchy. The novel breaks off with the landlady showing K. wardrobe after wardrobe of ornate, dark dresses: 'Are you amazed?' she asks K. 'No', he answers. 'I was expecting something of the sort; didn't I say you're not only a landlady, you're aiming at something else?' (*C* 412).

Kafka's relation with his parents was obviously part of his ambivalence toward clothing. They were after all professionals in the clothing business and, socially ambitious and conformist, knew the value of clothing in establishing social connections. Kafka's extended diary entries for 30 December 1911 and 2 January 1912 recount his earlier aversion to wearing the 'wretched clothes' his parents had made for him. Interestingly, Kafka locates the source of his physical ills in this clothing:

> I naturally noticed—it was obvious—that I was unusually badly dressed, and even had an eye for others who were well dressed, but for years on end my mind did not succeed in recognizing in my clothes the cause of my miserable appearance. Since even at that time [roughly age 14–16, the time of his first dance lessons], I was on the way to underestimating myself, I was convinced that it was only on me that clothes assumed this appearance, first looking as stiff as a board, then hanging in wrinkles. . . . As a result I let the awful clothes affect even my posture, walked around with my back bowed, my shoulders drooping, my hands and arms at awkward angles.

Kafka then recounts how his parents humiliated him in front of a tailor who had been called in to fit him for a black dress suit for dancing class:

> I was undecided, as I always was in such cases, they made me afraid that by a definite statement I would be swept away not only into an immediate unpleasantness, but beyond that into something even worse. So at first I didn't want a dress suit, but when they shamed me before the stranger by pointing out that I had no dress suit, I put up with having a tail coat discussed.

Progressively refusing his parents' suggestions one after the other, the young Kafka finally insists on having a high-buttoned, silk-lined tuxedo that the tailor declares impossible to sew. The tailor is dismissed, leaving the boy without a tuxedo and hence without access to the world of social *Verkehr* it symbolizes: 'I, under the reproaches of my mother, remained wearily behind, barred forever—everything happened to me forever—from girls, an elegant appearance and dances'.

II

A key source of information about Kafka's '*Jugendstil*' phase is his correspondence between 1902 and 1904 with his closest friend and fellow student, Oskar Pollak. Although heavily edited by Max Brod,[5] the letters provide a revealing portrait of Kafka at this time. In order to supplement this portrait, attention will also be focused on the *Jugendstil* cultural journal *Der Kunstwart* (*The Art Guard*), which Pollak and Kafka subscribed to and read regularly from their gymnasium years until 1904 or 1905. This journal offered Kafka an alternative to the *fin-de-siècle* conception of clothing and ornament of his parents' generation, providing him with the mask of a modern *Jugendstil* aestheticism that went

[5] Brod writes: 'At the time of the first publication of Kafka's letters in 1937, I omitted some unessential passages, quantitatively very little, and unfortunately can no longer fill these gaps since the original letters were probably lost during the German occupation of Prague' (*L* 425). Several reasons lead us to believe that Brod is less than candid. The first is his evident jealousy of Pollak; in his biography he admits that he learned 'with astonishment' that Kafka 'offered to send Pollak his literary manuscripts or read them aloud. Later, that never happened; one had to ask Kafka, press him urgently, before he showed anything from his work.' Brod may also have been uncomfortable with Kafka's amorous, courting tone (Pawel speaks of 'strong homoerotic impulses'), especially because he disliked Pollak's denial of his Jewish origins and *Deutschtümelei*. Finally, Brod was troubled by Kafka's self-hatred as a Jew and, convinced of Kafka's significance as a 'Jewish author', suppressed material that could be considered anti-Semitic or pro-German. (Thus he eliminated a reference in Kafka's travel diary to Walter Hasenclever as 'Jewish' and 'loud' (*Max Brod: Franz Kafka: Eine Freundschaft: Reiseaufzeichnung*, ed. M. Pasley (Frankfurt: Fischer, 1987), 239)). Add to this the political situation in which Brod edited the letters—the Nazis already in power in Germany and threatening to invade central Europe, Brod's compromised position as a Zionist, etc.—and one is forced to wonder how much of the early letters was censored and for what reasons. In any case none of Kafka's other letters was subjected to the same editing.

hand in hand with clothing reforms, nudism, rural artist communities, the arts and crafts movement, 'peasant' architecture, and a conservative German-national programme of cultural politics—all of which occupied Kafka's attention at this time and mark his distance from the paternal 'traffic of clothes'.

A basic theme in the letters to Oskar Pollak is the struggle between an unhealthy urban aestheticism and an idealized vision of rural industriousness. In one letter of 1903 Kafka tells his friend, who had recently left Prague for the country, that he is lucky to have

> good air for breathing in this green spring. Therefore it is presumptuous and a little sinful to write to you from the city, except to advise you, wise as city folks are where others are concerned, to throw yourself into agriculture. On the other hand, it is sensible and cautionary to have letters from the country written to oneself. (*L* 427)

When Kafka vacations with his parents in the country, he takes long solitary walks, watches cloud formations, sits in the garden with children, telling them fairy-tales, playing games, carving wooden objects, and, of course, writing. In the purple prose of the period, he celebrates the 'soil', the '*Scholle*', as the site of aesthetic experience:

> Or where I go through the fields which now lie brown and mournful with abandoned plows but which all the same glisten silvery when in spite of everything the late-afternoon sun comes out and casts my long shadow . . . on the furrows. Have you noticed how late-summer shadows dance on dark, turned-up earth, how they dance physically? Have you noticed how the earth rises toward the grazing cow, how trustfully it rises? Have you noticed how rich, heavy soil crumbles under too delicate fingers, how solemnly it crumbles? (Letter of autumn 1902)

The country is also the site of the 'healthy' classical German literary tradition that Kafka and Pollak prefer, as faithful readers of the *Kunstwart*, to the febrile, 'decadent' literature of the city.[6] When Pollak makes a pilgrimage to Goethe's house in Weimar in

[6] See Klaus Wagenbach's chapter on 'Prague at the Turn of the Century', in *Franz Kafka: Eine Biographie seiner Jugend* (Berne: Francke, 1958); English translation in Mark Anderson (ed.), *Reading Kafka: Prague, Politics, and the Fin de Siècle* (New York: Schocken Books, 1989).

the summer of 1902 and criticizes the 'national museum' set up there as a sacrilege of art, Kafka responds with considerable irony. Yet in all seriousness he rhapsodizes on the image of the rural, solitary Master: 'But do you know what really is the holiest thing we could have of Goethe's as a memento—the footprints of his solitary walks through the country—they would be it.'

Against this notion of the country as a space of freedom, literary inspiration, and aesthetic experience, Kafka poses the evil city, the bourgeois space of confinement, oppression, and corporeal inhibition. He complains of his 'bourgeois', *fin-de-siècle* desk in Prague which, with its ornate carvings and sharp edges, physically wounds his body whenever he tries to write something 'un-bourgeois', something Nietzschean and literary: 'It's a respectably-minded desk which is meant to educate. It has two horrible wooden spikes at the writer's knees. . . . If your body quivers ever so little, you inescapably feel the spikes in your knees, and how that hurts' (24 August 1902). In a revealing comparison, he calls Prague a 'little mother with claws', inviting Pollak to help him burn down the city that holds them prisoner (20 December 1902).

Kafka's celebration of German national tradition conceals a current of latent anti-Semitism, expressed as an antipathy for his father's unaesthetic world of trade and *Verkehr*. Prague is the site of 'Jewish' commerce and socialist politics where the peace of a Sunday afternoon is ruined by the noisy clerks with their 'red carnations and their stupid and Jewish faces' (9 November 1903). Like Hugo von Hofmannsthal, he stylizes himself as a child imprisoned in the city, catching only a glimpse of the street and its business transactions before turning back to his 'precious picture books' (1903). Or he longs for the peace of a rural Christian setting, which he idealizes in affected, dilettantish verse:

> Standing in the Christmassy square
> Of an ancient little town,
> The crèche's colored windows look out
> Upon the snowy ground.
>
> (Letter of 9 November 1903)

In this opposition between city and country, clothing occupies a crucial position. In a letter to Pollak of 20 December 1902,

Kafka includes a little prose capriccio entitled 'The Intricate Story of Shamefaced Lanky and Impure in Heart'. In this bizarre fictional encounter, an untruthful city-dweller and dandy who sports fashionable English neckties, a walking stick, and gleaming buttons on his vest visits a tall, awkward man who knits grey, woollen socks 'for the peasants'.[7] In a surrealistic trope, Kafka describes the dandy's language as a miniature replica of his smooth, shiny clothing: words emerge from his mouth in the shape of miniature dandies, 'fine gentlemen with patent-leather shoes and English cravats and glistening buttons'. For these little word-dandies, clothing represents a limit that cannot be crossed; when asked what 'blood of blood' is, one replies 'with a leer': 'Yes, I have English cravats.' Here the pun between 'with a leer' (*anzüglich*) and 'suit of clothes' (*Anzug*) turns the 'deep' question about blood back on itself. Reality stops at the shiny, fashionable surface: the deeper facts of the body, blood, or an interior emotional space have no meaning for these two-dimensional figures. Yet their erotic power is undeniable: 'Lanky also smiled, and his eyes crawled bashfully along his guest's glistening waistcoat buttons.' As the dandy speaks, his elegant words climb up on Lanky, 'tweaking and biting, and worked their way into his ears'. The city-dweller repeatedly jabs his walking stick into Lanky's belly, and the latter 'trembles' and 'grins'.

In this tense, erotically charged encounter, one can discern an anticipation of the same struggle between two competing modes of life that structure the full-fledged narrative *Description of a Struggle*, written several years later. What is striking in the 'Intricate Story' sent to Pollak—itself framed in the folds of a personal letter—is the centrality of the city/country distinction and the allegorical use of clothing. Kafka will continue this technique throughout all his writings, using it for instance in *The Castle* to distinguish castle from village, the silk garments of castle officials from the grey, loose-fitting and patched clothes of peasants.

[7] 'Für die Bauern.' The German word for peasant or farmer, *Bauer*, is etymologically related to the verb 'to build' or 'construct'. Kafka often uses the notion of construction for his own writing—hence the hidden but persistent connection between rural motifs and references to literary production.

III

As critics have noted, Kafka's formulation of the antagonistic relation between city and country is indebted to the aesthetic politics of the *Kunstwart*.[8] In his biography, Max Brod cites an unpublished letter to Pollak in which Kafka's debt to this journal is particularly evident:

> Just opposite the vineyard, on the country road, deep in the valley, stands a tiny cottage, the first and last in the village . . . Not even Schultze-Naumburg[9] could find a use for it, unless, at most, as a hideous warning. In all probability I and the owner are the only people who love it and weave our dreams about it . . . [All this] is like a dear, old peaceful German fairytale.[10]

Readers have since debated the extent to which Kafka's early self-consciously antiquated, precious style is due to a *Kunstwart* 'idiom'.[11] But this debate has served to camouflage an issue which Brod and most subsequent critics have been unwilling to acknowledge, namely, Kafka's identification with a German nationalist ideology and corresponding denial of his Jewish origins. What is surprising about these early letters is not so much their stylistic preciousness as the use of arguments and themes that will later be used by anti-Semitic German and Czech nationalists. Kafka's aversion to his father's 'Jewish' world of commerce, money, and urban 'traffic' surfaces in his remark about the 'stupid', 'noisy' Jewish clerks in Prague. But it also forms the subtext to what Brod dismisses as a passing *Deutschtümelei*: his celebration of the 'soil', his interest in agriculture, arts and crafts, his Germanic vocabulary (rather than Yiddish or the *mauschel*

[8] For a review of this criticism, see H. Binder (ed.), *Kafka-Handbuch* (Stuttgart: Alfred Kröner, 1979), i. 266–70.

[9] Reference here is to Paul Schultze–Naumburg's *Kunstwart* articles on German peasant architecture; see discussion below.

[10] *Franz Kafka: A Biography* (New York: Schocken Books, 1947; enlarged edn. 1960), 57.

[11] Max Brod first advanced this idea in his biography of Kafka (cf. pp. 54–60), which Klaus Wagenbach supported in 1958 (*Biographie seiner Jugend*, 106). Since then Harmut Binder has argued that the *Kunstwart* included essays by numerous contributors and could not have had a single, unified style. See Binder, *Kafka-Handbuch*, i. 266–70.

German spoken by German Jews like his father), his Goethe cult, and so on.[12]

The *Kunstwart* imparted to Kafka not just an idiom but an ethos of classical, High German culture which he ironized but never renounced.[13] Founded in 1887 by Ferdinand Avenarius, a nephew of Richard Wagner, the *Kunstwart* had a basically conservative if populist cultural mission. Unlike the avant-garde journals *Sturm* and *Aktion* that Kafka would come into contact with a decade later, it saw itself as the guardian of a classical Germanic heritage embodied in Dürer, Beethoven, Goethe, Schiller, Kleist, and Hebbel. In its vision of art as the source of spiritual and political renewal, it resembles other cultural journals founded in the same period, as well as such groups as the *Kunsterziehungsbewegung* and the *Werkbund*, German equivalents of William Morris's Arts and Craft Society.[14] Avenarius himself has been described as 'the typical representative of that well-meaning idealism common among the first generation of socialists, which expressed itself clearly in slogans like "art, music and knowledge for the people"'. Despite these aims, however, the journal's readership was limited largely to 'students and teachers of the middle and lower-middle

[12] See Wilfried Barner, 'Jüdische Goethe Verehrung vor 1933', in S. Moses and A. Schöne (eds.), *Juden in der deutschen Literatur* (Frankfurt: Suhrkamp, 1986), 127–51. As Barner notes, the Goethe cult was extremely strong among Jews at the turn of the century. Albert Bielschowsky was only one of many Jewish scholars to promote a 'national Goethe' in this period. His *Goethe: Sein Leben und seine Werke*, published in 1895 and reprinted 42 times until 1922, figured in the library of middle-class Germans and German Jews. His extended essay on Goethe's lyric poetry appeared in the *Kunstwart* in 1903.

[13] Pollak went on to become an art historian and specialist in baroque art in Prague and Italy (under papal protection). Kafka later experienced a religious awakening after his encounter with Buber and the Yiddish actors. But his rejection of Yiddish in his literary writings, his strict observance of classical High German, continued throughout his life. I come back to this question in my reading of 'Josephine the Singer'; see Ch. 8. On the problematic relations between Yiddish and German, see Sander Gilman's perceptive remarks on Kafka and Karl Kraus in his *Jewish Self-Hatred, Anti-Semitism and the Hidden Language of the Jews* (Baltimore: Johns Hopkins University Press, 1985).

[14] Friedrich Pecht began publishing *Die Kunst für Alle* in 1885; Otto Brahm founded the *Freie Bühne für modernes Leben* in 1890; Stefan George's *Blätter für die Kunst* (which Kafka greatly admired) first appeared in October 1892, proclaiming that 'art will have a magnificent rebirth'. As Fritz Stern has pointed out, these movements provide the context for the tremendous success of Julius Langbehn's *Rembrandt als Erzieher* (1890), which Avenarius hailed in the same year as 'proof' of their common aspirations. See Stern, *The Politics of Cultural Despair* (Berkeley, Calif.: University of California Press, 1961; repr. 1974), 158 and 174–5.

classes',[15] and its subsequent political evolution would veer distinctly to the right.

Avenarius had little appreciation of modern art and literature, and apart from a few decorative illustrations the *Kunstwart* cannot be considered a mainstream *Jugendstil* journal like *Pan*, *Ver Sacrum*, or *Jugend*. None the less, it fully embraced the *Jugendstil* notion derived from Morris and Ruskin of an organic unity between art and life: the aestheticization and simplification of modern industrial life would lead to social and moral renewal. (Avenarius was one of the co-founders of the *Werkbund*, which was predicated on this ethical fusion of art and politics). The journal thus devoted considerable space to the relations between art and rural life, to 'peasant' architecture, to handcrafts such as knitting, weaving, carving, and so on, and to rural artist communities like Worpswede and Hellerau.[16] Avenarius consciously played a mediating role between high and low cultures, attempting to bring the art of past eras to the 'people' (as in the form of quality reproductions of famous artworks), at the same time that he strove to raise folk art into acknowledged and respected visibility. Max Brod reports that Kafka had a *Kunstwart* reproduction of an engraving by Hans Thoma depicting a peasant working in the fields, which hung in his room for years.

Part of the *Kunstwart*'s social program was dedicated to reforming *fin-de-siècle* clothing into a 'modern style'. Paul Schultze-Naumburg, the art critic Kafka mentions in the above letter to Pollak, was a regular contributor to the *Kunstwart* and a close personal friend of Avenarius. Kafka was familiar with Naumburg's

[15] Paul Fechter, 'Ferdinand Avenarius', *Neue deutsche Biographie* (Berlin: Duncker & Humblot, 1953), 466.

[16] Kafka took an active interest in the latter community and visited Emile Jaques-Dalcroze's school there in 1914. as late as 1921 he still supported the pedagogical virtues of Hellerau and advised his sister Elli to send her 10-year-old son Felix there to protect him from the 'dirty' and 'squinting' spirit of bourgeois Jewish life in Prague: 'ten years without physical training, without hygiene, of a pampered life . . . caged with the grown-ups. [Felix] is vigorous, calm, bright, cheerful. Nevertheless these ten years have been spent in Prague where prosperous Jews are affected by a particular spirit from which children cannot be shielded. I am not referring to individuals, of course, but to this almost tangible general spirit, which expresses itself somewhat differently in everyone, in each according to his character, which is in you as well as in me—this small, dirty, lukewarm, squinting spirit. To be able to save one's own child from that, what good fortune!' (*L* 290–1).

Kulturarbeiten, popular cultural essays which appeared in the *Kunstwart* from 1899 to 1917 and promoted what might be broadly termed the *Jugendstil* aestheticization of everyday life. Two additional books entitled *Art and the Promotion of Art* or *Promoting Art in the Home*, took up issues such as 'l'art pour l'art', the 'aesthetics of the rental apartment', furniture, book design, clothing, jewellery, and generally any aspect of everyday life susceptible of aesthetic reform.[17]

In 1900 the topic of reform clothing was directly linked to the *Jugendstil*. Medical experts and feminists had already begun the fight against *fin-de-siècle* women's clothing; an international feminist congress denounced the corset as an 'instrument of torture' in 1896. In 1900 the Belgian *Jugendstil* artist Henry van de Velde organized an exhibition on 'The Artistic Improvement of Women's Clothing', calling for a modern *Reformkleid* that would unite aesthetic with social and medical considerations. The following year Naumburg organized a similar exhibition in Berlin dedicated to 'a new female garment'. And in 1903 a *Reformkleid* festival was held in Krefeld, over 100 women parading before the other guests in reform garments designed by leading *Jugendstil* artists of the period.[18]

In November 1903 Kafka attended a lecture in Prague by Naumburg on women's reform clothing, summarizing and discussing its contents in detail in a twelve-page letter to Pollak.[19] Although much of this letter was lost, the content of Naumburg's lecture can be surmised from his contemporary book, *The Culture of*

[17] *Kunst und Kunstpflege* (1901) and *Häusliche Kunstpflege* (1905).

[18] As Brigitte Stamm has noted, the reform clothing movement lasted only briefly and failed to compete with the capitalist fashion industry, the *Reformkleid* being by definition 'anti-fashion'. Of van de Velde she notes that he reflected 'the central concern of the New Style around 1900 to penetrate all aspects of life with art. He thus raised the creation of women's clothing into the realm of art and integrated the reform garment with the total work of art of the *Jugendstil*.' 'Berliner Chic', *Berlin um 1900*, exhibition catalogue (Berlin: Berlinsche Galerie, 1984), 114; cf. also her dissertation, *Das Reformkleid in Deutschland* (Berlin, 1976); H. van de Velde, *Die künstlerische Hebung der Frauentracht* (1900); Anna Muthesius, *Das Eigenkleid der Frau* (1903).

[19] (*L* 4267). Max Brod deleted much of this letter when he first edited the correspondence in the 1930s. Why he did so is all the more mysterious given the letter's overtly literary character, which Brod knew was linked to *Description of a Struggle* and *Meditation*.

the Female Body as a Basis for Women's Clothing.[20] A painter as well as an art critic, he had witnessed first-hand the physical deformities in his models caused by their corsets, the *bête noire* of all clothing-reform advocates at the turn of the century. Women's clothing since the Renaissance, he claimed, has always attempted to repress the body's natural lines into a 'Zerrbild' or caricature of the ideal:

> With few exceptions, women's attire from the fourteenth century until the present has been the means to change the body or make it appear differently from how Nature wished to use it for her many purposes. Its purpose was not to raise the body into an ever higher state of perfection but to distort it brutally into a caricature of the ideal. (14)

With abundant illustrations, photographs, and anatomical drawings, Naumburg then puts on a horror show of contemporary examples: waists laced into impossibly *petite* dimensions, rib-cages and breasts pushed above their natural positions, feet squeezed into elegant but overnarrow shoes. Like Oskar Bie, however, he takes this 'Ideal' not from Nature but straight from art history. Juxtaposing photographs of disfigured female bodies with classical paintings and sculptures of women dressed in loose, flowing gowns, Naumburg argues that women must free themselves from the fetters of contemporary fashion and adopt clothing that respects the body's anatomical needs. The body should be used as a basis, a *Grundlage*, for its clothing.

To this end Naumburg designed his version of the so-called reform garment or *Reformtracht*—a loose-fitting one-piece garment that hung from a woman's shoulders to her ankles and was fastened at the waist by a broad sash. A single undergarment or *Kombination* replaced the traditional corset, petticoats, and layers of woollen underwear. Naumburg patterned this reform garment after Greek models, apparently seeing no contradiction between this 'natural' dress and a highly stylized work of art. He also encouraged his readers to invent their own reform garments, for,

[20] *Die Kulture des weiblichen Körpers als Grundlage der Frauenkleidung*. Illustrated with *Jugendstil* designs by J. V. Cissarz, the book was published in 1903 in Leipzig by Eugen Dierderich. With Avenarius and Wolfgang Schumann, Diederich was one of the leading literary and art critics in Dresden at the turn of the century. Like Schultze-Naumburg, he would later evolve toward right-wing Germanic nationalism.

like the author of *Social Intercourse*, he saw fashion as the potential realm of individual, everyday creativity, of a spontaneous relation to art.[21]

At the turn of the century, Naumburg's clothing reform proposals had a sensible modernism to them that met with widespread approval, including Kafka's. Championing the body in its natural state, Naumburg was inevitably led to praise nudism or what in German was beginning to be called *Nacktkultur*, the 'culture' of nudism: 'Our lifestyle has tended to ignore or deny the naked body. Children in school are hardly ever taught about their own bodies, which are after all the material basis for their entire existence. Today the average person never sees the [undressed] body' (15). Kafka's lifelong interest in nudism dates from this same period. He visited rural nudist retreats such as Jungborn, practised nude swimming and sunbathing, and, as we shall see in the next chapter, did nude gymnastic exercises before an open window for many years.

This curious interest, so at odds with Kafka's dandyism and self-consciousness about his own body, stems from several different sources. On the one hand, the nudist movement was part of a historical reaction throughout northern Europe against the civilizing excesses, moral prudishness, and stylization of *fin-de-siècle* culture. This movement was often coupled with a Rousseauian return to Nature and anti-urbanism that especially appealed to the recently industrialized German and Austrian societies. And it appealed to Jews, who were often portrayed and saw themselves as 'deformed' by city life.[22] But Kafka's participation in this general revolt also had personal motives in his rejection of his father's fancy-goods business. It is surely no coincidence that he

[21] The mix of progressive and reactionary politics in Naumburg's theories should not go unnoticed. 'Ours is a battle for a more developed humanity', he wrote, that must be waged against 'decadence in all its forms: untruthfulness, nervous exhaustion, senility, perversity, and self-destruction' (*Die Kultur des weiblichen Körpers*, 12). Schultze-Naumburg took over direction of the Weimar architectural school in the late 1920s after the Bauhaus group had been forced out, writing Nazi propaganda treatises such as *Kunst aus Blut und Boden* and *Rasse und Kunst*.

[22] The critic of modern 'degeneration', Max Nordau (Max Südefeld), later became an important figure in the Zionist movement and called for the development of 'muscle Jews' capable of affronting the difficult physical life in Palestine. See Gilman, *Jewish Self-Hatred*, 291.

should take such an active interest in clothing reform, which aimed at eliminating precisely the kind of constraining, stylized, and 'unnatural' clothing accessories that were sold in his father's fancy-goods business. Off with the fashionable fetters of the soul, the material signs of the hated Prague, the father's *Geschäft* and morally unclean existence.

In addition to its political aims, the clothing reform movement also raised the question of artistic style, of a modern aesthetics of everyday life, of the *Jugendstil* body as a 'natural' work of art. In fighting against repressive clothing, Naumburg was not advocating mere simplicity or lack of style: just as the urban dandy turned his physical appearance into a theatrical, artistic spectacle, the author of *Promoting Art in the Home* wanted to make modern reform clothing into a popular, lived realm of art. Designed for the modern woman's life-style, functional for her work in and outside the house, the reform garment also provided a pleasing, aesthetic experience for both wearer and observer. Because it covered the body loosely, it could slide across the body's surfaces, adapt to its lines in a ceaselessly changing play or 'dance' of cloth against human form. Like Oskar Bie's aestheticized participants in the dance of modern *Verkehr*, Naumburg's reform-clad 'women of the future' resemble an ensemble of nubile dancers. 'Above all I have one image in mind', he writes:

> a dancing mass of people dressed in long, opaque robes which directly touch the 'naked' body so that its beauty moves together with the cloth folds, creating a new unity. Whoever has truly appreciated Greek sculpture like the Parthenon frieze will understand what unbelievably dreamlike beauty I have in mind. Of course, if corset and lace petticoat have to be worn underneath, all beauty will be lost. (*Kunst und Kunstpflege*, 55)

Naumburg's attention to the aesthetic possibilities of modern clothing differentiates him from those reformers who contented themselves with extolling the 'natural' beauties of the naked body. Adolf Just, the founder of the Jungborn nature retreat whom Kafka met in 1912 during his visit there, writes that 'the so-called reform garment, which I have helped introduce through my writings and personal example', was initially perceived as 'unaesthetic'—a charge he counters merely by noting that the body is more beautiful if left 'as Nature has formed it'.[23] A painter and an architect, Naumburg had a far more sophisticated eye for the aesthetic play of colour and material in clothing. Hence his relative tolerance for the 'follies of fashion', since fashion had recently introduced a wealth of colour and tasteful forms into German everyday life, thereby elevating the common (female) aesthetic sensibility:

For it is a fact that women's sense of colour, in so far as it is expressed in their attire, has been improving. The first step was the transition to colour, to a general enjoyment of colour, which produced a noticeable refinement. Moreover, this phenomenon is not limited to the ten thousand women of the upper classes; a refined sense of colour is spreading from the domain of high fashion to domestic interiors, middle-class houses and apartments. (*Kunst und Kunstpflege*, 55)

Naumburg's insistence on the democratic potential of reform aesthetics is consistent with the general attitude of the *Kunstwart* editors, who supported modern cultural and social reform while maintaining a conservative attitude to artistic tradition.[24] At the centre of their concern was the human body as an aesthetic surface. 'We appreciate in art the spiritual aspect of human beings', Naumburg announced,

but we appreciate it through the vehicle of the body. How false is the claim that a person's physical appearance is deceptive, that the external surface has nothing to do with the inside. On the contrary, I believe that the smallest spiritual particularity is expressed in the body. Every person wears precisely what he or she is, and only that, on public display. (*Häusliche Kunstpflege*, 125)

IV

Naumburg's conception of the body as a *Jungendstil* spectacle both coincides with and departs from Kafka's own fascination

[23] *Kehrt zur Natur zurück!* (Blankenburg in Harz: Verlag der Heilerdegesellschaft Luros, 1896; 12th edn. 1930), 220.

[24] In an article entitled 'Fashion and Reform Garment', Avenarius wrote that all fashions, even the most 'illogical', display a distinct aesthetic quality. 'I only know that we reformers wish for a *basis* of clothing that is reasonable, which therefore as the *expression* of reason is pleasing and which *simultaneously* allows for the development of the secondary aesthetic elements [*Nebenwerte*].' 21 (Apr. 1908), 7–8, Avenarius's italics.

with the body as an expressive surface. From his earliest writings to the last stories in *A Hunger Artist*, he never ceases to delight in depicting the human body and its capacity for gestural expression. At times the body disappears behind its clothed, ornamental surface, as in the opening pages of *Description of a Struggle*: 'The hostess stood in the middle of the room and made agile bowing movements, while the ornate folds of her skirt swing back and forth'.[25] In the same story Kafka is capable of undressing the human (female) body, turning it into an illuminated spectacle intensely observed by two male protagonists: 'Her neck was bare save for a black velvet ribbon around her throat; her loosely clothed body was stooped and kept stretching as she went down the stairs before us, holding the lantern low' (*CS* 10). With a few strokes of his pen he can sketch a girl's clothes and body in movement: 'The blonde with short, disheveled hair. Supple and lean as a leather strap. Coat, blouse, skirt, nothing else. Her stride!' (Diary entry in Jungborn, 12 July 1912). The common element here is that the body, however Kafka depicts it, is the site of performance and observation. The moving, gesturing (though not necessarily human) body is at the centre of his fictions, as it is in his materialist conception of writing and art. Almost without exception, his artist figures are artists of the human body: the circus rider (*Kunstreiterin*) in 'Up in the Gallery', the Hunger Artist, the trapeze artist in 'First Sorrow', even Josephine the singing mouse and K'.s two comical and uncanny assistants in *The Castle*, prose extensions of figures from the Variety and the Yiddish theatres. Kafka's presentation of the body is of course more complex, ironic, and, at times, aggressively unaesthetic than Naumburg's rather naïve unity of body and form. None the less, the latter's *Jugendstil* views provided him with a starting-point for an obsession with the body *in movement*, in the suggestive if ultimately undecipherable act of gesture and self-expression, that he never gave up.

It is at this point that one should mention Kafka's own *Jugendstil* drawings, which Max Brod published in posthumous editions of

[25] The published English version of this passage is flattened, and I therefore quote from Version B in the parallel edition of *Beschreibung eines Kampfes*, ed. Ludwig Dietz (Frankfurt: Fischer, 1969), 11, my translation.

his works. Virtually all of these drawings take as their subject human and animal bodies in motion. (No landscapes or still lifes by Kafka are known other than a sketch of Goethe's garden house in Weimar, which is in the process of burning down.) Kafka's 'stickmen' drawings, often reproduced on the cover of his writings, constitute a separate, non-*Jugendstilian* aesthetic. But other drawings, like the Japanese tumblers balancing on a ladder, or the rotund figure rendered with a single rapid line, display the chief characteristics of the *Jugendstil* aesthetic: flowing, virtually unbroken lines depict the moving body that verges toward the point of abstraction. In an influential and programmatic essay entitled 'The Art of Line' and published in *Ver Sacrum* in 1902, for instance, Franz Servaes argued that the chief merit of modern (i.e. *Jugendstil*) art was to have recognized 'the beauty of the *unbroken* line. . . . And thus it discovered in line the symbol of movement . . . Line is and will remain modern; it alone is the adequate expression of modern sentiment'.[26] This moving line, as in Kafka's drawings, tends toward the abstraction of modern dance, which itself is conceived of as the movement of abstract *Jugendstil* forms. 'Just as in Loie Fuller's [serpentine dances] the hemline of her dress curls and flows', Servaes recalls, 'so does the line in modern ornamental forms curve and bend, rise and sink in a movement that streams by, snake-like, impossible to grasp, held together merely by its own rhythm' (95).

The dance is in some ways the supreme art-form of the *Jugendstil*, one that engaged the human body and the play of line, form, colour, and music in an actual performance. Naumburg and Kafka both shared this idealized conception of the dance, which used the human body as a material surface, as a painting or sculpture come to life and set into movement. The serpentine dances of Loie Fuller; Isadora Duncan's combination of ballet, Greek gymnastics, and long flowing clothing; Emile Jaques-Dalcroze's gymnastic dances for large groups, all caught their attention and are part of the same *Jugendstil*, modern sensibility announced by Servaes.[27] In his study of the counterculture

[26] Reprinted in J. Mathes (ed.), *Theorie des literarischen Jugendstils*, 96–8, my translation.

[27] Oskar Bie's conception of modern 'traffic' is of course intimately related to dance.

movement in Ascona, the 'home of modern dance', Martin Green notes:

> One of the earliest photographs of Monte Verita shows the colonists wearing reformed dress, hand in hand for a round dance. . . . People discussed Darwin's *Expression of the Emotions in Man and Animals* (1872), which contained photographs by Reijlender, and talked about unconscious body gestures. Then Spencer's *First Principles* . . . posited rhythm as universal in nature. Above all, Nietzsche had given Zarathustra dance songs, and in *The Birth of Tragedy* had described a god-like dancer who becomes a work of art, in whom the productive power of the whole universe is manifested.[28]

An enthusiastic reader of Wagner and Nietzsche, Isadora Duncan predicted in 1903 the emancipation of woman and female beauty through the 'Dance of the Future': 'Oh, she is coming, the dancer of the future: the free spirit, who will inhabit the body of the new woman: more glorious than any woman who has yet been: more beautiful than . . . all women of past centuries—the highest intelligence in the freest body!'[29] Green comments, 'Isadora strove to idealize the music, not to mirror or echo it . . . She was a *Seelentänzer*, a "soul dancer", to use the term of the times' (*Mountain of Truth*, 170).

Kafka particularly admired the dancer's *absorption* in the artistic process. When Diaghilev's Russian ballet performed in Prague in 1913, he saw the dancers as the embodiment of technical mastery and artistic perfection: 'last night the Russians were magnificent. Nijinsky and Kyast are two flawless human beings; they are at the innermost point of their art; they radiate mastery, as do all such people' (letter to Felice Bauer of 19 January 1913). He also took an interest in experimental dance forms, visiting the Dalcroze school in Hellerau in 1914 and writing with uncommon enthusiasm about Dalcroze's use of 'rhythm gymnastics', which alone surpassed in his view the beauty of the Russian ballet. As Green notes, 'Dalcroze aimed at a spiritualization of the body, at having

[28] *Mountain of Truth: The Counterculture Begins, Ascona, 1900–1920* (London: University Press of New England, 1986), 169. Kafka will later come into contact with one of the most famous members of the Ascona movement, Otto Gross. See Green, *Mountain of Truth*, 40–3, and Ch. 6 below.

[29] Gordon McVay, *Isadora and Esenin* (Ann Arbor, Mich.: Ardis, 1980), as quoted by Green, *Mountain of Truth*, 169.

freedom, health, nature, triumph over the artificial clothes and shoes and postures and hair styles of 1900. This was *Seelentanz*' (*Mountain of Truth*, 170).

In Kafka's literary writings, dance is repeatedly associated with the notion of beauty and freedom. Gregor Samsa's insect legs 'dance . . . as if set free' in the opening, lyrical moments of his metamorphosis. In a rare verse passage in the fourth octavo notebook, Kafka draws on the notion of 'soul dance' to celebrate the moving body in bucolic freedom:

> Little soul,
> you leap in the dance,
> lay your head in warm air,
> lift your feet out of gleaming grass,
> which the wind sets into gentle motion.
> (DF 108)

In elliptical, almost haiku form, these lines invoke the dance of a pure body, one that has been freed from its urban clothing and can move with the rhythm of Nature. It is the dance that all of Kafka's imprisoned protagonists long to perform, and which we generally witness only through its absence.

Kafka also introduced other types of performance which, like the dance, foreground the body as an object of aesthetic interest. The gymnast, acrobat, trapeze artist, circus horse-rider, singing mouse, or hunger artist—these figures have all externalized their art into visible corporeal display. What interests Kafka in these figures is the impersonality of a body that has been subjected to constant training and exercise, a body that is 'flawless' because it has been absorbed by the artistic process itself. In dance and other visual spectacles of the body, the literal identification between artist and artwork works to efface the performer's individual 'personality'. Thus the French critic Mauclair could describe Loie Fuller's dance as a 'poème dégagé de tout appareil du scribe'. And as Paul Valéry remarked of her serpentine dances, she withdrew from the work, burying the human form in masses of silk and lighting effects, achieving an impersonal discontinuity with Nature.[30] In

[30] Both references are taken from Frank Kermode's 'Poet and Dancer before Diaghilev', *Partisan Review* (Jan.–Feb. 1961), 69.

all of Kafka's artist figures, the question of psychological depth has been abandoned, their 'inner' truth revealing itself in corporeal performance.

Kafka's heterogeneous mix of circus performers, dancing and singing dogs, gymnasts, and Japanese tumblers corresponds to a similar conception of 'lived' art promoted by the *Kunstwart* contributors. Naumburg pleaded for instance for a 'Variety theatre of the future', a music-hall in which dancers, trapeze artists, wrestlers, and clowns would be recognized as 'true' artists. 'Couldn't the artistic form of the performances and other qualities offered by the Variety have an elevating effect?' he asks. The music-halls 'should dress their athletes and gymnasts in such a way that the movement of their muscles . . . is brought out' (*Kunst und Kunstpflege*, 51). He prefers spectacles of the body in motion to static, 'boring' contests of physical strength. And he regrets that trapeze artists perform at such heights that 'the actual motif, the body, is no longer visible' (52). Singling out the clowns, mime artists, trained dogs and apes of the music-hall who, in their own peculiar way, have realized the *Jugendstil* fusion of life and art, body and artwork, Naumburg dreams of the ideal, 'undogmatic' stage of the future:

> At times I dream of a future music-hall, of an 'undogmatic stage' raised to the level of art where beautiful, amusing, interesting, and exciting events can be represented that would be out of place in respectable plays with plots and action. . . . Then what appears to us today as the evil enemy of art may appear as one of the most important aids toward artistic development. (59–60)

In a sense he could not know, Naumburg was anticipating Kafka's literary version of this variety show. In tandem with much of the literary and artistic impulses of the turn of the century, from Hermann Bang's trapeze artists in 'Four Devils' to Picasso's or Rilke's circus figures, Kafka will be increasingly drawn to such 'unrespectable' milieux, to the melancholy world of the circus, the music-hall, the cabarets. The Yiddish theatre of Yitzak Löwy, with its pantomime, folk-songs, dances, and emphatically gestural acting, will provide him with an additional variation of this spectacle of the artistic body in motion. Even when the setting is not explicitly theatrical, his protagonists often behave like performers from the circus or the music-hall, with dubious artistic and social status. Hence the synchronized movements of the seven 'artistic dogs' in 'Investigations of a Dog', reminiscent of the trained dogs of the Variety, but also true artistic masters who have something of Nietzsche's musical, Dionysian spirit:

> [S]even dogs stepped into the light. . . . They did not speak, they did not sing . . . but from the empty air they conjured music. Everything was music, the lifting and setting down of their feet, certain turns of the head, their running and their standing still, the positions they took up in relation to one another, the symmetrical patterns which they produced by one dog setting his front paws on the back of another and the rest following suit until the first bore the weight of the other six . . . great masters all of them, keeping the rhythm so unshakably. (*CS* 281)

Kafka is not always so lyrical. The human acrobats and circus performers who once seemed to him a model of artistic freedom and absorption are often depicted in an increasingly ironic light. Red Peter, the circus ape in 'A Report to an Academy' who still remembers his freedom as an untrained, undomesticated animal on the Gold Coast, has only scorn for the European Variety theatre:

> In variety theatres I have often watched, before my turn came on, a couple of acrobats performing on trapezes high in the roof. They swung themselves, they rocked to and fro, they sprang into the air, they floated into each other's arms, one hung by the hair from the teeth of the other. 'And that too is human freedom', I thought, 'self-controlled movement'. What a mockery of holy Mother Nature! Were the apes to see such a spectacle, no theatre walls could stand the shock of their laughter. (*CS* 253)

Of course, it is not enough to point out the thematic continuity between Kafka and the *Kunstwart*'s *Jugendstil* aesthetics. One also needs to examine how he transformed these motifs for his own purposes, setting them into the complex situations of his stories and novels. This will be the task of the readings of individual texts offered in the subsequent chapters of this book. Here I have attempted to show that the *Jugendstil* initially provided Kafka with an alternative to *fin-de-siècle* 'decadence' and the 'traffic' of clothes, with an artistic and social ideal that sought to liberate the body from its material fetters, transforming it into a beautiful, healthy organism, a 'lived' artwork. However far Kafka eventually moved from this *Jugendstil* vision, he never gave up the notion of the body as the primary object of artistic expression and self-representation. Simpler 'modern' clothing, reform garments, the naked healthy bodies of gymnasts and swimmers, the self-absorbed bodies of dancers and circus animals—this broad range of 'body artists' exercised an unmistakable influence on his own writing, if often as a Utopian, unrealized ideal or, like the blooming Grete in *The Metamorphosis* and the panther at the end of 'A Hunger Artist', as a bitter emblem of contrast. As we shall see in the following chapter, the figure of the gymnast becomes an explicit model for him as he attempts to discipline his body into something more than an ornamental surface of *Jugendstil* line and colour—something he calls a writing 'organism', a 'machine'.

3

Body Culture: J. P. Müller's Gymnastic System and the Ascetic Ideal

> For those who are at once the priests and the victims [of dandyism], all the complicated material conditions to which they submit, from an impeccable toilet at every hour of the day and the night to the most perilous feats of the sporting field, are no more than a system of gymnastics designed to fortify the will and discipline the soul.
>
> (Baudelaire, 'The Painter of Modern Life')

I

THE *Jugendstil* impulse to aestheticize the body was intricately related to another movement, at once complementary and antagonistic to this aestheticization, that sought to vitalize, harden, cleanse, and 'modernize' the body. In the *Kunstwart*'s issue of August 1904, under the title 'Body Culture', a certain Heberlin objects to *fin-de-siècle* 'decadence', to the woman 'who can neither stretch upwards nor bend to the floor', to the dandy 'who uses only cars and lifts rather than his legs', to all creatures physically debilitated by modern forms of urban life (410). He also rails against the deformation of the body brought about by clothing, against the 'stiffening and crippling of [women's] hips and feet', which is only part of a more general, physically inhibiting process of socialization (411). To counteract these symptoms of decadence he recommends to his readers an American exercise manual that sets forth a 'complete system' of 'psychic, aesthetic and physical culture'.[1] His aim is to improve not only the health of the individual but that of the entire nation, whose 'folk body' is

[1] *Dynamic Breathing and Harmonic Gymnastics: A Complete System of Psychical, Aesthetic and Physical Culture* (New York: G. Stebbins, 1893).

threatened with 'degeneration' (*Entartung*): 'If things continue as they have, our race will degenerate, nay, it is already deep in the process of degeneration, and . . . if things continue thus, salvation will be impossible' (414).[2]

Similar ideas, if not always couched in the same racial and proto-fascistic language, were extremely common in Kafka's circles. The *Neue Rundschau*, the foremost literary journal of the time which Kafka read regularly after 1903, also addressed the theme of *Körperkultur*. In 1908 Norbert Jacques described a modern dwelling that was divided into two parts: 'one serves the gymnastics of the body, the other the gymnastics of the soul'.[3] This turn-of-the-century habitat encourages the harmony of body and mind, of physical and spiritual cultures: 'Thus a programme of physical culture leads to two results: it cleanses and purifies the body while making it more beautiful. It has a beneficial effect on one's inner life and provides visual pleasure to one's companions' (927).[4]

In a recent study on German nationalism and sexuality, George Mosse has interpreted the 'rediscovery of the body' at the turn of the century as a reaction against 'bourgeois respectability'. Unlike the writers and artists of the decadent movement, who rebelled by cultivating an aesthetically stylized, artificial way of life, the proponents of the emerging physical culture movement

[2] The political consequences of such rhetoric are well known. On the one hand it coincided with the development of a German nationalist, right-wing cult of physical 'regeneration', which went back to *Turnvater* Jahn's gymnastic clubs and concluded with the racial policies of the Third Reich. But Zionist groups also espoused a similar programme of physical regeneration. See George Mosse, *Nationalism and Sexuality: Respectability and Abnormal Sexuality in Modern Europe* (New York: Howard Fertig, 1985); Kohn, 'Father Jann and the War against the West', in *The Mind of Germany: The Education of a Nation* (New York: Harper & Row, 1960); S. Gilman, *Jewish Self-Hatred: Anti-Semitism and the Hidden Language of the Jews* (Baltimore: Johns Hopkins University Press, 1985); G. Baioni, 'Zionism, Literature and the Jewish Theater', in M. Anderson (ed.), *Reading Kafka: Prague, Politics, and the Fin de Siècle* (New York: Schocken Books, 1989).

[3] 'Ein modernes Gebäude', 926.

[4] One should also note the numerous articles in the *Selbstwehr* (*Self-Defence*) about the Jewish gymnastic associations in Prague in the first decades of the century. Max Nordau's call for a new generation of 'muscle Jews', liberated from centuries of debilitating ghetto life and capable of enduring physical hardship in Palestine, was part of a widespread interest in Zionist circles for a physical regeneration of Jews.

championed the naked, unadorned body as the symbol of personal freedom, purity, and youth. 'Its champions', Mosse notes,

> refused to hide their bodies as society demanded, and instead sought to expose them to the healing power of the sun and the rhythms of nature. . . . Those who led this revolt were for the most part young, and their rebellion went beyond books and journals to inspire youth movements, sports, and eventually an entire new national consciousness.[5]

For Mosse this athletic revolt against bourgeois convention is separate from decadent or modernist movements, and heralds the National Socialist cult of nature and classical beauty. In fact, the body culture movement drew support from a broad political and cultural spectrum that included not only right-wing German nationalists, but also Social Democrats, anarchists, Zionists, and 'decadent' or 'modernist' artists and writers.[6] The Prague circle of Jewish writers was no different. Max Brod, whose early writings were written in the purple hues of *fin-de-siècle* decadence, recalls the frequent outings he made to the countryside in the first decade of the century with his friends and future modernist writers, Kafka and Franz Werfel:

> Kafka and I were avid hikers. Every Sunday, often Saturdays as well, we were in the forests surrounding Prague whose beauty encouraged a cult of innocence and enthusiasm. . . . We swam in the forest streams, for Kafka and I lived then in the strange belief that we hadn't possessed a countryside until a nearly physical bond had been forged by swimming in its living, streaming waters. . . . Soon Werfel was introduced into our secret clan of nature worshippers. One beautiful summer Sunday we took the train to the pure silver waters of the Sazawa, undressed in the middle of a forest, in nature (which we greatly preferred to the civilized swimming establishments), listened to the resounding new verse of [Werfel's] *World Friend* as naked river and mountain gods, and swam for hours in the rushing waters. This sublime, Hellenic summer day lingers forever in my memory.[7]

[5] *Nationalism and Sexuality*; 48–50.

[6] Thus the Young Vienna circle of aesthetes—Hofmannsthal, Hermann Bahr, Adrian—were also passionate cyclists who took long trips together in the neighbouring countryside. Stefan George, who more than any other figure helped introduce the French 19th-century 'decadents' Baudelaire and Mallarmé into contemporary German literature, also insisted on a neo-Hellenic ideal of physical beauty and discipline as the basis for a new literary classicism.

[7] *Streitbares Leben* (Frankfurt: Insel, 1979), 22–3.

If this portrait seems incongruous with the conventional image of Kafka and his life in Prague, it is in part because critics have worked with ideological schematizations like Mosse's, dismissing Kafka's interest in physical culture and the various aspects of the naturalist movement as a personal quirk or *Reinheitsfanatismus* (as Wagenbach termed it) that has little to do with his writing.[8] Even as familiar an observer as Max Brod, while allowing that Kafka 'was always interested in *Naturheilkunde* in all its various forms, such as the raw food diet, vegetarianism, Mazdaznan, nudism, gymnastics and anti-vaccinationism', declared such interests to be 'beyond' rational analysis.[9]

In fact, if there is a single element of continuity in Kafka's writing, it is his preoccupation with the body—what he perceives as a debilitated, 'decadent', inferior body—and a corresponding interest in programmes of physical renewal, diet, fresh-air and sun cures, and natural healing. What for Werfel and Brod was only a passing youthful flirtation with physical culture, for Kafka remained a lifelong belief that bordered on a religion. The following chapter will attempt to probe the relationship between Kafka's writing and his interest in physical culture. Beginning with his perception of his own body as unhealthy and debilitated, I will sketch his effort to remedy this problem through various methods of physical culture, focusing on his commitment to J. P. Müller's programme of home gymnastics and his trip to the Jungborn sanatorium in the Harz mountains in 1912. A final section will trace the motivic as well as stylistic effect that 'body culture' had on his writing, concluding with a brief discussion of the related

[8] See *Franz Kafka: Eine Biographie seines Jugend* (Berne: Francke, 1958). Kafka's other biographers—H. Binder, E. Pawel, R. Hayman—are similarly dismissive about this point.

[9] See his commentary to Kafka's Jungborn diary of 1912. Brod also notes that Kafka's 'attitude to the "natural health methods" and reform movements of a similar nature was one of very intense interest . . . Fundamentally he saw in the efforts to create a new healthy man, and to use the mysterious and freely proffered healing powers of nature something extremely positive which agreed with many of his own instincts and convictions, and which he widely put into practice too. He slept with the window open all the year round. When you went to his place to see him, the cool fresh air there was a thing that struck you. He always wore light clothing, even in winter, went for long periods without eating meat and drank no alcohol' (*Franz Kafka: A Biography* (New York: Schocken Books, 1947; enlarged edn. 1960), 109–10).

turn from *Jugendstil* to avant-garde modernism in German and Austrian culture in this period.

II

Throughout his life Kafka was plagued by poor physical health and a perception of his body as physically inadequate—too weak, too thin, too tall for the requirements of writing. Moreover, he felt that there was a direct relation between his body and his development as a writer. On 22 November 1911 he noted in his diary:

> It is certain that a major obstacle to my progress is my physical condition. Nothing can be accomplished with such a body. . . . [It] is too long for its weakness, it hasn't the least bit of fat to engender a blessed warmth, to preserve an inner fire, no fat on which the spirit could occasionally nourish itself beyond its daily need without damage to the whole. How will the weak heart that lately has troubled me so often be able to pound the blood through all the length of these legs? . . . Everything is pulled apart throughout the length of my body.

This perception is aggravated by a sense of his body's fragmentation, of the discrepancy between consciousness and individual body parts. 'How far away, for instance, are the muscles of my arms', he writes in his diary in 1911. His attention focuses on individual corporeal details: 'The lobe of my ear felt fresh, rough, cool, succulent as a leaf, to the touch' (spring 1910, *D1* 11). But this attention leads only to despair: 'I write this very decidedly out of despair over my body and over a future with this body'. On 20 October 1911, he reports that 'I am probably sick, since yesterday my body has been itching all over', again focusing on his body's lack of unity: 'Also the connection between stomach and mouth is partly disturbed, a lid the size of a gulden moves up or down, or stays down below from where it exerts an expanding pressure on my chest'.[10]

Precisely because of this sense of the body's fragmentation there arises a will to piece the body together, to restore the

[10] Much of this sort of material was removed by Max Brod when he first edited Kafka's diaries, as the recent critical edition of the *Tagebücher*, ed. H.-G. Koch, M. Müller, and M. Pasley (Frankfurt: Fischer, 1990), has revealed.

harmony of its missing unity. Elias Canetti, one of the few critics attentive to the corporeal dimensions of Kafka's writing, remarks that Kafka 'is attracted to what the practitioners of natural healing recommend, because of their conception of the body as a unity; he concurs wholeheartedly in their rejection of therapy for particular organs'. Hence also his interest in 'swimming, exercising naked, leaping wildly up the stairs at home, running, long walks in the country which enable him to breathe freely'—'every activity', as Canetti remarks, 'that demands and restores unity of the body'.[11]

Like most boys in German-speaking countries at the turn of the century, Kafka learned to do gymnastics or *turnen* in school. 'They put me through a thorough course of gymnastics', he writes in an autobiographical fragment of 1910, 'and if I have nevertheless remained rather small and weak, that just couldn't be helped' (*D1* 22). He continued to practise these callisthenics and acrobatics (*turnen* implies both) after graduating from high school, either in one of Prague's public *Turnhallen* or on the gymnastic apparatus set up in bathing establishments. During a trip to Paris in 1911, for instance, he performed a series of acrobatic manœuvers on a knotted rope hung over the water, as Max Brod admiringly noted in his diary.[12]

Beginning sometime around 1908 or 1909 and continuing through the years of his major literary works ('The Judgment', *The Metamorphosis*, *Amerika*, and *The Trial*), Kafka also followed the exercise programme of the Danish gymnast and pedagogue J. P. Müller, performing them twice a day, naked, in front of an open window in his bedroom. Kafka continued the Müller exercises for many years, although he probably stopped them at the outbreak of his tuberculosis in 1917. When a version of the system for women was published in 1913, he sent a copy to Felice, pedantically insisting that she follow the exercises to the letter: 'I absolutely insist upon the Müller exercises, I am mailing the book today; if they bore you, it shows you are not doing them

[11] *Kafka's Other Trial* (New York: Schocken Books, 1974), 28–9.

[12] Cf. *Max Brod: Franz Kafka: Eine Freundschaft: Reiseaufzeichnungen*, ed. M. Pasley (Frankfurt: Fischer, 1987), 123. Kafka's diary entry for the same incident (which was omitted from the English edition) has a slightly sinister ring to it and makes no mention of his own performance: 'In a swimming school a knotted rope hangs over the water for gymnastics.'

properly; try hard to do them exactly as prescribed' (*F* 304). Three years later, in November 1916, he still felt they were important, insisting that 'these exercises cannot be improvised; they have to be studied, have to be studied beforehand' (*F* 510).

First published in Denmark in 1904, and in Germany the following year, *My System* resembled other programmes of physical renewal at the turn of the century in its comprehensiveness. More than just a set of callisthenics, it proposed a *Weltanschauung*, a philosophy of life designed to improve the well-being of both individual and society, offering suggestions about diet, clothing, hygiene, sports, medicine, mental as well as physical health, aesthetics, and ethics. Like the *Kunstwart* author Heberlin, Müller had a moral mission that was directed against the deleterious effects of *fin-de-siècle* culture. 'There are people of both sexes', he writes in the introduction,

> who coquettishly indulge their infirmities and try to make themselves interesting in the belief that their pale and sickly appearance is an undeniable sign of their aesthetic and spiritual inner qualities. . . . A portion of the authors of our *belles-lettres* have done incalculable harm to the young people in our society by systematically championing, through personal example as well as through their writings, a mixture of exclusively intellectual culture, physical weakness, and moral sickness. Fortunately, there are signs that the worst effects are over. And thus we who work for the physical and therefore moral progress of society may now expect to find an audience.[13]

While Müller addressed himself to a broad audience, he was particularly concerned with the 'victims' of modern urban life such as office workers, whose unhealthy and sickly appearance he describes with evident relish:

> The typical office worker in big cities is often a sad sight. Hunched over in early years, his shoulders and hips made crooked by the awkward position at his desk, his face pale, pimply, and powdered, his thin neck sticking out of a collar that a normal man could use as a cuff, his foppish, fashionable suit rotating around pipe-cleaners that are supposed to be arms and legs.

Müller also addressed himself to intellectuals and artists, whose 'spirit works in higher spheres' and who tend to neglect their

[13] *Mein System* (Copenhagen: Holger Tillge, 3rd edn. 1905), 7. All translations are my own.

bodies. Noting that the majority of composers and writers die 'in their thirties', he laments that many literary and musical treasures have been lost because 'these geniuses had no thought for the health of their bodies' (40–1).

The success of Müller's manual, which went through five printings in the first few months of publication, reveals the need for such reform programmes at the turn of the century. Kafka shared this contemporary enthusiasm. His ambivalence about the physical effects of urban life, already strong in his university years, no doubt increased in 1907 when he began full-time employment as an office worker for the Workmen's Compensation Institute. If one adds to this his perception of himself as a 'Western Jew,' whose supposedly enervated, 'decadent' physique was a common theme among anti-Semites as well as Zionists in the contemporary press, one can begin to understand Kafka's long-standing attachment to Müller's system.[14] Although his thinking about physical culture, nudism, diet, and medicine may not necessarily stem from this programme, he certainly received systematic guidance from the Danish athlete in his effort to improve his physical condition. In any case, their agreement on a number of issues is striking and deserves to be looked at more closely.[15]

Consider for instance Müller's concern with the body's intake of food and air: 'Many people make themselves sick by committing mortal sins against hygiene—those who always wear a corset and carry a parasol, who stuff themselves daily with strong drinks and heavy, undigestible food, and constantly breathe into their lungs and bloodstream the pestilent air that they themselves and others, sitting in the same room, have exhaled and depleted of oxygen' (8). He recommended a diet of raw vegetables, fresh fruit, milk, and cheese; alcohol, strong spices, rich sauces, and

[14] Kafka describes himself in a letter to Milena Jesenská of November 1920 as 'the most Western-Jewish' of the 'Western Jews' in his circle (*M* 217).

[15] Max Brod erroneously dates the beginning of Kafka's interest in naturalism to his visit to the Warnsdorf garden city in 1911, where the industrialist Schnitzer recommended 'sleeping with the windows open, sun-bathing, working in the garden, joining . . . a club for natural healing' (*Biography*, 109). Kafka's first references to Müller date from 1909, and he may have been familiar with the latter's views earlier.

large quantities of meat and fish were to be avoided. Less was better than more: 'There are more people who slowly eat themselves to death, than there are who die of hunger. So you should always eat less than you think is filling . . . a good portion of the food can be expelled undigested' (28). Modifying Feuerbach's dictum that 'Man is what he eats' (*der Mensch ist, was er ißt*), Müller writes that '"Man is how he eats" or "how he digests".' Prophetic words for the likes of Gregor Samsa or the Hunger Artist!

Like other contemporary movements of physical culture, Müller's ideal is not the muscular frame of the body builder but the beauty of the Greek athlete—a naked, desexualized, agile, 'clean' body in symbiotic relationship to the 'movement of Nature'. The cover of his exercise manual depicts a Greek sculpture of *The Scraper*, a nude athlete cleaning himself after competition. This neo-classical ideal forms the basis of his vitalistic philosophy:

> Use fresh air and cold water, let the sun shine on you and don't let a single day pass without setting every muscle, every organ of your entire body, if only for a short while, in vigorous motion. To remain stationary is against the law here, as in all of nature, and leads to decay and an early death. Movement is life; it increases and preserves the vital forces to a normal, advanced end to life. (9)

Generally moderate in his reform proposals, Müller displays an almost fanatical obsession with cleanliness. He conceives of the body's surface as a living sponge, capable of absorbing atmospheric impurities and secreting its own refuse, which needs to be removed immediately to prevent reabsorption (17). For this reason he insisted that his exercises be done in conjunction with wet-towel rubbings and a bath to free the body from dirt, dead skin cells, sweat, and other 'poisons', as well as to stimulate cardiovascular circulation and the internal organs. The bath was to be taken with cold water ('the best for one's nerves') which, if one wished, could be freshened with a handful of table salt (61).

Anyone familiar with Kafka's frequent complaints about the weakness of his blood, heart, lungs, digestive tract, and 'nerves' will recognize the appeal Müller's exercises must have held for him. The Danish athlete was promising a corporeal Elysium—a strong, healthy, resistant organism in which separate organs and body parts would function as a unified whole. But he was also offering another path of revolt against the bourgeois 'respectability' of Kafka's parents, against the 'traffic of clothes'. Indeed, Müller's system was directed as much against bourgeois clothing as it was for an improvement in the body's physical health and appearance. 'Mornings, get out of bed,' he instructed the reader at the beginning of his descriptions, 'and put on your trousers (or reform underwear) and sandals! . . . Evenings or while changing during the day, take your clothes off!' (47) Müller also had a number of specific suggestions concerning the reform of contemporary clothing that did not differ significantly from those of Schultze-Naumburg or the Jungborn nudists. He objected to the corset, to tight-fitting collars, garters, socks, and shoes as detrimental to circulation of the blood. He preferred cotton and linen to wool because these materials allowed the body to 'breathe'. He advocated wearing a minimum of clothing at home, sleeping with open windows even in cold weather, and practising outdoor sports such as swimming and hiking, if possible in the nude. The underlying premiss of his system was that the body was its own best garment. Exposed regularly to the elements, it would gradually develop from an emaciated, enervated state until it could withstand the brightest sunlight and coldest temperatures.

In sum, *My System* seems to have provided Kafka with a sensible programme of exercise, hygiene, and diet which he felt would counteract the unhealthy aspects of his life in Prague; a programme that would unify, strengthen, 'reform' his body for the physical demands of his writing. Whether it actually improved his health is a matter of speculation. It did not prevent the outbreak of his tuberculosis, and Kafka probably had to renounce the cold baths and nude exercises in front of an open window in 1917, when his tuberculosis was diagnosed. But he remained committed all his life to the nude fresh-air sessions and vegetarian fare that Müller recommended, the rigours of the exercise system giving way to more tranquil cures in sanatoria. His letters to Milena Jesenská from Merano in 1920 report that he spent much of the day sunning himself nude in the garden. Even at the end of his life, in the sanatorium in Kierling where his weight had shrunk to less than 50 kilograms, Kafka rested 'half-naked on the balcony' in the vain hope of curing himself by natural means.

III

Kafka's trip to Weimar, Leipzig, and Jungborn in the summer of 1912 was undertaken in the dual spirit of literary creation and body culture.[17] The first part of the journey was no doubt organized by Brod and had a professional aim. In Leipzig they visited the young editors Ernst Rowohlt and Kurt Wolff, Brod arranging for publication of a literary anthology of Prague writers[18] and paving the way for that of his friend's first book, *Meditation*. In Weimar they visited the naturalist writer Johannes Schlaf (who spoke to them about his geocentric astronomical theories), Goethe's house, and the national literary archives. For the second half of the trip Kafka travelled alone to a place that can scarcely have appealed to his Zionist friend: the nature retreat Jungborn (Fountain of Youth), where *Naturheilkunde* and body culture were practised as a religion with distinctly Christian overtones.[19]

Founded by Adolf Just in 1896, Jungborn was famous for its naturalist philosophy of spiritual renewal through physical culture. Guests slept in open-air huts or in the grass, did group callisthenics in the nude every morning, sang Christian hymns in open-air religious services, took natural spring waters and mud baths, and attended lectures on vegetarianism, clothing reform, and natural medicine. Martin Green has recently noted that Adolf Just

[16] Unpublished letter of May 1924 to his parents, recently discovered in Prague.

[17] Kafka visited other *Naturheil* health centres, including the Erlenbach sanatorium in Switzerland and the garden city Warnsdorf in 1911 (cf. *L* 73–5 and Brod, *Biography*, 109). Full documentation exists however only for the trip to Jungborn.

[18] *Arkadia*, published in 1913, would include Kafka's story 'The Judgment'.

[19] In Warnsdorf too naturalism took on a religious aspect. The industrialist Schnitzer, who examined Kafka there and supposedly discovered poisons 'in his spinal marrow and almost up to his brain', explained the Bible from a vegetarian standpoint. As Kafka reported to Brod after returning to Prague: 'Moses led the Jews through the desert so that they might become vegetarians in these forty years. Manna as a meatless diet. The dead quails. The longing for the "fleshpots of Egypt." Even more clearly, in the New Testament Jesus addressed bread with the words, "This is my body"' (Brod, *Biography*, 109).

was the most moral and spiritual of these [nature cure] doctors. He had suffered from nervous diseases in the 1880s, and in 1896 opened the Jungborn Anstalt in Eckertal in the Harz, where men could live a paradisal life in nature. His book of that year, *Kehrt zur Natur zurück!* (Back to Nature), was a great success . . . Just said everyone should be his own doctor and make use of the four great therapeutic means that nature supplies—mud, diet, light and air baths, and the cold rubdown. Just's medicine was explicitly Christian, he quoted from the New Testament and called Jesus the first nature cure doctor. His book's subtitle runs, in translation, *The True Natural Method of Healing and Living and the True Salvation of the Soul—Paradise Regained.*[20]

In this rural Christian setting, Kafka took part in the *Naturheil* activities with the other (mostly non-Jewish) guests during the day, reserving his evenings for reading and writing. His diary from this period gives us a sampling of the Jungborn philosophy. From a lecture on clothing reform he notes on 9 July: 'The feet of Chinese women are crippled in order to give them big buttocks.' From the same lecture, given by a doctor and follower of Mazdah (the god of Zoroastrianism), he quotes: '"Though your toes may be completely crippled, if you tug at one of them and breathe deeply at the same time, after a while it will straighten out." A certain exercise will make the sexual organs grow. . . . It is impossible to clean the kind of clothes we wear today!'

Although reluctant to show himself completely naked, Kafka participated in the morning washings and callisthenics, which the guests did as a group outdoors: 'This morning: washing, setting-up exercises, group gymnastics (I am called the man in the swimming trunks), some hymn singing, ball playing in a big circle . . . Pitched hay in the afternoon' (*D2* 303). The nudity of the other guests bothered him, as is clear from his rather testy entry for 11 July: 'When I see these stark-naked people moving slowly past among the trees . . . I now and then get light, superficial attacks of nausea. . . . They come upon you so silently. Suddenly one of them is standing there, you don't know where he came from. Old men who leap naked over haystacks are no particular delight to me, either'. The following day he notes: 'With Dr. Sch. (forty-three years old) on the meadow in the

[20] *Mountain of Truth: The Counterculture Begins, Ascona, 1900–1920* (London: University Press of New England, 1986), 159.

evening. Going for a walk, stretching, rubbing, slapping and scratching. Stark naked. Shameless.'

One should not fail to note the incongruity of Kafka's presence at Jungborn; after all, the writer who had discovered the Yiddish theatre and his own Jewishness with such enthusiasm the year before was hardly a likely candidate for Just's Christian revivalism. Further, the nudity at Jungborn can only have been a source of embarrassment for the physically self-conscious Kafka, who was always reluctant to stand out as a Jew in Christian circles. (This may be the real reason for his unwillingness to shed his trunks.) He also had to endure the proselytizing efforts of the other guests, including a land surveyor from Silesia who belonged to a Protestant revivalist movement, to whom Kafka steadfastly maintained that there was 'no prospect of grace' for him at the time, referring instead to his own 'inner voice' (14 July).

However uncomfortable or out of place Kafka may have felt at Jungborn, the overall tenor of his remarks is distinctly positive and gives us an indication of the strength of his opposition to Prague, the office, and his 'confinement' in his parents' apartment at this relatively late stage in his life. Jungborn gives him a sense of 'wonderful freedom', of pleasant 'independence', as he writes to Brod on 9 July. He can lean against the door of his cabin 'like a houseowner', can read at his leisure, without being disturbed by the noise in the family apartment in Prague, can 'walk alone in the woods or lie in the meadows'. His reading includes Flaubert and Goethe, and one night he dreams that he heard Goethe reciting 'with infinite freedom and spontaneity' (diary entry for 10 July). He has brought with him his own literary Bible, Flaubert's *L'Éducation sentimentale*, which he reads at night alongside Just's Christian tracts and chapters from the Old and New Testaments. Most of all he is free to write. The 'inner voice' he refers to above is clearly his literary imagination, which he hopes will be stimulated by the Jungborn setting. He has brought with him the first draft of his 'American novel', which he works at throughout his stay.

As it turned out, Kafka's expectations were not immediately fulfilled. The first letter to Brod of 9 July notes that although the 'independence' at Jungborn gives him 'an inkling of America' (a curious but unmistakable reference to his novel), and although he has taken long solitary walks in nature, 'none of this stimulates the desire to write. If that is on its way, at any rate it hasn't yet arrived in the mountains'. The next day he is overjoyed to receive a poem Brod has written for him and writes back that it 'will remain the adornment of my hut, and when I wake up at night . . . I will read it by candlelight'. On the other hand, he is 'hapless and sad' at his inability to drive his novel forward: 'I get in a tangle with the very first sentences I want to write. I have already discovered that I must not let the dreariness of what I have already written deter me.'

Part of Kafka's problem was the food at Jungborn, which he felt upset the delicate balance between writing and eating. In a passage that reveals his physical conception of the writing process (and points to works like *The Metamorphosis* and 'A Hunger Artist'), he claims:

My chief affliction consists in my eating too much. I am stuffing myself like a sausage, rolling in the grass and swelling up in the sun. I have the silly idea of wanting to make myself fat, and from there on curing myself in general . . . *There is definitely a connection that my scribbling goes more slowly than in Prague.* (*L* 80, my emphasis)

Here we find one of the chief conflicts in Kafka's life, one that he was never able to resolve and was part of his own *Hungertod*. On the one hand he felt he had to nourish, strengthen, 'fatten' the body with healthful food and natural cures to 'engender a blessed warmth, to preserve an inner fire'. On the other his own writing 'organism' insisted on an ascetic dieting that made his body ever thinner, lighter, less substantial, until it became as ethereal as 'music'.

Near the end of his stay at Jungborn, Kafka concludes that he has written only 'in a lukewarm bath', not with the true fire of inspiration; he has not experienced 'the eternal hell of real writers' (letter of 22 July). He refuses to show Brod the manuscript of his novel, 'which is being worked in small pieces, more strung together than interwoven', and may cost him his 'sanity'. Three weeks after arriving in Jungborn he returns to Prague—physically renewed, his 'craving for people' satisfied, but without any of the tangible literary results he had hoped for. Although he could not know it at the time, he was close to experiencing the 'hell of real writers'. But that would erupt in Prague, in the heart of urban and familial *Verkehr*.

IV

Kafka's interest in Müller's system and the Jungborn *Körperkultur* is more than a biographical curiosity. To measure its true importance, one would need to write a phenomenology of the body in his texts, as well as—and perhaps more crucially—a phenomenology of his texts *as* a body, as a linguistic corpus with its specific energies, rhythms, movements, and stylistic 'hygiene'.[21] Admittedly, on a strictly motivic level little of Müller's health regime or Adolf Just's rural paradise appears as such in Kafka's literary texts.[22] For the most part his protagonists remain trapped within the 'traffic of clothes'—in the dark, airless, cramped spaces of the city, their bodies disfigured or deformed. And they are almost always clothed. But as Adorno noted in another context, Kafka's work is like the negative of a Utopian photograph: one must read it in reverse, as the depiction of what the author struggled *against* in the social world, not what he dreamed of privately.[23]

None the less, there is one figure which testifies to Kafka's interest in body culture that is not merely transformed into its ironic negative: the writer as gymnast or acrobatic *Turner*. This figure appears suddenly and inexplicably at the end of 'The Judgment', which Kafka wrote in September 1912, little more than a month after returning to Prague from Jungborn. The story is well known and has been subjected to so much critical scrutiny that there is no need for a full analysis here. But one should note that, like almost all his works, the text is structured by the opposition between paternal *Verkehr* and filial isolation. At the beginning of the story Georg Bendemann is about to take over

[21] Cf. the articles by M. S. Pasley in Anderson (ed.), *Reading Kafka* and H. Lehmann in G. Kurz (ed.), *Der junge Kafka* (Frankfurt: Suhrkamp, 1984).

[22] An exception is the 'Nature Theatre' chapter of *Amerika*, whose outdoor setting and Christian resurrection symbolism bear a vague relationship to the Jungborn experience.

[23] Cf. T. Adorno, 'Notes on Kafka', in *Prisms*, trans. S. and S. Weber (Cambridge, Mass.: MIT Press, 1983), 252–5.

his father's business and, through his impending marriage, his father's sexual role in the family. In other words he is poised to enter the 'traffic of clothes', understood in the sense of the German term *Verkehr* outlined in Chapter 1. This notion finds graphic condensation in one terrifying image, a *Schreckbild* which literally drives Georg to his death—that of his father lifting his nightshirt above his knees in imitation of Georg's fiancée's purported sexual advances:

> 'Because she lifted up her skirts,' his father began to flute, 'because she lifted her skirts like this, the nasty creature,' and mimicking her he lifted his nightshirt so high that one could see the scar on his thigh from his war wound, 'because she lifted her skirts like this and this you made up to her. (*CS* 85)

Confronted with this doubly terrifying image of paternal authority and female sexuality, Georg is driven from the room by primal instincts to the river ('es trieb ihn zum Wasser'). Yet instead of leaping wildly from the bridge as one might expect, he executes an artful gymnastic 'turn' of the body: 'He swung himself over, like the accomplished gymnast he had once been in his youth, to his parents' pride . . . and let himself drop. At that moment an unending line of traffic was streaming over the bridge.'

How should one interpret this curious and seemingly unmotivated figure of the gymnast? On the one hand the horizontal explosion of city traffic (*Verkehr*) across the bridge; on the other the artful performance of the gymnast (and model child). The answer, I would suggest, lies in Kafka's own activity as a writer. At the end of this night of inspired composition, having experienced for the first time the fire of true literary creation, Kafka sees himself as the literary gymnast, sure of his technique, certain also of the quality of the text he has just finished writing, perhaps about to stand up and perform the Müller gymnastic exercises before going to bed. The traffic that streams across the bridge is not just an image of urban life, but the liberated energy of the writer, the *Verkehr* of literary creation. Georg Bendemann plunges to his death, but the gymnast-writer comes to life. And in this moment he becomes again the model son of his parents' wishes, 'a son after [the father's] own heart'.

This reading is supported by a series of references to the writer as gymnast or acrobat that recur throughout Kafka's writing from 1910 until his death. Crucial to this figure is the capacity for aerial ascension. Already in early texts like 'The Tradesman' or *Description of a Struggle*, we have seen how vertical movement is associated with the flight of artistic imagination (the shopkeeper who fashions an embellished speech as he rises in the lift, the protagonist of *Description* who climbs the Laurenziberg and engages in a series of literary capriccios). But in the gymnast the human body itself has become the artwork. More radically than the Jugendstil dancer, the gymnast possesses a pure body, the sign of which is his ability to perform without solid ground under his feet, to rise into the air, twisting and turning his disciplined, light, 'clean' body into a variety of forms. The *Turner* or gymnast is a *Luftmensch*, whose primary abode is not amidst the 'traffic' of everyday social relations but above and outside this world, suspended in mid-air. He thus comes to stand in Kafka's work for an ideal artistic economy, an entity that relies on a minimum of force for maximum expressivity and that has freed itself from the constraints of a material existence.

The above German terms bear on Kafka's conception of the acrobatic writer and require elucidation here. The word for gymnastics, *turnen*, although historically related to 'Turnvater' Jahn and the development of a nationalist gymnastics movement at the beginning of the nineteenth century, is etymologically related to the notion of 'turning' (as the English cognate suggests) and thus lends itself as a figure for literary metaphors and 'turns of phrase'. What the *Turner* accomplishes with agile turns of the body in midair is achieved by the writer through turns of language: tropes, *Rede-wendungen*, rhetorical figures. Thus Kafka associates the image of the turning body with notions of performance, play, *Spiel*, amusements, and the like—all as figures for the ethereal, non-workaday activity of art and writing, his literary gymnastics.

But the gymnast is also related to the *Luftmensch* (literally 'air person'), a term Max Nordau used in a famous essay of 1901 to designate East European Jews without employment or fixed abode who were forced to beg for a living.[24] Kafka, following his encounter with the *Luftmenschen* of the Yiddish theatre, takes the term literally, depicting the artist as a 'groundless' being, often an animal rather than a human being, who hovers in the air. His aerial ascension is proof not of artistic discipline and purity, but of social and ethical senselessness. Thus the floating canine protagonists in 'Investigations of a Dog' are *Luftmenschen* or rather *Lufthunde*, whose artful, acrobatically co-ordinated movements provoke the narrator's genuine admiration. Yet the 'superb sureness' of the dogs' corporeal movements, the 'wonder' of their ability to float through the air, is undercut by the senselessness of their existence: 'They have no relation whatever to the general life of the community, they hover in the air, and that is all, and life goes on its usual way; someone now and then refers to art and artists, but there it ends' (*CS* 294).

The first of Kafka's many references to *turnen* as an ideal of literary creativity occurs in his diaries in early 1910. Complaining of his 'unhappiness' and his 'inability to write', he imagines Japanese acrobats 'who scramble up a ladder that does not rest on the ground but on the raised soles of someone half lying on the ground, and which does not lean against a wall but just goes up into the air'. 'I cannot do this', he laments (*D1* 12). Kafka is so taken with this image that he interrupts his written description with a drawing, capturing in a few strokes of his pen the graceful insubstantiality of the admired acrobats. Consider also the equestrienne or *Kunstreiterin* in 'Up in the Gallery', the two-paragraph story Kafka published as part of the *Country Doctor* collection in 1917. The German term makes clear that this female acrobat is an artist, literally an 'art rider', horses and riders often symbolizing

[24] Steven Aschheim writes in *Brothers and Strangers: the East European Jews in German and German Jewish Consciousness, 1800–1923* (Madison, Wis.: University of Wisconsin Press, 1982) that Nordau, in his address to the Zionist Congress of 1901, 'popularized that peculiarly Jewish notion of the *luftmensch*. Today it has come to mean a kind of spiritual, rootless intellectual figure, but this is not the meaning that Nordau originally gave to it . . . *Luftmenschen* were an entire class of grown, tolerably healthy men who were unemployed and wandered around in the hope of obtaining a piece of bread by the end of the day . . . the Jews of the ghetto had become a *Luftvolk*—they had no capital for the present and no reserves for the morrow' (87).

literary inspiration in Kafka's work.[25] The first paragraph depicts her as 'frail' and 'consumptive', forced to execute the same performance before an insatiable public and whom the lonely gallery spectator finally rescues (though only in his imagination). The second paragraph depicts her as she 'actually' is: the ideal, ethereal exemplar of artistic body culture, a beautiful lady who 'floats in between the curtains', mounts and rides the horse with consummate 'artistic skill', performs her great aerial turn on the horse, dismounts, and exults in her ovation. Here the image of a gravity-defying, acrobatic turn of the body is set in the context of performance and public spectacle, which itself becomes a figure for Kafka's own gracefully cadenced, 'turning' text.

One of Kafka's last stories, 'First Sorrow', takes up the 'art' of trapeze acrobatics hailed by Schultze-Naumburg, here described as 'one of the most difficult humanity can achieve'. Again we are presented with the example of a *Turner*, the acrobatic body offered as artistic spectacle high above the ground of quotidian experience. And again this art is set against the horizontal *Verkehr* of the world below him—the vexing but unavoidable train rides between performances, and the generally vulgar realm of the impresario. By contrast the world of the trapeze is depicted as 'beautiful' in the reform sense of the term: 'it was quite healthful up there, and when in the warmer seasons of the year the side windows all around the dome of the theater were thrown open and sun and fresh air came pouring irresistibly into the dusky vault, it was even beautiful' (*CS* 446). And yet the trapeze artist who lives almost completely within the realm of art is a melancholy, suffering figure, obsessed by the idea of always holding only 'the one bar in my hands' and who asks himself how he can go on living. As in the 'Investigations of a Dog', the ideal of corporeal freedom and the artist's superior distance above society (his 'height') merge with the problem of a 'groundless' existence. Art is a superfluous, 'suspended' activity that denies the artistic

[25] M. S. Pasley writes that 'the metaphor "horse" for "story" or "rider" and "horse trainer" for "narrator" runs through all Kafka's writings'. 'Die Handschrift redet', *Franz Kafka: der Process*, Marbacher Magazin, No. 52, 1990. See especially the horses that emerge from a pigsty in 'A Country Doctor'.

Luftmensch a firm place in the world. His only connection is the wooden 'bar' in his hands, manifestly a symbol for the writer's pencil.

Interestingly enough, the notions of body culture and the gymnast-writer are at work even in texts that superficially seem to have nothing to do with them. Gregor Samsa in *The Metamorphosis* is a perfect specimen for Müller's regime. A salesman whose health has been undermined by office work and 'constant traveling' (*Verkehr*), by 'bad and irregular meals', he wakes up to find his body transformed into something monstrous. But, oddly enough, once he overcomes his initial shock and accepts his new form, this strange body has an unusual agility, quickness, and lightness. He experiences a sense of 'physical comfort', noting with joy that his many legs are 'completely obedient' and even strive to 'carry him forward in whatever direction' he chooses (*CS* 102). He discovers that his body allows him to climb the walls and hang from the ceiling where he rocks to and fro in a state of self-absorbed contentment. He resembles in other words the artistic *Turner*, with all the social isolation and ethical senselessness that this existence implies. But like the gymnast he can fall from a great height without harming himself, his hard shell (like Müller's 'muscle corset') protecting him from the fall. Gregor's demise also takes place in conformity with Müller's warnings. Deprived of fresh air, sunlight, and fresh food, his room and body covered with filth, Gregor eventually succumbs to the closure of his petty bourgeois, *fin-de-siècle* environment. His sister Grete however blossoms with new strength, as if their bodies were in a negative symbiotic rapport, one waxing as the other wanes. At the story's conclusion she is in perfect health and performs what might well be an exercise taken from Müller's exercise manual: 'At the end of their journey [Grete] sprang to her feet and stretched her young body' (*CS* 139).

Consider finally the infrequently read text 'The Aeroplanes in Brescia', Kafka's account of an aviation competition he witnessed while on vacation in Italy and which he published in the Prague newspaper *Bohemia* in September 1909. Already in this early piece Kafka sees a similarity between the writer and the air-borne pilot, describing the French aviator Rougier sitting 'at his control board like a writer at his desk'.[26] Rougier 'ascends in small circles, flies over Blériot [his competitor], turns him into a spectator and never stops climbing upward' (24). Like the trapeze artist in 'First Sorrow' who performs at such a height that he disappears from view, Rougier 'turns' higher and higher with his machine until one thinks that 'his position can only be determined by the stars' (25). Substitute the aeroplane for the hardened, disciplined body of an acrobatic *Luftmensch*, the aviator's circles for the gymnast's corporeal 'turns' high above the ground, and one can recognize an extreme version of Kafka's writing ideal at this time: the ascetic body that 'turns' around itself, oblivious to its public, rising into the air until, inexplicably, it disappears and is forgotten. Here, as in Kafka's overtly fictional texts, 'traffic' provides the horizontal ground for the artist's vertical ascension. 'Rougier is still climbing, but we travel deeper and deeper into the *campagna*' (25).

V

The importance of *Körperkultur* for Kafka's writing is not limited to the motif of the *Turner*, but forms an essential part of his notion of a strong, self-absorbed writing 'organism'. On 3 January 1912 he noted in his diary a spontaneous ascetic impulse in his body toward this ideal:

> It is easy to recognize a concentration in me of all my forces on writing. When it became clear in my organism that writing was the most productive direction for my being to take, everything rushed in that direction and left empty all those abilities which were directed toward the joys of sex, eating, drinking, philosophical reflection and above all music. I dieted in all these directions. . . . My development is now complete and, so far as I can see, there is nothing left to sacrifice.

Later that same year, after the breakthrough experience of 'The Judgment', Kafka had time only for the essential activities of office work, eating, sleeping, and . . . the Müller exercises. In a letter to Felice Bauer of 1 November 1912 he noted that his mode of life 'is devised solely for writing, and if there are any changes,

[26] *Die Aeroplane in Brescia*, with an afterword by Reinhard Lettau (Frankfurt: Fischer, 1977), 24.

then only for the sake of perhaps fitting in better with my writing'. His daily schedule is as follows:

> From 8 to 2 or 2:30 in the office, then lunch till 3 or 3:30, after that sleep in bed . . . till 7:30, then ten minutes of [Müller] exercises, naked at the open window, then an hour's walk . . . then at 10:30 . . . I sit down to write, and I go on, depending on my strength, inclination, and luck, until 1, 2, or 3 o'clock, once even till 6 in the morning. Then again [Müller] exercises, as above, but of course avoiding all exertions, a wash and then, usually with a slight pain in my heart and twitching stomach muscles, to bed.

Kafka's ascetic, even monastic devotion to literature later proves to be the prime obstacle to marriage. In a now famous letter to Felice Bauer of 14 August 1913 (at the end of which he insists she follow Müller's *System für Frauen*!), he declares himself to be 'made of literature': 'I have no literary interests, but am made of literature, I am nothing else, and cannot be anything else'. The ideal of body culture has turned the body itself into literature.

In Kafka's radically ascetic devotion to art one can recognize the ideal of the 'l'art pour l'art' movement, which sought to constitute art as an autonomous realm 'above' empirical bourgeois existence. Flaubert, Nietzsche, Stefan George, the young Hofmannsthal, and Thomas Mann had all given Kafka the belief in art as a religion and justification for life. The writer was to serve this religion by dedicating himself completely to his craft as an ascetic, bachelor-artist. Kafka pushed this ideal to a radical, self-denying extreme. By 1912 he had largely discarded the more obvious trappings of *fin-de-siècle* aestheticism. Gone were the top hats, silk cravats, the dandy's interest in 'gentlemen jockeys', the taste for rare books and the habit of speaking in hushed tones; but the impulse to merge with his writing remained. In other words, the core of the aestheticist philosophy was still intact, although around it had arisen the notion of the strong, clean, functional, modernist body of the *Turner* fully absorbed by the physical demands of writing.

This focus on body culture and the corresponding purge of what might be loosely termed 'ornament' had far-reaching implications for Kafka's literary style. The drastic change in his writing that took place between 1907 and 1912 cannot be discussed fully here; it will be treated in Chapter 7 in connection with 'In the Penal Colony', where the problematic of the body as a writing *machine* is explicitly developed. Here one can observe simply that the stylistic change from early texts like *Description of a Struggle* or the self-consciously literary letters to Oskar Pollak to 'mature' works like 'The Judgment' or *The Metamorphosis* is one of progressive 'ascesis': *Jugendstil* ornament, precious phrasings and antiquated spellings, musical embellishments, bizarre or far-flung metaphors, and other features of his early writing are purged for the sake of a rigorously limpid, modern German in dramatic narrative form. To put it in terms of body culture: the written corpus sheds its *fin-de-siècle* 'clothing' in order to stand on its own, 'naked', as pure literature.

As we have seen, Kafka's attempt to reform his body physically was part of a broad cultural movement in northern and central Europe at the turn of the century. The stylistic *ascesis* he subjected his writing to is paralleled by a similarly ascetic movement in literature, architecture, and other arts, a turn away from the flowery, baroque adornment of *fin-de-siècle* culture to an unadorned, 'muscular' neo-classicism that later became known as modernism. Adolf Loos's 1908 architectural manifesto against the *Jugendstil*, 'Ornament and Crime',[27] is only one in a series of phenomena signalling a break with nineteenth-century forms for a modern 'anti-style' of non-ornamental, unadorned functionalism. Modern bodies, buildings, artworks, and texts were all to conform to an aesthetics of functional purity. Kafka's characteristic prose style is a significant part of that series.

Like all artistic developments, even those that advertise themselves as radical departures from the past, the modernist rejection of *fin-de-siècle* ornament went through various stages. The *Jugendstil* is here clearly a transitional movement. Linked to aestheticism by its winding, vegetal arabesques, it also anticipates the unadorned functionalism of modernism in its emphasis on youth, nudity, vitality, and open geometric forms. Of course, what appear to the later cultural historian as distinct phenomena coexist in a

[27] See ch. 7 and my discussion of 'In the Penal Colony'.

confusing welter to the contemporary observer; in the first decade of this century, 'decadent' eroticism, *Jugendstil* aestheticism, and neo-classicizing forms of body culture appeared as interrelated aspects of a modern revolt against bourgeois tradition. The three corresponding impulses in Kafka's early development that I have attempted to depict in these first three chapters, while not entirely contemporaneous, none the less largely coexist until 1910–12, at which point they would seem to disappear. The burden of the following five chapters, all of which are organized as formal readings of individual works but which also draw on contemporary historical sources, will be to demonstrate the legacy of *fin-de-siècle* ornament and aestheticism in the stories and novels written after the breakthrough of 'The Judgment' in late September 1912, texts that form the basis of Kafka's reputation as one of the arch-modernists of German and European fiction.

4

Kafka in America: Notes on a Travelling Narrative

> Given that all objects are located in a continuously changing time and illumination, and we spectators no less so, we always encounter these objects in a different place.
>
> (Kafka, 'Über Apperzeption')

> Le moral, c'est le travelling.
>
> (Jean-Luc Godard)

I

No, Kafka never went to America. But he did imagine it and, as we know, gave an astounding presentation of this new world—though perhaps not the world we commonly mean when we say 'America'—in his first novel, *Der Verschollene*, which Max Brod later published under the title of *Amerika*. In scope, style, and subject-matter the novel differs sharply from his earlier work, most of which is set in the European context that Kafka knew first hand. Why did he choose America, and especially New York, as a subject of representation for his first sustained literary project? What did this city represent to him? And what bearing did the notion of 'America' or 'New York' have on the literary texts he had already written?

The key to these questions is again the notion of *Verkehr*, which in this novel (unlike the commerce of fancy goods in earlier texts) retains the primary significance of 'traffic'. Kafka was fascinated by the movement of traffic in the modern city and, more important, by the aesthetic spectacle and metaphysical dilemmas this movement implied. This fascination coincides with a general shift in European art, philosophy, and science that was taking place at the turn of the century: a shift away from the representation of people and things securely rooted in a stable, constant environment, and toward a relativized perception of things in motion, of subtle or unconscious displacements of energy, fluctuating or ephemeral patterns of circulation and exchange. Increasingly, artists, philosophers, and scientists were turning to the analysis of phenomena that earlier generations would have avoided as too unstable, transitory, intangible or illogical to capture in a stable representation, be it artistic or scientific. What French Impressionist painters had achieved and made into a cliché as early as the 1880s continued to dominate other fields of thought throughout the *Jahrhundertwende*. As cursory, almost random examples of this tendency—all of which Kafka had direct knowledge of—one might single out Einstein's theory of relativity; or Brentano's phenomenological analyses; or Freud's charting of the displacements of unconscious psychic energies; or Mach's use of statistical analysis to account for sense impressions and to refute the idea of a stable, unifying 'ego'.[1]

In *Meditation* and *Description of a Struggle*, as we have seen, the notion of *Verkehr* already subsumes a variety of meanings that include not only traffic, but commerce, exchange, circulation, social and sexual intercourse. It also implies the metaphysical and epistemological destabilization of modern life, the literal representation of traffic serving as a 'vehicle' for a more general concern with the problem of appearance, with the place of the subject in a merely apparent or *scheinbaren* world, and with the grounding of discourse in such an unstable terrain. To put it most simply and abstractly: in his early work Kafka is always concerned with the apparent groundlessness of material reality, that is, with *things in motion*.

A rare insight into Kafka's thinking about this problem while still a student can be gleaned from his unfinished theoretical essay

[1] Einstein was professor of physics at the University of Prague and briefly frequented the Fanta salon, where he met Brod and Kafka (H. Binder (ed.), *Kafka-Handbuch* (Stuttgart: Alfred Kröner, 1979), i. 289). Brentano, whose work inspired Husserl, had many disciples in Prague, including Anton Marty, whose influence on Kafka is documented (K. Wagenbach, *Franz Kafka: Eine Biographie seiner Jugend* (Berne: Francke, 1958), 113–17; Binder, *Kafka-Handbuch*, i. 75–6). Ernst Mach, with Freud perhaps the key scientific figure in Vienna in terms of his influence on contemporary literature, also taught in Prague; one of his disciples there was Adolf Gottwald, Kafka's science teacher in the gymnasium (Wagenbach, *Biographie seiner Jugend*, 54).

'On Perception' ('Über Apperzeption'), which Max Brod first published in his history of the Prague circle in 1966, but which has been strangely neglected by subsequent research. A polemic response to Brod's articles on aesthetics in *Die Gegenwart* of 17 and 24 February 1906, the five philosophical propositions in Kafka's essay insist that perceptions are always 'new': 'for given that all objects are located in a continuously changing time and illumination, and we spectators no less so, we always encounter these objects in a different place'. Hence perception is not a state but a movement—'Apperzeption ist kein Zustand, sondern eine Bewegung'. Kafka then attempts to illustrate this proposition with the example of a person without any sense of place ('ganz ohne Ortsgefühl') who comes to Prague as if it were a foreign, unknown city and who therefore cannot perceive it.[2]

The big city—*die Großstadt*—was a common theme in German literature at the turn of the century, and New York often served the European imagination as a hyperbolic version of its own urban and futurist tendencies. Oskar Bie's celebration of Berlin and Paris in his essay *Social Intercourse*, as we have seen, inevitably led him to New York, 'the world city of American life itself', whose tremendous quotidian movement was known to earlier cultures only during religious holidays.[3] But whereas Bie and Schulze-Naumburg in his *Kunstwart* essays tend merely to aestheticize urban existence, Kafka insists on the depersonalizing, dispersive effects of the city on individual consciousness. Karl Rossmann is in fact a character without any 'sense of place' who arrives in a foreign city and, because he cannot perceive it, is 'dispersed' by its vast, impersonal energies. Yet Kafka never overtly sentimentalizes his plight. The narrative voice remains impassive, seemingly non-judgemental, content to register and describe rather than condemn or celebrate—as if it had taken on something of the mechanical, depersonalized quality of *Verkehr*

[2] *Der Prager Kreis* (Stuttgart: Kohlhammer, 1966), 94–5, my translation. Brod had maintained in his articles that 'the category "beautiful" should simply be replaced by the category "new"', and that a 'new perception' (*neue Apperzeption*), subjectively reworked, would constitute 'the essence of beauty'. He sees in Kafka's counterargument an affinity with Schopenhauer's notion of a 'will-free intellect' as well as Hofmannsthal's Lord Chandos 'Letter'. Cf. 93–4.

[3] *Der gesellschaftliche Verkehr* (Berlin: Gurlitt, 1905), 7.

itself. In this respect he differs from the majority of his contemporaries, whose vision of the big city is filtered through an emotional, sentimental register of individual 'loneliness' or 'alienation'. Consider by way of contrast the following passage from Max Brod's early *Jugendstil* novella, 'The Carina Island' (1906):

From the infinite silence of the night emerged a humming, constantly interrupted tone . . . like a mysterious pulsing of millions of restless hearts, like a profound lament of unfulfilled beings. Their hearts break, the human beings all go to their perdition. . . . But the tone of profound lament survives in all eternity. It is the magic nocturnal song of the big city, an endless murmuring melody which the lonely man, shuddering, hears in the valley of houses from his distant spot on a mountain face.[4]

A glance at Kafka's figuration of the big city in his earlier texts provides an instructive contrast to *Amerika*. With its ornate traffic, the modern city in *Description of a Struggle* offers a giant stage for theatrical performance, quotidian mini-spectacles, street 'happenings'. But accident and randomness break into this stylized, mechanized realm, unmasking its disordered temporality, violence, and falsehood. 'Isn't it true that these Paris streets suddenly fork out in different directions?' asks the Supplicant anxiously. 'They're turbulent [*unruhig*], aren't they? Not everything is in order there—how could it be? Sometimes there's an accident, people gather together from side streets with that big city stride that hardly touches the pavement . . . they breathe fast and crane their tiny heads forward' (*CS* 43). The big city as a theatrical, depersonalized space marked by its 'traffic' and hence by the problem of 'accident'—of *Unfall*, but also contingency (*Zufall*), chance, and death—this, roughly speaking, is the double optic through which Kafka's early texts view the modern world.

Kafka's interest in traffic and travel in the literal sense plays a key part in his thinking through 1912 and the writing of *Amerika*. During his summer vacations in 1909, 1910, and 1911, he travelled to Italy and France with Max Brod, conceiving with him the idea of launching a series of budget travel guides. (Called 'On the Cheap', it was meant as a rival to Baedeker.) No doubt with

[4] 'Die Insel Carina', in *Experimente* (Berlin: Axel Juncker, 1907), 33–4, my translation.

Goethe and Flaubert in mind, both of them kept a travel diary of their impressions during these trips that was meant to foster their literary work. They also began a novel about a railway journey entitled *Richard and Samuel*, each of them writing alternate chapters in order to create a 'stereoscopic' narrative perspective in keeping with the traveller's own movement and changing point of view. And one of Kafka's first published texts, 'The Aeroplanes in Brescia', records his perception of modern aerial *Verkehr* at an aviation contest in Italy in 1909, comparing one of the aviators to a 'writer at his desk'.

The trips to Milan and especially Paris in 1911 gave Kafka the opportunity to test the validity of his literary depiction of *Verkehr* against a true European metropolis. Not surprisingly, much of his Paris diary is devoted to the city's traffic network, understood in a broad but literal sense—subway lines, railroad tunnels, and street maps, but also water pipes, telephone and bell 'systems', messengers. (*D2* 280). It also focuses on the uncertain position of foreigners (observers who are 'ganz ohne Ortsgefühl') negotiating this traffic for the first time. Thus Kafka notes that:

> You recognize strangers by the fact that they no longer know their way the moment they reach the top step of the subway stairs; unlike the Parisians, they don't pass immediately from the subway into the bustle of the street. In addition, it takes a long time, after coming up, for reality and the map to correspond. (*D2* 281)

These scattered notations culminate in the diary's final entry—the five-page literary sketch of 11 September 1911 which narrates a traffic accident Kafka witnessed in front of the Opéra. As a literary work, the account is unsuccessful and loses itself in an undramatic, detailed elaboration of the spectators' responses to the accident. But it does reveal the focus of his literary imagination on traffic shortly before beginning the first version of *Amerika*. Indeed, the attention to the various stories provoked by the accident (rather than to the accident itself) indicates an attempt to weld together the subject of *Verkehr* and literary narration. This tactic however leads to a personalization of traffic and a rather traditional attempt at characterization—precisely the opposite of what he had already achieved in his earlier texts and would insist on a year later in depicting 'das allermodernste New York'—the 'most up-to-date New York' (letter to Kurt Wolff of 25 May 1913).

II

Before turning to Kafka's depiction of *Verkehr* in *Amerika*, it is worth noting that his epistemological attention to things in motion tends to efface the objects of representation, as we can see in his earliest 'American' text, 'The Wish to Be a Red Indian'. First published in *Meditation* and probably written around 1908, it consists of the following hypothetical, unfinished sentence:

> If one were only an Indian, instantly alert, and on a racing horse, leaning against the wind, kept on quivering jerkily over the quivering ground, until one shed one's spurs, for there needed no spurs, threw away the reins, for there needed no reins, and hardly saw that the land before one was smoothly shorn heath when horse's neck and head would be already gone. (*CS* 390).

The peculiar movement of this text results in a progressive effacement of the ostensible object of representation, a process that operates as much on the level of images—the disappearance of rider, horse, and American plain (the 'quivering ground')—as on the grammatical and syntactical level of subjunctive verbs and unfinished hypothetical clauses. The text proposes itself as the possibility of an image ('If one *were only* an Indian . . . on a racing horse') that its own subsequent movement then retracts or suspends: 'no spurs . . . no reins . . . horse's neck and head . . . already gone'. The reader is left with no rider, no horse, and certainly no specific, geographically situated image of 'America', only a 'smoothly shorn heath' that one can hardly perceive.

The same is true on a larger, more complex scale of Kafka's first novel, which, as we know from his letter of 11 November 1912 to Felice Bauer, he intended to call not *Amerika* but *Der Verschollene*. The difference between these two titles merits some reflection. Unlike most novels of the nineteenth century, Kafka's texts are rarely located in a geographically or temporally specific landscape—a fact obscured by Max Brod's decision to publish the novel with the title that has since become famous. Everything in this text—and in a sense still to be defined, especially the novel's *Verkehr*—argues against this nominal localization. The actual title *Der Verschollene* defies any simple English translation: in German it indicates an unnamed person who has got lost in obscure circumstances and whose existence hangs in doubt. This loss is often the result of an accident (ship passengers lost at sea are *verschollen*) and can refer to persons as well as objects (like the first version of Kafka's novel). Etymologically, the title suggests a progressive silencing (from the verb *verschallen*, 'to die out').

Critics have overlooked the fact that Kafka probably derived the title for his novel from Arthur Holitscher's *Amerika: Heute und morgen* (*America: Today and Tomorrow*), a series of travel reports that was first published in the *Neue Rundschau* shortly before Kafka began work on the second version of his novel.[5] Holitscher's work also begins with the journey by ship to New York. Shortly before docking, he receives a telegram which prompts him to make the following observation:

> Up above on the sun deck, in this bizarre yellow city of smoke-stacks, windbreakers with gaping jaws, ventilators, swaying lifeboats and humming cables sits the little brown house [the ship's telegraph office] that establishes the bond between us, the missing ones [*uns Verschollenen*] and the secure world.[6]

But whereas Holitscher confidently asserts the stability of this connection, Kafka undermines it, seizing on the notion of a sustained *Verschollen-Werden*—an effacing and silencing of the object of representation—that becomes the actual subject of his novel, its starting-point but also its destination. Holitscher's book names and describes America, tours the famous landmarks and buildings, repeatedly seeks to situate both writing subject and reader in the new world. In one episode he takes the lift to the top of the Woolworth building, then the tallest edifice in the city, from which point he gives a panoramic description of New York

[5] The influence of this work in other regards has of course long been established; cf. G. Loose, *Franz Kafka und Amerika* (Frankfurt: Klostermann, 1968) and W. Jahn, *Kafkas Roman 'Der Verschollene' ('Amerika')* (Stuttgart: Metzler, 1965). Holitscher's travelogue first appeared in instalments in the *Neue Rundschau* in 1911 and 1912, in book form in the S. Fischer Verlag, Berlin, in 1912. Kafka later acquired the 2nd edition of this book (1913), which is the edition quoted here.

[6] The German text reads: 'Oben auf Sonnendeck . . . steht das kleine braune Haus, das die Verbindung herstellt zwischen uns Verschollenen und der sicheren Welt' (26).

and a brief history of his stay—there is the harbour where I arrived, there is my hotel. An anti-tourist guide, Kafka's novel works instead to undermine Karl Rossmann's position in the world, to deterritorialize and disfigure America's identifying signs, to un-name and silence the named. Thus, as in the text 'The Wish to Be a Red Indian', the reader is confronted with an image of America that presents itself with uncommon force and vividness, only to erase itself in a series of ambiguous, contradictory, anti-mimetic gestures.

In *Der Verschollene*, Kafka accomplishes this erasure primarily through the thematic and structural device of *Verkehr*. The novel presents itself as a text in motion, as a travelling narrative. Each chapter offers a new form of 'traffic' that propels the protagonist relentlessly into new circumstances: the steamship in the opening chapter gives way to the complex traffic patterns of New York City, to automobile and pedestrian movement along the highway, to the vertical *Verkehr* of the thirty lifts in the Hotel Occidental, to the sexual traffic in Brunelda's apartment, the race-track in Clayton, and finally to the train that leads to the Oklahoma 'Nature Theatre' (described as being perhaps a 'wandering circus'). Kafka's narrative is literally *unterwegs*, 'on the road', as a new mode of transport supplants the previous one in projecting the novel into an endless and in a certain sense timeless space of the 'American' continent.

A few examples of how this traveling text works to destabilize and defamiliarize Karl Rossmann's perception of the world will prove useful. The novel begins with Karl's sudden expulsion from his own family for having fathered the illegitimate child of the family's maid; that is, it begins by severing its protagonist from the network of familial, social, and linguistic relations that in more traditional novels customarily situates characters and events in a distinct milieu. Scarcely any reference is made throughout the novel to this past life, and the few tangible remains Karl has of it (notably his father's army suitcase and a photograph of his parents) are lost along the way.[7] Cut loose and cut off from his

[7] One apparent exception is Karl's memory of his rape-like seduction by Johanna Brummer, which he recalls only when his uncle pulls out a letter he has received from the maid. The way she is referred to, however, confirms the effacement of Karl's past:

past, Karl is free to experience a kind of rebirth in new, unfamiliar surroundings. But before he has time to adjust to these surroundings, to establish himself in a new set of personal and professional ties, the initial gesture of expulsion that sets Karl's voyage and the text into motion is repeated. The stoker, the uncle, Mr Pollunder and Clara, Robinson and Delamarche, the head cook and Theresa at the Hotel Occidental—all these characters momentarily allow Karl into their world only to expel him from it into another set of foreign circumstances. Like the text itself, Karl remains *unterwegs*, always on the outside, constrained to keep moving in a permanently renewed condition of exile that is reinforced by allusions to Adam and Eve's banishment from Paradise and the Jews' historical flight from Egypt (as in the chapter entitled 'The Road to Rameses').

The law of this type of narrative thus initially seems to be that characters do not return or, if they do, that their reappearance will not add up to any final effect or resolution of plot. Banished from one circle of relations to the next, Karl encounters in random fashion the aptly named vagabonds Delamarche and Robinson (the latter clearly a reference to Defoe's '*verschollene*' hero lost at sea). They too have been truncated from their past, placed in a foreign world, and forced to wander the streets. Karl and the reader never learn about their past in a way that would make their present situation, actions, and character intelligible. The novel does not project them into the future, but into an endless present, a temporal mode unorganized by any stable origin or destination. As a result, the reader must judge these characters on the basis of extremely vivid but fragmented descriptions that never turn into a cumulative history or story. In this sense the reader is in Karl's position *vis-à-vis* his uncle's unintroduced guests: 'For Uncle Jacob hardly ever said even a passing word about any of his acquaintances and always left it to Karl to figure out by his own observation whatever was interesting or important about them' (*A* 49).

'Karl had no feelings for Johanna Brummer. *Hemmed in by a vanishing past*, she sat in her kitchen beside the kitchen dresser' (*A* 27, my emphasis). Here, at least, the effacement of personal history is the result of sexual trauma and repression.

The curious flattening of character that results from this narrative technique is of course part of the peculiarity of Kafka's fictions as a whole and marks the distance between them and the psychological realism of nineteenth-century novels. Kafka's characters emerge in vivid, sharp detail—often 'present' like photographic likenesses as they execute some striking gesture—but only as partial, flat surfaces without the depth of a past history or individual psychology. This technique might be likened to portraits by Gustav Klimt in which a particular realistic anatomical detail, usually the face, is isolated against a two-dimensional gold surface. Kafka's characters are temporally flat—cut out of a historical continuum and presented to us as isolated, tantalizingly vivid, but finally opaque objects of interpretation.

The same destabilization of character in Kafka's novel also undermines his depiction of America as an identifiable, geographically defined location. Here the first disorienting image of Kafka's novel—the Statue of Liberty holding a sword rather than a torch—stands as a warning against those readers who would enter Kafka's 'America' as if it were a garden of mimesis. For after referring to this disfigured but still recognizable monument, Kafka's text stubbornly refuses to name any famous street, building, or tourist sight that would allow its readers to recognize and find themselves in the space Karl Rossmann traverses. The Hotel Occidental, Butterford and Rameses, Clayton and the Theatre of 'Oklahama' (as Kafka spelled it in the manuscript)—the few places marked with a proper name are so improbable, contradictory, or imaginary that they seem to constitute a mythical rather than a referentially verisimilar landscape. Indeed, in this improbable landscape even Kafka's apparent mistakes seem to take on a bizarre, 'postmodern' logic.[8] A bridge leads from Manhattan to Boston (rather than Brooklyn) and hangs over the Hudson (rather than the East River); Karl pays for a meal with pounds rather than dollars; a hotel only five stories high has thirty lifts and thousands of employees; a modern country house outside New York is slowly revealed to contain a Gothic labyrinth of

[8] Postmodern in the sense of Robert Venturi's *Complexity and Contradiction in Architecture* (New York: Museum of Modern Art, 1966), in which he argues for the deliberate juxtaposition of conflicting styles.

unlit corridors, a marble chapel, and bedrooms guarded by liveried servants bearing candelabra.

Unmarked or deliberately obscure transitions between scenes and chapters heighten the narrative's disorienting effects. Although Karl's journey begins in New York, we are never told where his uncle's apartment is situated. During the two months of his stay he lives in a confined, unidentifiable space that has nothing to do with 'New York'. Thus, when Karl looks at the city from a distance with Delamarche and Robinson during their 'March to Rameses' in chapter 4, his vision is oddly abstract, empty. His companions, however,

> clearly saw much more; they pointed to right and to left and their outstretched hands gestured over squares and gardens *which they named by their names.* They could not understand how Karl could stay for two months in New York and yet see hardly anything of the city but one street. And they promised, when they had made enough money in Butterford, to take him to New York with them and show him all the sights worth seeing. (*A* 112, my emphasis)

Needless to say, the text leaves the reader in Karl's position of disorientation: we know only that Robinson and Delamarche name the sites, not what they are called.

Similarly, when Karl leaves New York for Mr Pollunder's country house, he falls asleep during the ride and hence cannot tell how far or in what direction he has travelled. The dark, endless corridors of this house prevent him from finding his way in it, and when he finally escapes he chooses a 'chance direction' (*eine beliebige Richtung*') and sets out on his way. His random encounter with Delamarche and Robinson results in their march to Butterford, which is unexpectedly interrupted when Karl finds refuge in the Hotel Occidental. Banished from the hotel, Karl is driven to what he infers to be a distant street outside the city that, against the recommendations of his friend the head cook, he has refused to visit. The transitional sentence between chapters 6 and 7 is typical of Kafka's use of *Verkehr* to propel his travelling narrative forward: 'It looked as if an accident were inevitable, but the all-embracing stream of traffic quietly swept into itself even the arrowy thrust of their vehicle' (*A* 207).

The cumulative result of Karl's movement, which he experiences passively as a series of 'accidents', chance encounters, or forced and aimless departures, is to drive him further and further from any known point of origin and reference. Again, Karl's predicament is largely akin to that of the reader as the narrative moves implacably ahead, abandoning unnamed places and inscrutable characters for new ones, apparently following a random, unpredictable course and without posting identifiable spatial and temporal signboards.[9] Karl never engages in introspection, rarely thinks back over the course of his adventures in order to give them some coherence or meaning, passively endures the accidents and adventures that befall him and propel him forward. Thus he never learns from his experiences, but re-experiences the same events in a timeless, deterritorialized present. Despite being the father of a child, fundamentally he remains a child and is treated as such by the characters around him.[10] Even the few exceptions to this rule confirm its general validity. For instance, when Karl suddenly reveals his identity as a German from Prague in the fifth chapter, the head cook introduces herself as Grete Mitzelbach from Vienna, claiming to have worked in the 'Golden Goose' restaurant in Karl's home town. But this brief moment of recognition, of a shared past and 'territorialization' of the narrative, is immediately retracted: '"The old Golden Goose," Karl said, "was torn down two years ago"' (*A* 134). The cook's name is never repeated, and the fact of their shared past has no further bearing on subsequent events.

The last completed chapter of the novel, ironically entitled 'A Refuge', departs from the literal meaning of *Verkehr* as traffic but rejoins it on the secondary level of *Geschlechtsverkehr*—the 'traffic' or 'commerce' of the sexes. The chapter introduces a formidable

[9] This movement appears to have something in common with the 'random' or at least unprogrammed mode in which Kafka wrote his longer narrative. As Malcolm Pasley has suggested, 'Kafka's narratives, including his novels, essentially arose without a specific or premeditated goal, without any predetermined plot line or choice of characters, arose simply *along the way*.' 'The Act of Writing and the Text: The Genesis of Kafka's Manuscripts', in M. Anderson (ed.), *Reading Kafka: Prague, Politics, and the Fin de Siècle* (New York: Schocken Books, 1989), 246.

[10] '"You're still only a child, Rossmann," said Robinson . . . "You've still a lot to learn"' (*A* 231).

protagonist named Brunelda, a 'great singer'[11] who lives in an apartment filled with a disturbing mass of crates, dirty clothes, curtains, rugs, flasks, cushions, perfume bottles, used plates, and silverware. The first thing Karl notices are the crates; the next reference is to Brunelda's fancy clothing, a 'delicate yellow hem of lace' which he stares at until she yells at him to stop. The overtly sexual character of Brunelda's clothing is repeatedly emphasized: it is what she uses to enslave her male admirers and what the narrator uses to mark her as both sexually attractive and repulsive to Karl.[12] The identification of clothing and a degrading form of sado-masochistic sexuality culminates in the description of Brunelda's bed, which is a giant mound of dirty clothes, blankets, curtains, and rugs (*A* 261).

As critics have noted, the events that take place in Brunelda's apartment bear a strong resemblance to traumatic moments of Kafka's childhood that he describes in the 'Letter to His Father'. Karl's exclusion from her bedroom on to the balcony recalls for instance the famous incident of the 'Pavlatsch' when, as a young child, Kafka was exiled from his parents' apartment for crying for water during the night.[13] What has not been noted, however, is the affinity between Brunelda's apartment and the fancy-goods store where Kafka watched his father tyrannize his employees. Brunelda herself wears many of the fancy goods sold by Hermann Kafka: the parasol, lace undergarments, and toiletries that she uses for sexual gain all belong to the paternal realm of 'gallant wares'. Her apartment seems to be an amalgamation of the father's shop and the family's cluttered apartment. The unpacked *crates* of belongings (once referred to as an entire 'wagon load')

[11] Brunelda's former profession, gargantuan physical dimensions, and unrestrained libido make it clear that Kafka remembers his evening lectures in Jungborn: 'Recently [the doctor] declared that breathing from the diaphragm contributes to the growth and stimulation of the sexual organs, for which reason female opera singers, for whom diaphragm breathing is requisite, are so immoral' (letter to Max Brod, 17 July 1912).

[12] '"Wait, I'll make you a little more comfortable," said Delamarche anxiously, and he undid a few buttons at her neck and pulled her dress open at the throat so that part of her breast was laid bare and the soft, yellowish lace border of her chemise appeared. "Who is that, said the woman suddenly, pointing a finger at Karl, "why is he staring at me with such a wild look?"' (*A* 225).

[13] See H. Binder's extended discussion in his *Kafka-Kommentar* (Munich: Winkler, 1976), ii. 422–51.

especially evoke a commercial rather than merely domestic environment. At one point Brunelda throws an expensive porcelain object (also a piece of fancy goods) on the floor in a gesture that repeats, in exaggerated form, Hermann Kafka's treatment of his employees: 'But once . . . when [her husband] left an absolutely priceless piece of porcelain, Brunelda must have recognized it somehow, for she flung it on the floor at once, stamped upon it, spat on it and did other things to it as well, so that the servant could hardly carry it away for disgust' (*A* 236–7). Kafka writes in the 'Letter to His Father': 'For instance, the way you would push goods you did not want to have mixed up with others, knocking them off the counter . . . and the assistant had to pick them up' (*DF* 161). Hermann Kafka's habit of calling the employees 'mangy dogs' or 'paid enemies' is also repeated by Brunelda: 'Now send these apes packing', she says to Delamarche in front of her servants.[14] The subsequent image unites three aspects of paternal *Verkehr*—money, sex, and clothing accessory: 'Then Brunelda took Delamarche's hand and drew it down to the purse she wore at her belt; Delamarche put in his hand and began to pay off the servants; Brunelda did nothing but stand there with the open purse at her waist. (*A* 239).

Here, too, the effect of *Verkehr* is to disrupt Karl's vision and understanding of his surroundings. Brunelda's apartment is dark and dusty, crucial events take place behind screens or underneath bedclothes or while Karl is on the balcony, and the giant singer's body itself becomes an obstacle to rather than an object of vision. In one scene the protagonists gather on the balcony to watch a political rally on the street below, Brunelda insisting that Karl use her binoculars. He declines, but she insists, shoving the glasses in his eyes in a scene that is as comic as it is brutal, and that again makes clear Karl's symbolic blindness:

> 'I can't see anything', he said, trying to get away from the glasses, but she held them firmly, and his head, which was pressed against her breast, he could move neither backwards nor sideways.

[14] Robinson glosses the scene for Karl: 'Apes—that's what [Brunelda] called the servants; you can imagine the expression on their faces.' The Muir translation of 'fools' for Kafka's 'Affen' has been altered to follow the German. Their version repeatedly minimizes the text's graphic sexuality; for instance, when Karl sees a man squeezing a woman's 'breast' in the apartment opposite Brunelda's, the Muirs translate 'waist'.

> 'But you can see now', she said, turning the screw.
>
> 'No, I still can't see anything', said Karl . . .
>
> 'When on earth are you going to see?' she said and turned the screw again; Karl's whole face was now exposed to her heavy breath. 'Now?' she asked.
>
> 'No, no, no!' cried Karl. (*A* 252)

The unfinished state of Kafka's manuscript makes problematic any speculation about the conclusion of Karl Rossmann's adventures and the absolute linearity of the narrative. In the afterword, Max Brod suggests that Kafka intended to conclude the work on a note of reconciliation, allowing Karl 'to find again a profession, a stand-by, his freedom, even his old home and his parents, as if by some celestial witchery' (*A* 299). But even if this were his intent, one can see how the logic of a linear, travelling text would conflict with such a magical (not to say conventional) conclusion, a conflict that may well have contributed to Kafka's inability to finish the novel. In any event the very last lines reiterate the theme of a disorienting, dispersive *Verkehr*, set this time in the 'Wild West', and on a distinctly sinister note:

> The first day they travelled through a high range of mountains . . . narrow, gloomy, jagged valleys opened out and one tried to follow with a pointing finger the direction in which they lost themselves; broad mountain streams [plunged] underneath the bridges over which the train rushed; and they were so near that the breath of coldness rising from them chilled the skin of one's face. (*A* 297–8)

In October 1914, two years after abandoning the manuscript, Kafka wrote the chapter entitled 'The Nature Theatre of Oklahoma' that attempts to conclude without stopping the movement of *Verkehr*. Karl Rossmann takes a job as a technical worker under the pseudonym of 'Negro', in a travelling theatre or 'Wandercircus'. With this artistic *Aufhebung* of Karl's identity—'Negro' seems less a pseudonym than the lack of a name, a black hole in the narrative—Kafka apparently has effaced the last identifying marks of property that defined Karl Rossmann with respect to the 'secure world'. Without a name, without material possessions (he spends his last dollar on the train fare to Clayton), 'Karl' is now truly *verschollen*.

This effacement of the writing subject has an unmistakable political subtext, for Kafka was clearly interested in portraying the situation of the poor, the unemployed, the homeless, as the basic feature of immigrant life in America. As recent studies have shown, he drew on František Soukup's socialist lectures in Prague for the description of striking workers, political demonstrations, and general living conditions for foreigners who had been brutally displaced from their homeland.[15] Holitscher, a socialist Jew whose travelogue is keenly sensitive to the plight of immigrants and former slaves in America, included a photograph of a lynched Black man with the ironic caption 'Idyll in Oklahama'.[16] But this socio-political rootlessness (the *Lumpenproletariat* exemplified by Delamarche and Robinson, and finally all the members of the Nature Theatre) merges with the problem of a metaphysical *Bodenlosigkeit*, with the groundlessness of Karl's existence in a world of changing appearances, unstable impressions, accident, and death: a world of 'traffic'. It is at this point, in the notion of *Verkehr*, that the novel's political content intersects with its aesthetic and epistemological structures.

III

Considerable distance separates Kafka's text from traditional novels of the nineteenth century, which—whether written by

[15] Kafka apparently drew heavily from Soukup's *Amerika: Rada obrazu americkeho zivota* (*America: A Series of Pictures of American Life*), which is unfortunately unavailable in English or German translation. From the few passages Binder quotes in his *Kommentar zu den Romanen* (Munich: Winkler, 1976), however, we can see that Soukup's class portrait of American life also stresses the element of 'traffic'; consider for instance the following description of New York light: 'One, two, a hundred, a thousand—suddenly all the streets start burning and New York is swimming in a sea of light waves . . . from the roofs to the sidewalks everything is a single giant orgy of electric light rays. And everythiing is in constant motion and flux' (as quoted in Biinder, *Kommentar*, 100). Kafka attended Soukup's lecture and slide presentation of 'America and its Civil Servants' on 1 June 1912 in Prague. See also A. Wirkner, *Kafka und die Außenwelt* (Stuttgart: Klett, 1976), and G. Loose's *Franz Kafka und Amerika*.

[16] Holitscher also misspelled Oklahoma this way—further indication that *Amerika: Heute und morgen* served Kafka as a source. Holitscher often notes the similar social plight of Jews and Blacks in America, which may have led Kafka (although he says Karl Rossmann is not Jewish) to a symbolic identification of Karl's final predicament with that of Black Americans—hence the pseudonym 'Negro'.

Jane Austen, Balzac, Fontane. or the young Thomas Mann—are organized according to the notion of property. By property narrative I mean any text that works to establish the identity of its protagonists, as well as the stability of those narrative structures through which that identity is apprehended, by encircling its protagonists in a network of property relations. Property is not just land or economic wealth, but all the advantages and attributes that generally accompany it: a proper name, first of all; a house and land, perhaps an aristocratic residence bearing the same name; a wife and children also marked with this name; a line of ancestors and descendants that makes the protagonist's identity accessible as a form of historical, psychological, or epistemological property. Situated in a precise historical and geographical space, the property narrative is concerned with determining the origins of its protagonists, the motives for their behaviour, the consequences of their decisions. The persons and places it represents are offered to the reader as stable, ultimately knowable objects of perception; are offered to us as a form of narrative property that we can acquire and make our own.

The modernist travelling narrative—like *Der Verschollene*—denies this form of consumptive reading because it is always in motion, is always one step ahead of its reader, never turns around to question its own origins or motives and allow the reader to catch up with it. The pleasure it offers is random, vicarious, shifting. A travelling text works to destabilize the identity of the protagonist as well as the genealogical structures through which this identity is normally presented. The protagonist has no property, is always on the road, never knows what is about to happen, and never asks why he is there at all. The proper name is tenuous, thin, disguised, or unimportant, for its bearer is continually forsaking the place where it is recognized. Desire is not fixed to a specific object, intent on possessing this object, or amassing with it various forms of property, but is itself on the road, merging with the crowd, getting lost in traffic, moving on.[17]

[17] See Leo Bersani's notion of 'wandering desire' in his study *Baudelaire and Freud* (Berkeley, Calif.: University of California Press, 1977).

1. Kafka as a student, with the cabaret waitress Hansi Szokoll, the 'Trocadero Valkyre'.

2. Kafka as a high-school student.
'What you write about the young writer is interesting, but you exaggerate the points of similarity. I merely try casually and in a hit-and-miss way to dress well . . .' (Kafka to H. Weiler, 1907)

3. Kafka as a student, with his 'Madrid uncle', Alfred.

4. Interior of Hermann Kafka's fancy-goods shop. 'The way you wrapped up a parcel or opened a crate was a spectacle worth watching, and all in all certainly not the worst school for a child.' (Kafka in the 'Letter to his Father')

5. 'A Conflict in Fashion', Bruno Paul, *Simplicissimus*, 1902. The original caption read: 'The reform garment is above all hygienic and keeps the body fit for its maternal tasks. . . . As long as you wear that rag you'll never be able to get pregnant!'

6. Woman's undergarment by American reformer Maria M. Jones, 1869.

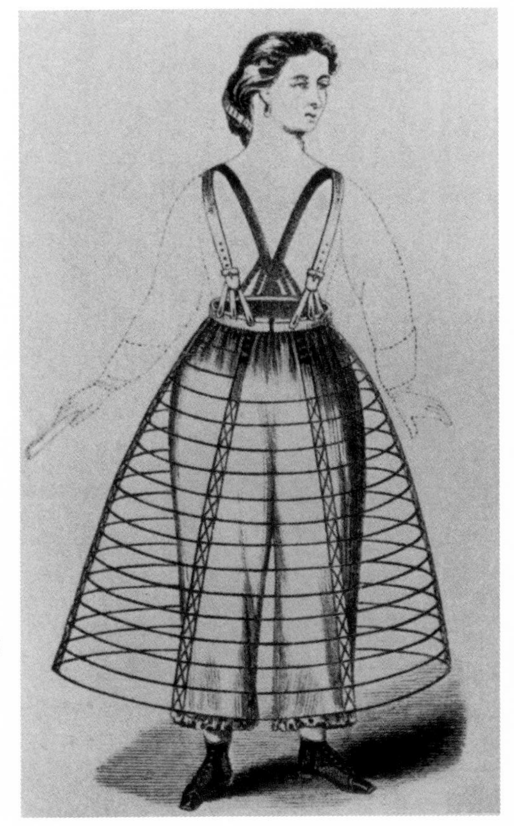

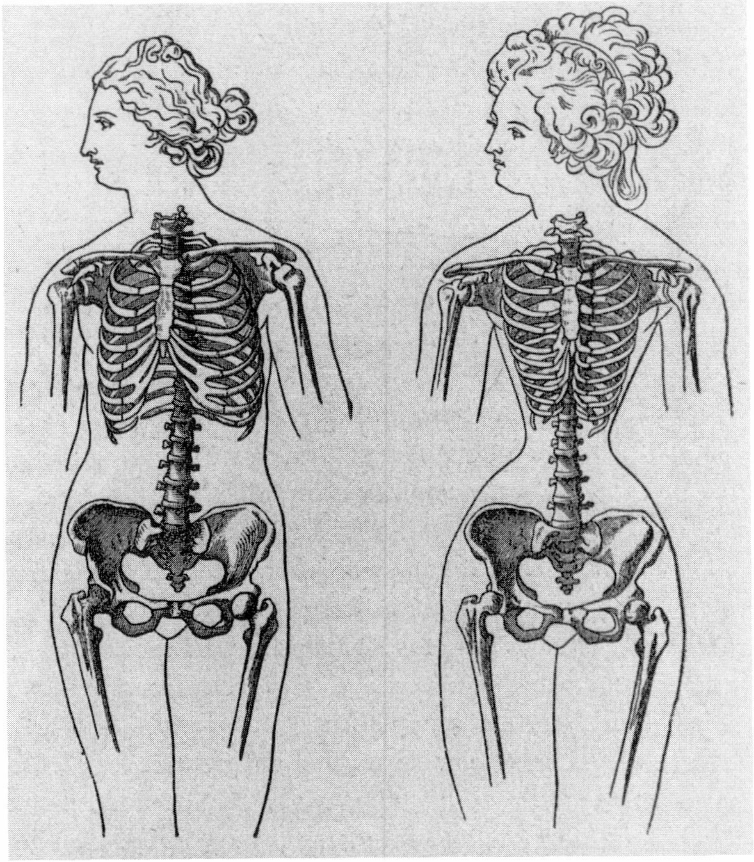

7. Normal female ribcage without (*left*) and with corset. A popular image in debates about women's clothing at the turn of the century.

8. Reform dress after a sketch by P. Schultze-Naumburg. Kafka attended a lecture by Naumburg on the reform of women's clothing in 1904.

9. Woman in reform dress *c.*1900, designed by Belgian architect Henry van de Velde. Jugendstil furniture and cloth patterns by van de Velde in background.

10. Jugendstil cover of the *Kuntswart* (*Art Guard*), the journal Kafka subscribed to from *c.*1900 to 1904.

Wagner-Heft.
MIT BILDER- UND NOTEN-BEILAGEN.
BEZUGSPREIS 3M. VIERTELJ. EINZELHEFT 60 PF.
KUNSTWART
RUNDSCHAU UEBER
DICHTUNG, THEATER
MUSIK UND
BILDENDE KÜNSTE
JAHRG. 15
HERAUSGEBER
FERDINAND
AVENARIUS
HEFT 18
VERLAG VON
GEORG·D·W·CALLWEY
IN MÜNCHEN
ZWEITES JUNIHEFT 1902
AUSLIEFERUNG FÜR BERLIN: GEORG SIEMENS.

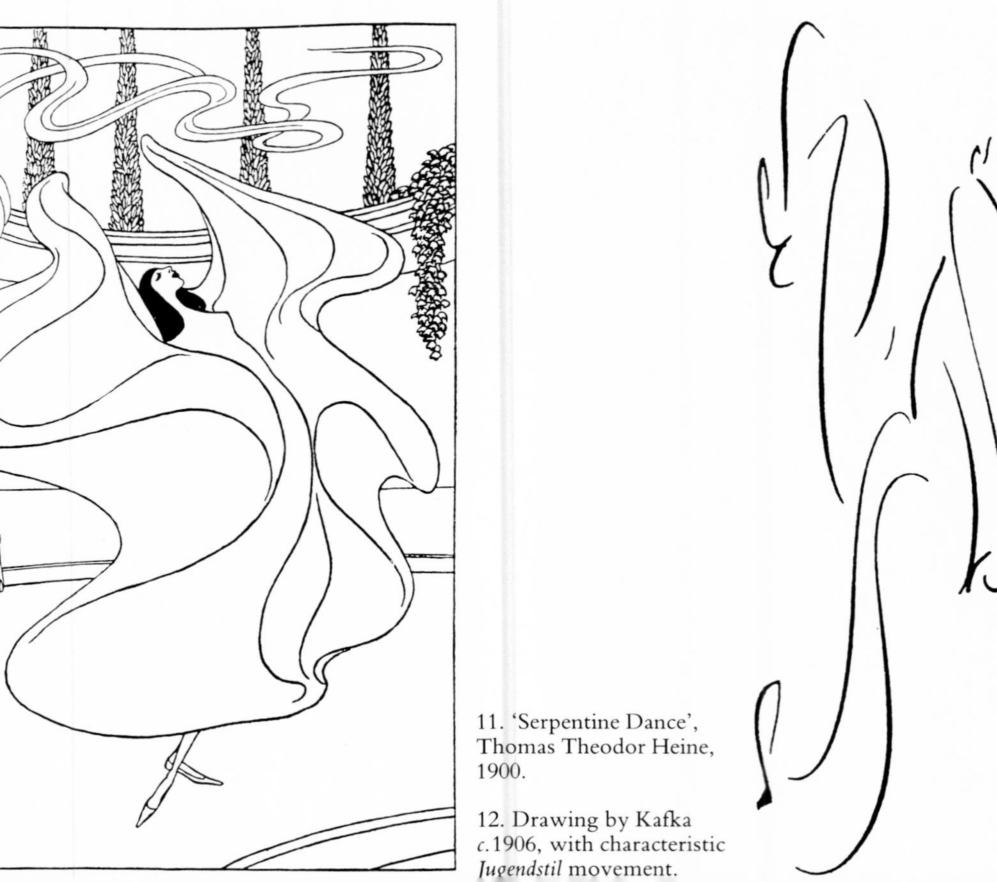

11. 'Serpentine Dance', Thomas Theodor Heine, 1900.

12. Drawing by Kafka *c.*1906, with characteristic *Jugendstil* movement.

13. Group of dancers in neo-Classical reform clothing performing Jaques-Dalcroze's 'rhythmic gymnastics'. Kafka admired the Dalcroze method and visited his school in the artist colony in Hellerau.

14. Dalcroze dancers performing a 'Seelentanz'. 'Little soul, you leap in the dance, lay your head in warm air, lift your feet out of gleaming grass.' (Octavo notebook)

15. Cover of Adolf Just's *Kehrt zur Natur zuruck!* illustrating a Jungborn cabin.

16. Cover of J. P. Müller's gymnastics manual, whose method Kafka followed from *c.*1908 to 1917. 'What piece of furniture [for our flat] will be needed? A folding screen, of course, or a mat, in order to do Müller exercises. In order to do them naked, with the window open, and so prevent the people opposite from joining in the exercises.' (Kafka to F. Bauer, 25 May 1914)

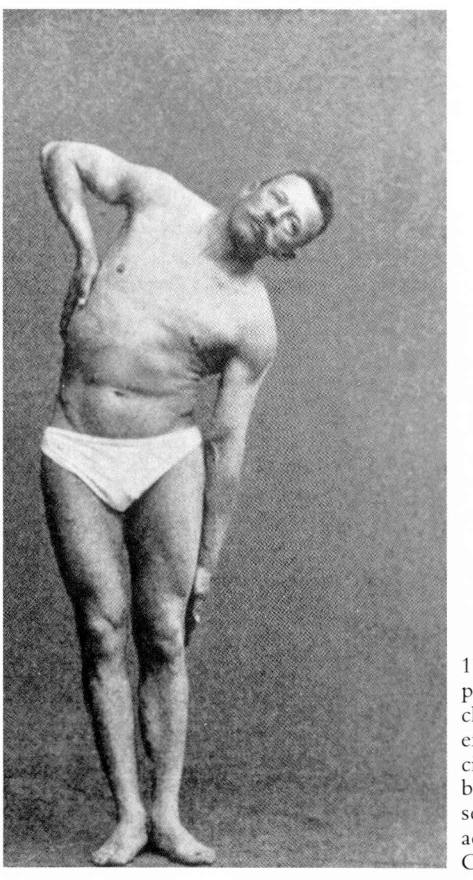

17. & 18. The Danish pedagogue Müller in a characteristic 'towelling' exercise meant to improve circulation and clean the body. Müller often struck sculptural poses in accordance with his neo-Classical aesthetics.

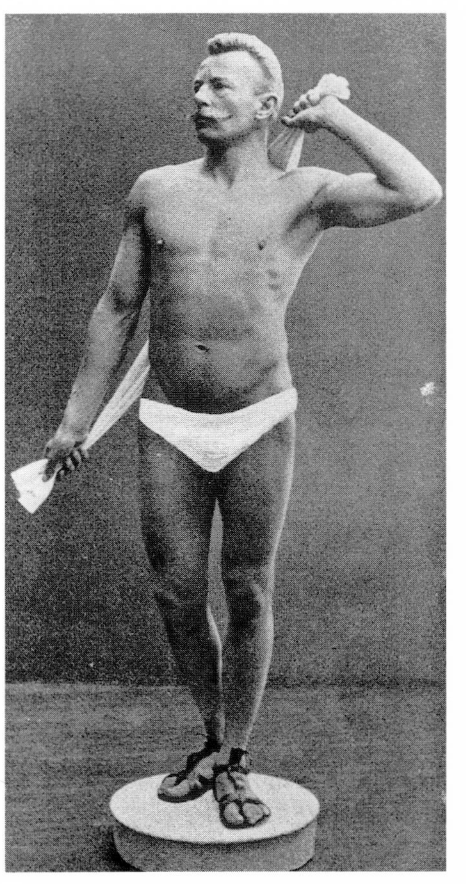

19. 'The Hunt' by the Prague artist Alfred Kubin *c.*1900–1. 'Perhaps I will someday find words for saying again what your work has meant to me.' (Kafka to Kubin, 22 July 1914)

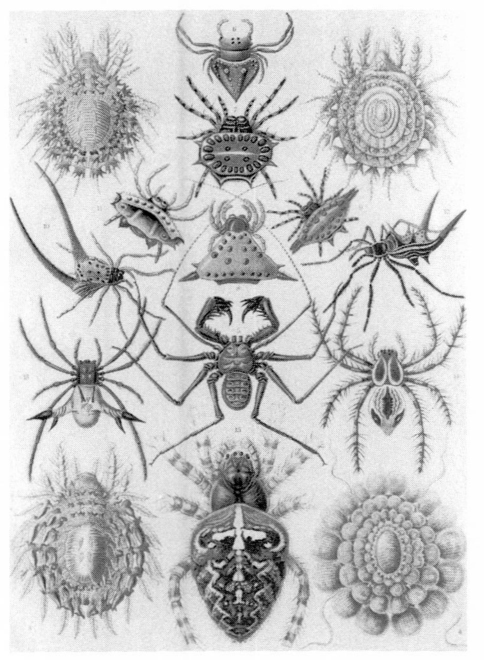

20. Illustrative plate from Ernst Haeckel's *Kunstformen der Natur*, 1899–1903, whose stylized representations of plant and animal forms provided a handbook of motifs for *Jugendstil* artists.

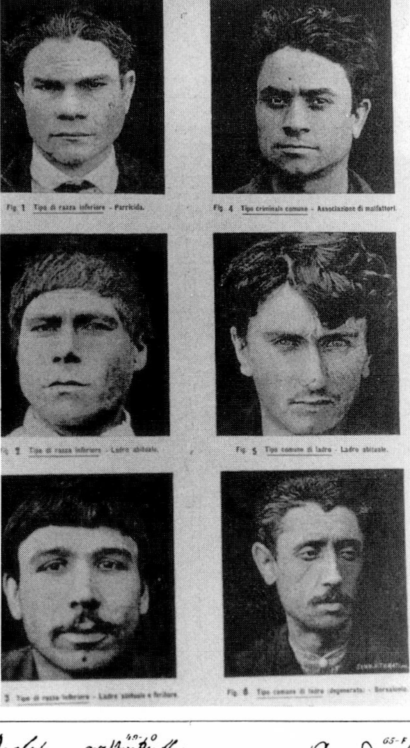

21. 'Criminal' physiognomies, from Cesare Lombroso's *Criminal Man* (*L'uomo delinquente*, 1875).

22. Facsimile of 'criminal' signatures from Cesare Lombroso's *L'uomo delinquente*, 1875. The letter O signifies murderer, L thief, T con man, F counterfeiter, B robber.

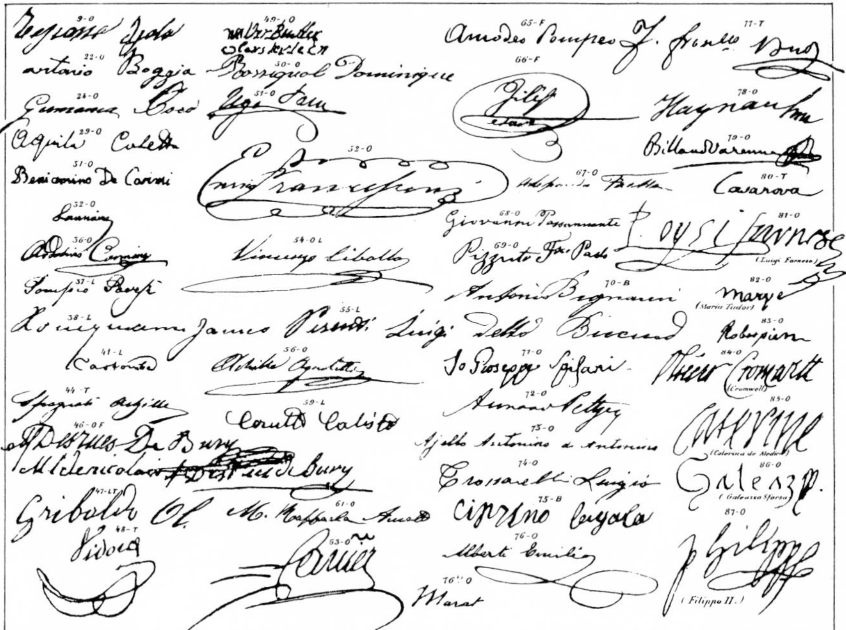

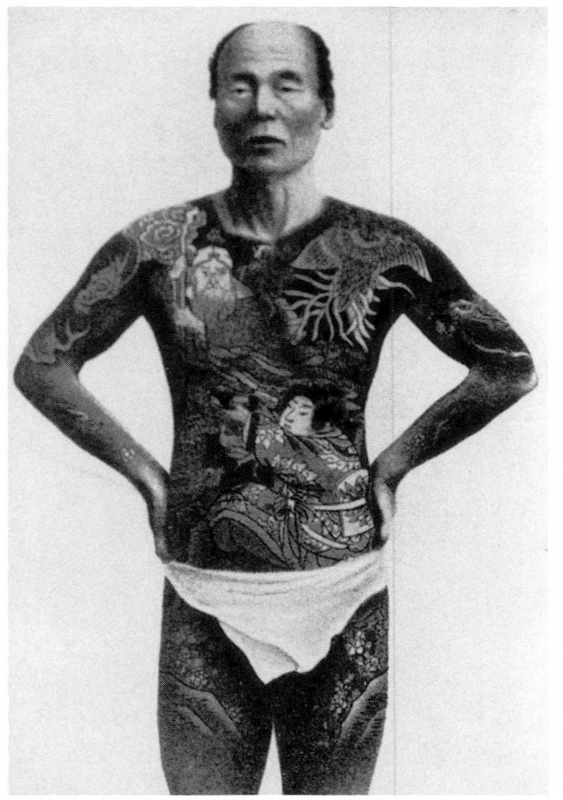

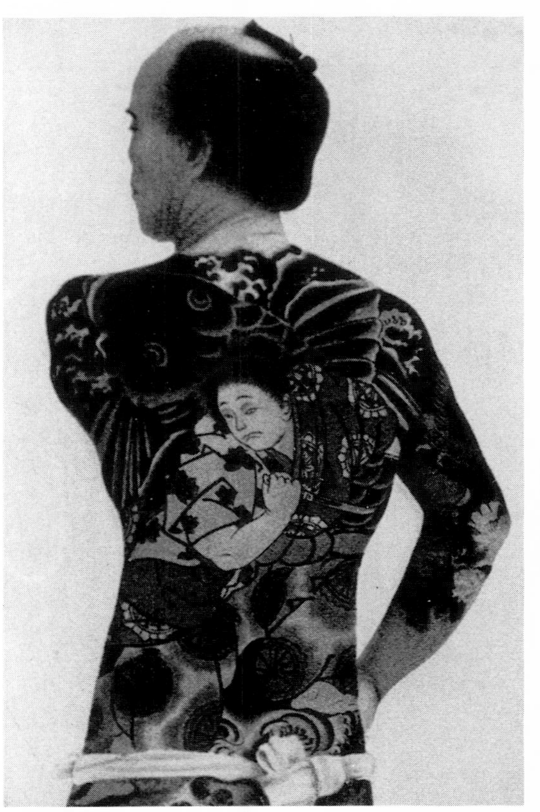

23. & 24. Japanese man with 'tattoo suit'.

25. Cover illustration by Heinrich Vogeler for Hugo von Hofmannsthal's verse play 'The Emperor and the Witch', 1900.

26. Page from *Die neue Rundschau* in 1904. Kafka read this journal regularly from 1904.

Kleider

Oft wenn ich Kleider mit vielfachen Falten, Rüschen und Behängen sehe, die über schönen Körper schön sich legen, dann denke ich, daß sie nicht lange so erhalten bleiben, sondern

[63]

27. Page from the first edition of *Meditation*. 'No doubt the typeface is a little too consciously beautiful, and would be more appropriate to the tablets of Moses than to my little prevarications.' (Kafka to F. Bauer, 8 November 1912)

Nr. 2 WIEN 15. OKTOBER 1903 Preis 20 h

DAS ANDERE

EIN BLATT ZUR EINFUEHRUNG ABENDLAENDISCHER KULTUR IN OESTERREICH: GESCHRIEBEN VON ADOLF LOOS 1. JAHR

TAILORS AND OUTFITTERS
GOLDMAN & SALATSCH

K. U. K. HOF-LIEFERANTEN
K. BAYER. HOF-LIEFERANTEN

KAMMER-LIEFERANTEN
Sr. k. u. k. Hoheit des Herrn Erzherzog Josef etc. etc.

WIEN, I. GRABEN 20.

Société Franco-Autrichienne
pour les arts industriels

MÖBELSTOFFE

LYONER SEIDEN- UND SAMT-BROKATE

ECHTE UND IMITIERTE GOBELINS

ENGLISCHE UND FRANZÖSISCHE TEPPICHE

STICKEREIEN UND APPLIKATIONEN

SPITZENVORHÄNGE

WIEN, I. Karntnerstrasse 55, 1. Stock

Société Franco-Autrichienne

28. Cover of Adolf Loos's short-lived journal *Das Andere*, which appeared in 1903 as a supplement to Peter Altenberg's *Die Kunst*.

29. Cover of Karl Kraus's satirical journal *Die Fackel*.

Nr. 3 Wien, Ende April 1899

DIE FACKEL

HERAUSGEBER:

KARL KRAUS.

ERSCHEINT DREIMAL IM MONAT.

PREIS 10 KR. WIEN.

Nachdruck nur mit Angabe der Quelle »DIE FACKEL« erlaubt.

30. Kafka, 1906.

Clearly linked to the development of the big city, late capitalism, and increasingly fluid, shifting forms of property, the travelling narrative has become a privileged mode of narration in twentieth-century literature. In German and Austrian literature, the conflict between property and travelling narratives can be illustrated in the difference between Thomas Mann's *Buddenbrooks* and Robert Musil's *Man without Qualities*. Mann's novel turns obsessively around the family name, house, property, and ancestral line, even though it is ultimately concerned with the breakdown and decline—the *Verfall*—of this tradition. By contrast, Musil's novel begins with the description of random atmospheric conditions and a traffic accident in a modern city, two mathematical figures that serve to introduce a protagonist defined negatively—as the absence of 'qualities' (or 'properties'), as a life suspended in the 'subjunctive' mode.

The montage novels of Döblin and Dos Passos, Butor's *La Modification* or Handke's *The Wrong Move* (*Falsche Bewegung*) provide further examples of a widespread modernist tendency in European and American literature to use the theme of 'traffic' to create a destabilized, shifting mode of narration opposed to the nineteenth-century novel's insistence on narrative 'property'. This literary tendency inevitably merges and in some cases collaborates with similar efforts in cinema. Perhaps the most radical use of travelling narratives has been made by filmmakers such as Jean-Luc Godard, Werner Herzog, and Wim Wenders, whose films repeatedly thematize mechanized forms of travel as a self-reflexive gesture toward the moving, unstable nature of cinematic representation. The Godard quotation with which this essay began its itinerary—'Le moral, c'est le travelling'—provides the most succinct definition of this kind of wandering text. Subject, camera, and projected image are all implicated in the traffic of travelling images.

V

At this point, and by way of conclusion, I would like to return to Kafka's text and discuss two specific instances of his presentation of New York traffic. This will have two functions: first, it will provide an illustration of the destabilizing, anti-mimetic effects of *Verkehr* that I have attempted to describe generally; and second, it will introduce an additional element to Kafka's use of a 'travelling' narrative, one that I feel marks it as a peculiarly modern text.

The first chapter of *Der Verschollene* takes place on board the ship that has brought Karl Rossmann to America. Our first view of New York occurs midway through the chapter when the novel's young protagonist looks through the windows of the captain's office at the harbour traffic.

> Meanwhile outside the windows the life of the harbor went on; a flat barge laden with a mountain of barrels, which must have been wonderfully well packed, since they did not roll off, went past, almost completely obscuring the daylight; little motor-boats, which Karl would have liked to examine thoroughly if he had had time, shot straight past in obedience to the slightest touch [*Zuckungen*, jerky movements, twitches] of the man standing erect at the wheel. Here and there curious objects [*eigentümliche Schwimmkörper*] bobbed independently out of the restless water, were immediately submerged again and sank before his astonished eyes; boats belonging to the ocean liners were rowed past by sweating sailors; they were filled with passengers sitting silent and expectant as if they had been stowed there, except that some of them could not refrain from turning their heads to gaze at the changing scene. A movement without end, a restlessness transmitted from the restless element to helpless human beings and their works! (*A* 17)

This passage seems to be the reworking of a dream Kafka noted in his diary shortly before beginning the novel. There Kafka labels the New York harbour traffic an 'ungeheuer fremdländischer Verkehr', literally a 'monstrous foreign traffic', claiming it to be more interesting than the traffic on a busy Paris boulevard.[18] But here the movement, flux, appearance, and effacement of traffic in the city is further destabilized by the water on which spectator and spectacle are located. Various moving vehicles and floating objects come into Karl's view and then disappear. The reasons for their movement, their origins and destination, remain hidden.

[18] See the entry for 11 Sept. 1912.

Karl perceives only a fragment of their trajectory, which has been cropped randomly by the position he happens to occupy in the cabin and can see through the porthole. These objects hence appear opaque to him: the logic behind the arrangement of the mountain of barrels, the identity of the strange 'Schwimmkörper' bobbing in and out of sight, the thoughts of the 'expectant passengers' who have been 'stowed' like inanimate objects—everything in this scene is silent, unexplained, distant, and obscurely indifferent to his presence. The traffic unfolds without Karl's participation; he experiences it as a passive and distant spectator. And yet Karl is also on water, is himself a part of the 'movement without end' that transmits its own restlessness (*Unruhe*) to 'helpless human beings and their works'.

At the same time, the unstable, inscrutable motion of this harbour traffic provides a highly vivid, illuminated scene. Framed by the windows of the captain's office, the traffic offers itself as an image momentarily isolated from Karl's immediate surroundings. But this image is not frozen: it passes by, is succeeded by another, which in turn also disappears and is replaced. What Karl sees, in other words, is a succession of moving images that is strikingly cinematic. The autonomous, disembodied movement of these images, their indifference to any spectators, even the passing shadow cast by the barge that momentarily darkens the office and makes it like a movie theatre—all these elements contribute to a cinematic perception of the harbour traffic.

The same cinematographic quality—cinematographic in the sense of a tension between vivid, framed images and their self-cancelling movement—marks the description of the street traffic that Karl perceives from the sixth-floor balcony of his uncle's apartment:

A narrow balcony ran along the entire front wall of Karl's bedroom. But what would probably have been the highest vantage point in Karl's home town here offered little more than the view of one street which ran perfectly straight between two rows of squarely chopped buildings and therefore seemed to be fleeing into a great distance where the massive outlines of a cathedral loomed up in a dense haze. And mornings and evenings and in the dreams of the night a never ending traffic [*Verkehr*] pulsed along this street which, seen from above, looked like an inextricable confusion, for ever newly improvised, of distorted human figures and the tops of moving vehicles of all types, and from which arose a new, variegated, wilder confusion of noises, dust and smells, all of which was seized and penetrated by an intense light that was dispersed, carried off and then reflected back again by the multiplicity of objects, a light that appeared so palpable to the mesmerized eye that it seemed as if every instant a huge plate of glass covering the entire street were being shattered with tremendous force again and again. (*A* 38–9)

This image of 'New York'—the only detailed image the reader is ever given—again presents the spectacle of an infinite, 'never ending', mechanical traffic. The syntactical structure of this last, unusually long sentence is, I think, intentionally complex. The proliferation of dependent clauses, the doubling of the word 'mixture', the shifting focus of attention as one subject replaces the next, all lead to a linguistic confusion that reinforces the impression of an infinitely complex, vital, unchartable line of traffic that is no doubt meant to convey the bewilderment of Kafka's foreign protagonist observing the city for the first time. Seen from such a height, the pedestrians seem disembodied, distorted. The moving vehicles exist only synecdochically, as flat, rectangular tops without human agents to control their motion. Haze, noises, dust, smells assault Karl's senses. Even the New York light[19]—the same element that illuminates the image Karl is observing—is so intense that it actually disrupts an accurate perception of the street. But most of all the movement of this spectacle—the constantly shifting, discontinuous, self-improvising quality of images that flee into a hazy distance outside Karl's field of vision—undermines and deterritorializes this vision of 'America'. Karl's eyes are 'betört', confused, deluded.

We should also note the unusual spatial organization of this scene. Kafka does not situate his protagonist high enough above Manhattan to perceive what is after all one of the most formally ordered cities in the world. In this respect he differs from Holitscher who, in his American tourist book, climbs from the confusion of a busy street to the top of a skyscraper where he surveys an

[19] See Soukup's description of the New York light in note 14 above.

ordered, Cartesian grid of named streets, buildings, parks, and monuments. To Holitscher, the city presents itself as a map in which he can retrace his steps, read and relive the brief history of his visit, in short, situate himself spatially and temporally in a foreign world (*Amerika: Heute und morgen*, 57–61). Karl Rossmann is given only the perception of a single, unnamed street whose relation to the rest of New York is never disclosed.[20] What would have provided the 'highest vantage point' at home in Prague—a panorama of a totality to be observed, studied, measured, represented—here offers a fragmented image without relation to a surrounding whole.

And yet, despite the elusive, fragmented nature of its contents, the image of this traffic is marked by its visuality. The image is again framed: at the front edge by Karl's balcony; to the left and right by the buildings that have been 'squarely chopped off'; at the top edge, less emphatically, by the outlines of the cathedral. The traffic thus flows before him in an 'absolutely straight' line of moving images—again, like a ribbon of celluloid images passing before the eye of the projector. The context for vision and representation is also affirmed by the curious metaphorical appearance of a giant plate of glass, as if to evoke a projector, a lighted shop-window or a painting under glass. But the intensity of the light, the violent energy of *Verkehr*, cannot be contained in a stable representation: 'a light that appeared so palpable to the mesmerized eye that it seemed as if every instant a huge plate of glass covering the entire street were being shattered with tremendous force again and again.' As in a painting by Magritte, the glass of representation shatters, leaving Karl and the reader figuratively blinded.

Whether or not Kafka was aware of the cinematographic quality of these passages is unimportant, for his formulation of

[20] In establishing Kafka's use of Holitscher's book, Hartmut Binder makes the absurd claim that the street Karl sees is Broadway (*Kommentar*, 99). Not only does Kafka's description not match the picture of Broadway on p. 49 in Holitscher's book (the cathedral is missing, the street is open on one side, etc.), but it deliberately denies a perception of the street as named, situated locale. Binder's general project of anchoring Kafka's text in a biographical, referential context frequently goes against the grain of the text's tendency toward 'namelessness', and in this respect he repeats Brod's emblematic error of naming the novel *Amerika*.

Verkehr already implies a cinematic apprehension of reality. Edgar Allan Poe, in describing the flow of a London crowd perceived from a café window in his story 'The Man of the Crowd', presented an equally cinematographic image some forty years before the invention of film. What is striking, however, is the similarity between these images of American traffic and Kafka's own comments on cinema in his diaries and letters. The common element is *Unruhe*, the restless, rapid movement of images that 'blind' the spectator by preventing any stable, controlled act of perception. In reference to his visit to the Emperor's Panorama in Friedland in 1911, the year before he began his American novel, Kafka noted in his diary: 'The pictures [of the panorama are] more alive than in the cinema because they offer the eye all the repose [*Ruhe*] of reality. The cinema communicates the restlessness [*Unruhe*] of its motion to the things pictured in it; *the eye's repose would seem to be more important*' (*D2* 241, my emphasis).

Kafka's ambivalence toward the cinema—on the one hand, his undeniable fascination with its photographic realism, on the other his discomfort with the speed of these images' succession on the screen—may well explain why he chose 'the most modern New York' as the site for Karl Rossmann's exile. For if New York is defined by its 'traffic', by the relentless movement of its framed images, the city offers itself as an eminently cinematic space. The dominant metaphor for Prague in *Description of a Struggle* is theatre; New York, with its highly developed technology, requires the cinema. No doubt inspired by the American movies he and Max Brod saw in Prague and Paris, Kafka imagines 'America' through the grid of film, as if the only adequate mode of transmitting its unstable, complex *Verkehr* were through an artistic medium itself in motion, travelling. But to thrust Karl Rossmann into such a cinematic space is to condemn him to the nightmarish observation of a world that will not stand still and that is profoundly indifferent to his presence—as indifferent as film and projector are to the spectators in a cinema. Karl comes to America thinking he will observe, learn, understand, *see* it. Instead, the images move too quickly, peripheral phenomena distract him, and when he looks again the images have left the screen. Karl sees everything in America as if for the first time, which is to say that he sees nothing at all.[21]

Other critics, notably Wolfgang Jahn in the first book-length study of *Der Verschollene*, have noted the cinematographic quality of Kafka's first novel.[22] The montage-like narrative, the openness and freedom of movement from chapter to chapter, distinguish it from the claustrophobic landscapes of *The Trial* and *The Castle*. In the above remarks I have tried to show that the cinematic aspect of *Der Verschollene* extends beyond the montage arrangement of specific scenes to the general problematic of *Verkehr*, indeed, that these scenes emerge from the logic of a 'travelling narrative'. This logic permeates the novel's structure, making each individual scene, image, and detail part of a phenomenological description of the act of seeing,[23] or rather, the ultimately impossible act of viewing a world caught in a self-cancelling motion that is 'forever newly improvised'. Image, frame, light, movement—these are the constitutive ingredients for Kafka's presentation of 'America', as we can now see in rereading the novel's celebrated opening figure: 'As Karl Rossmann . . . stood on the liner slowly entering the harbor of New York, a sudden burst of sunshine seemed to illumine the Statue of Liberty, so that he saw it in a new light, although he had sighted it long before. The arm with the sword rose up as if newly stretched aloft' (*A* 3). Karl, the ship, the light, even the statue—all are depicted in the process of movement. Nothing is still or familiar in America, not even its most celebrated monument. Kafka did not have to travel to New York to write this passage. As he is said to have remarked

[21] In a working-class district of Prague there was a cinema called 'Bio Slepcu', Cinema of the Blind, because the concession belonged to the association supporting the blind. Gustav Janouch reports Kafka's response to this name as follows: '"*Bio Slepcu!*" Every cinema should be called that. Their flickering images blind people to reality' (*Conversations with Kafka*, 2nd edn. trans. G. Rees (New York: New Directions Books, 1971), 147).

[22] *Kafkas Roman 'Der Verschollene' (Amerika)*; see also his 'Kafka und die Anfänge des Kinos', *Schiller Jahrbuch*, 6, (1962), 353–68. Hanns Zischler documents Kafka's early interest in film as well as his gradual ambivalence for the medium in 'Masslose Unterhaltung: Franz Kafka geht ins Kino', *Freibeuter*, 16 (1983), 33–47.

[23] I am indebted to Herbert Blau for stressing the 'act of seeing' in Kafka's novel. Cf. also Anne Hollander's excellent discussion of the cinematic quality of Flemish painting in 'Moving Pictures', *Raritan*, 3 (winter 1986), 82–102.

to Gustav Janouch: 'One takes a photograph of things in order to get them out of one's mind. My stories are a way of closing my eyes.'[24]

[24] *Conversations with Kafka*, 31. Note also Kafka's reported claim to Janouch that 'we Jews are not painters. We cannot depict things statically. We see them always in transition, in movement, as change. We are storytellers' (132).

5

Sliding Down the Evolutionary Ladder? Aesthetic Autonomy in The Metamorphosis

Was he an animal that music moved him so?

(*The Metamorphosis*)

I

A FEW years ago an art gallery in New York created a mild sensation by dousing a number of human models, clothes and bodies, in green paint and hanging them on its bare white walls. Although the models adopted various poses, they made no attempt to deny their living status, and interacted freely with the bemused public. Somewhat at a loss to describe the artwork, which apparently was not for sale, the media spoke of 'Dada', 'performance', and 'action' art. Franz Kafka's literary masterpiece of 1912, *The Metamorphosis*, enacts essentially the same scenario when its human-sized bug hero climbs the wall of his bedroom and usurps the aesthetic space occupied by a gilt-framed photograph, hugging his flat body against the glass until it 'completely covers' the picture. When his mother, less blasé than a New York audience of the 1980s, enters the room, her senses are overwhelmed. She perceives only a huge brownish spot against the flowered wallpaper and, crying out 'Oh God! Oh God!', falls into a dead faint. No avant-garde artist of the modern period could ask for a more satisfying public response.

Since the story's initial publication in 1915, few if any readers of *The Metamorphosis* have wished to recognize Gregor Samsa's metamorphosed body as an aesthetic form. For Kafka's early public the bug was simply too repulsive, and was explained away with allegorical notions like 'alienated labor' or 'unconscious self-loathing.'[1] Further, although Günther Anders in an early and quite perceptive essay interpreted Gregor Samsa as a *Luftmensch* and 'artist' figure,[2] and although subsequent critics have seen a parallel between Gregor's isolated condition and Franz Kafka's monk-like dedication to his writing,[3] readers have been hard put to reconcile this aesthetic dimension with the specificity of Gregor's outward form. In fact, close scrutiny of the story has led critics to deny that the bug has any reliable visual specificity at all: actual descriptive details are scant and contradictory, and since the story is narrated largely from Gregor's perspective, his own body tends to disappear from the reader's view. The opening designation of Gregor as an 'ungeheure Ungeziefer' or 'giant vermin' is notoriously ambiguous, for *Ungeziefer* refers to a broad range of animal parasites rather than a single type, *ungeheuer* ('monstrous') is by definition vague, and the 'un-' prefixes in both words double the term's lack of specificity into a kind of negative infinity. Significantly, when the cleaning lady calls to Gregor with the precise term *Mistkäfer* (dung beetle), he refuses to respond. Thus abstractly

[1] For an overview of the secondary literature on *The Metamorphosis*, see S. Corngold's *The Commentators' Despair: The Interpretation of Kafka's 'Metamorphosis'* (Port Washington: Kennikat Press, 1973) and P. Beicken's *Franz Kafka: Eine kritische Einführung in die Forschung* (Frankfurt: Fischer Taschenbuch, 1974), 261–72. One of the earliest interpretations of the story in psychoanalytic terms was by H. Kaiser, whose 'Franz Kafkas Inferno: eine psychologische Deutung seiner Strafphantasie' appeared in the official psychoanalytic journal *Imago* in 1931. A large number of critics have taken over Kaiser's notion of a 'punishment fantasy', including H. Tauber, H. D. Luke, C. Neider, W. Sokel. For Marxist readings of the story, see K. Hughes (ed.), *Franz Kafka: an Anthology of Marxist Criticism* (Concord: University Press of New England, 1981).

[2] 'Because Gregor Samsa wishes to live as an artist (i.e. "free as air" [*wie ein Luftmensch*], he is considered in the eyes of the respectable, down-to-earth world, to be a "bit of an insect"; thus, in *The Metamorphosis*, he wakes up as a beetle, whose idea of happiness is to be clinging to the ceiling.' *Franz Kafka*, trans. A. Steter and A. K. Thorlby (London: Bowes & Bowes, 1960), 43. See also the historical meaning of *Luftmensch* discussed in Ch. 3.

[3] Corngold offers the suggestive hypothesis that Kafka's experience of writing 'The Judgment' in September 1912, the story which 'came out of [him] like a real birth, covered with filth and slime' (*D1* 278), is the implicit biographical meaning of *The Metamorphosis*. See the expanded version of his essay 'The Metamorphosis of the Metaphor', in *Franz Kafka: The Necessity of Form* (Ithaca, NY: Cornell University Press, 1988). P. Cersowsky notes interestingly the tradition of metamorphosis into an animal as 'an extreme image of the melancholy disposition', thereby linking Gregor to the melancholy 'decadent type'. See *'Mein ganzes Wesen ist auf Literatur gerichtet'* (Würzburg: Königshausen & Neumann, 1983), p. 76.

or negatively defined, the bug would seem to have no discernible form, and to the reader at least it remains a visual cipher.

This critical tendency to de-emphasize the bug's status as a visual object of representation reached its most extreme and brilliant limit in Stanley Corngold's influential essay 'The Metamorphosis of the Metaphor'.[4] Drawing on Anders's insight that Kafka often literalizes metaphors as the basis for his central images and plot lines, Corngold interprets Gregor's form as primarily linguistic and rhetorical rather than visual. Because the text circumvents the dialectical relationship of metaphor, insisting that Gregor *is* a bug but without denying him specifically human traits, the monstrous vermin form functions as a 'mutilated metaphor, uprooted from familiar language' (59), an 'opaque sign' (56). Anything disturbing about his appearance arises primarily from a disturbing use of rhetorical structure, an 'unclean' mixing of the metaphor's human tenor and its material vehicle:

> It appears, then, that the metamorphosis in the Samsa household of man into vermin is unsettling not only because vermin are disturbing, or because the vivid representation of a human 'louse' is disturbing, but because the indeterminate, fluid crossing of a human tenor and a material vehicle is in itself unsettling. (56)

Such interpretations have an indisputable hold on Kafka's story and, I suspect, are ultimately correct. Kafka knew that his story was a kind of literary tease, that it depended on the reader's imagination to visualize what is only suggested by the text. When confronted with his editor's plan to illustrate the bug for the cover of the first edition, his response was unambiguous: 'The insect itself cannot be depicted' (letter of 25 October 1915). He proposed instead the image of a half-opened door with only darkness behind it—the bug itself remains unseen and the reader must perform the same act of imagination that is required by the text in the passage from linguistic sign to mental image. Kafka's suggestion was in fact taken up, and a black-and-white illustration by Ottomar Starke adorned the story's first edition in Kurt Wolff's series *Die weißen Blätter*.

[4] First published in 1970, the essay was reprinted in an expanded version in *The Necessity of Form*, which is the edition quoted here.

None the less, one cannot help feeling that such critical and authorial strictures have something of a magician's legerdemain—Now you see him, now you don't—and hide as much as they reveal. Although the text is a verbal artefact which expertly subverts the metaphorical function of language, it also requires the reader to make a sustained effort to visualize the bug within a minutely described environment. Moreover, such strictures obscure the fact that the text repeatedly displays Gregor's body as a visual object of unusual power—a scandalous, grotesque object difficult to behold, yes, but one that is attributed with an undeniable aesthetic function, as in the scene when Gregor hangs himself on the wall in front of his mother and sister. Indeed, the basic movement of all three sections of the novella consists in covering and uncovering Gregor's body, like a monster at a fair or a sacred icon.

Accordingly, this chapter will attempt to describe Gregor's form in visual and aesthetic terms, even when the text itself leaves these terms vague or obscures their reference. Two avenues of interpretation will be followed: a historical, deliberately digressive approach that compares Kafka's use of the vermin image to contemporary developments in science and literature; and a textual reading in terms of the problematic of *Verkehr*, clothing, and corporeal gymnastics that I have delineated in the preceding chapters and on which *The Metamorphosis*, perhaps more crucially than any of Kafka's other writings, depends.

II

Kafka's most famous text has been with us so long that it is easy to forget the audacity of using a human-sized cockroach as the main figure in a literary text. Nothing in the classical literature of animal fables or even in the Romantic literature of the uncanny or the grotesque is quite like *The Metamorphosis*, with its mixing of the monstrous and the everyday, the repulsive and the beautiful.[5]

[5] In his *Introduction à la littérature fantastique* (Paris: Éditions du Seuil, 1970), Todorov rejects an affiliation with the fantastic, noting that Kafka's text proceeds in an opposite movement: 'Le récit fantastique partait d'une situation parfaitement naturelle pour aboutir au surnaturel, *la Métamorphose* part de l'événement surnaturel pour lui

And yet there is precedent for Kafka's modernist masterpiece in the scientific and aesthetic discourses of the *fin de siècle*. His story is about a metamorphosis from human to animal form, and like all his animal narratives it arises from—and in reaction to—the ubiquitous presence of Darwin's theory of evolution.[6] The idea of 'metamorphosis' was in the air. Goethe's *Metamorphosis of Plants* and the *Metamorphosis of Animals* were held in high regard in scientific circles as Romantic harbingers of Darwin's own writings. German scientists like Ernst Haeckel and Wilhelm Bölsche propagated Darwin's teachings in Germany, not only in their research but in popular lecture series and *Volksausgaben* for a broad audience; Haeckel held an influential lecture on the evolutionary theories of Goethe, Lamarck, and Darwin in 1882, a year before Kafka's birth. Largely because of Haeckel's efforts, Darwin's evolutionary monism gained increasing currency in German-speaking countries, as all life forms were understood to be united in a great chain of being stretching from single-celled plasma to the highest primates.

Such theorizations found their equivalent in art and literature of the period. The *Jugendstil*, with its proliferation of swirling plant, mineral, and animal forms, espoused a monistic philosophy of an all-permeating life force, of organic change and becoming. Not infrequently, *Jugendstil* artists drew inspiration from contemporary scientific representations, which increasingly emphasized unusual, unknown, exotic, or otherwise bizarre forms of the natural world. Haeckel's *Kunstformen der Natur* (*Art-forms of Nature*, 1899–1903), which included 100 colour illustrations of protozoa, ocean sponges, medusas, coral, tropical birds, flowers, and exotic insects, served as a veritable handbook for the *Jugendstil* movement.[7] In his foreword he notes that the higher forms of plants and vertebrate animals that had dominated scholarly and artistic attention until the nineteenth century have given way to 'strange

donner, en cours de récit, un air de plus en plus naturel; et la fin de l'histoire est la plus éloignée qui soit du surnaturel' (179).

6 See Margot Norris's discussion of Darwin and Nietzsche in relation to Kafka in *Beasts of the Modern Imagination* (Baltimore: Johns Hopkins University Press, 1985).

7 See Jörg Mathes, introduction to *Theorie des literarischen Jugendstils* (Stuttgart: Reclam, 1984), 32.

and marvellous forms'.[8] Addressing himself explicitly to contemporary artists, he promises that his book will bring these hidden treasures to light, thereby providing them with a 'rich supply of new and beautiful motifs'.[9]

Haeckel's work had a twofold importance for literary and visual artists at the turn of the century. First, it offered them spectacular new material—vivid colors, flowing lines, translucent textures, grotesque and fantastic creatures from another realm of experience—that could be used in representations of organic and inorganic forms. It thus helped to enlarge the canon of aesthetically valid subjects, treating what might have been dismissed as ugly, overly stylized, bizarre, or lowly organisms as beautiful aesthetic forms in their own right. On a theoretical level, Haeckel promoted the notion of an originary *Kunsttrieb* or artistic impulse that could be found in all of nature. Attempting to explain the remarkable sensuous beauty, symmetry, and variety of even the most primitive organisms, he posited a 'soul' within each cell that constantly struggled for 'plastic' definition and self-realization: 'One can describe the artistic impulses of protists as "plastic cellular instincts", for they stand on the same rung of the soul's activity as the well-known instincts of higher, multiple-celled animals and plants' (12). The will to art not merely as a democratic possibility but as a biological necessity arising from the depths of every living organism—here was a philosophy for turn-of-the-century reformists and educators.

Kafka's first encounter with these ideas came in the *Gymnasium*. Under the influence of his science teacher Adolf Gottwald, a convinced Darwinist, he read the author of *On the Origin of Species* at age 16. And according to his classmate Hugo Bergmann, he read Haeckel's *Welträtsel* (*The Riddle of the Universe*, 1899) with 'unusual enthusiasm' in the same period.[10] A few years later he

[8] Foreword to 1st edn., *Kunstformen der Natur* (Leipzig: Bibliographisches Institut, 1899).

[9] As it turned out, Haeckel was richly rewarded for his efforts. In his 1913 introduction to *Die Natur als Künstlerin* (*Nature as Artist*) (Berlin: Vita), he remarks that since the publication of his earlier work he has received numerous pieces of furniture, dishes, cups, and pillows, all 'tastefully embellished with the charming forms of the above-mentioned protists' (12).

[10] As quoted by K. Wagenbach, *Franz Kafka: Eine Biographie seiner Jugend* (Berne: Francke, 1958), 60.

would find similar ideas in the literary writings of Hugo von Hofmannsthal and his friend Max Brod. The ornamental exoticism that one finds in their early work, as indeed that of the entire *fin-de-siècle* and *Jugendstil* generation, is sustained and legitimized by their naturalist curiosity in contemporary evolutionary theories linking plant, animal, and human intelligence.[11] Brod's early novellas abound in vegetable and animal exotica whose *correspondance* with the human soul he attempts to convey by an abundance of synaesthetic tropes. The following description from his 'Carina Island' (in which he portrays Kafka as a detached, melancholy aesthete) gives us a typical sampling:

> It was a forest full of passion through which we strode. In the deep tranquillity and solitude, magnificent magnolia trees put forth their blossoms like large, violet bowls of porcelain. Humming-birds flashed through fragrant symphonies of scarlet and snow-white oceans of flowers, through palagonitic bushes and lilies and begonias. Giant silk-like moths spread their shimmering wings, butterflies showed off their violet and emerald-blue shades of colour. Giant beetles, which looked like precious jewels or like foliage, crept their way through the oily, red soil.[12]

Hofmannsthal also echoes Haeckel's monistic exoticism in his early *Jugendstil* story 'Fairytale of the 672nd Night' (1895), when the main protagonist recognizes in the ornaments of his plush, *fin-de-siècle* furniture 'a magic image of the intertwined wonders of the world'. In these carved ornaments he sees 'the forms of animals and the forms of flowers and the merging of flowers with animals; the dolphins, lions, tulips, pearls and acanthus . . . It was a great heritage, the divine work of all generations and species.'[13] In his Lord Chandos 'Letter' written seven years later, the emphasis on ornamental flora and fauna shifts to less exotic, indeed 'insignificant' creatures; but Haeckel's influence is still evident in the

[11] Maurice Maeterlinck, whose writings played a key role in Symbolist and *fin de siècle* literary movements, was an amateur zoologist and botanist who dedicated several works to minute descriptions of ants, bees, and the *intelligence des fleurs*; he felt that their activity revealed a sense of order and beauty, an innate 'artistic instinct'. Other writers, notably Jens Peter Jacobsen (a trained botanist who translated Darwin into Danish), Joris-Karl Huysmans, and Octave Mirbeau in France, developed similar ideas about natural evolution in their works.

[12] 'Die Insel Carina', in *Experimente* (Berlin: Axel Juncker, 1907), 46.

[13] 'Das Märchen der 672. Nacht', in J. Mathes (ed.), *Prosa des Jugendstils* (Stuttgart: Reclam, 1982), 41–2.

fluid, evanescent passage between them and the protagonist's human consciousness. The text, which Kafka knew and valued, is particularly relevant to *The Metamorphosis*:

> In these moments an insignificant creature—a dog, a rat, a beetle, a crippled appletree, a lane winding over the hill, a moss-covered stone—mean more to me than the most beautiful, abandoned mistress of the happiest night. . . . [Such creatures] can become the vehicle of a divine revelation . . . of my flowing over into those creatures, or my feeling that a fluid of life and death, dream and waking, flowed into them for an instant—but from where?[14]

Kafka's story is another matter, of course. His beetle does not crawl through the earth of Brod's exotic tropical island but through the drab, petty bourgeois apartment of a European city. And unlike Hofmannsthal, who keeps Chandos's mystical revelation within a human framework, Kafka reverses the camera angle, forcing us to see not so much the insect as the world of higher primates from the insect's perspective. Moreover, Gregor's metamorphosed body does not cater to contemporary aesthetic taste for stylized exotica. Like the cockroach that Kafka mentions in the 'Letter to His Father', the vermin form in *The Metamorphosis* is meant to sting and bite its audience, to upset traditional aesthetic notions with a scandalous, 'inhuman' otherness. Frau Samsa's reaction—her appeal to 'God' as well as her fainting—is again exemplary.

As an assault on conventional bourgeois taste, the novella thus definitely belongs within the canon of Expressionist and avant-garde modernism, rather than in *fin-de-siècle* 'decadence' or the *Jugendstil*. Its closest visual counterpart is to be found in the early drawings of Kafka's Prague contemporary and acquaintance Alfred Kubin, whose allegorical symbolism often relies on a similar grotesque crossing of human and abstract insect-like figures. But like Kubin's zoological fantasies, Kafka's story draws on the visual forms promoted by *fin-de-siècle* scientific and literary discourse, on 'strange and marvellous forms' from a radically other realm of experience. More crucially, it insists on

[14] 'Ein Brief', as reprinted in U. Karthaus (ed.), *Impressionismus, Symbolismus und Jugendstil* (Stuttgart: Reclam, 1977), 148–50, my translation. The above quotations appear in three separate passages but all refer to the same mystical, unutterable experience.

what one might well call the animal's 'humanness', which emerges most poignantly in his relation to art. Just as Haeckel recognized in single-celled protozoa a human 'soul' and a primal *Kunsttrieb*, so does *The Metamorphosis* endow a lowly, potentially repulsive form with a human consciousness and a will toward art. However grotesque and 'other' the *Ungeziefer* may appear to the Samsa family, the text's true subject (as in Kafka's other animal stories) is the condition of being caught between human and animal forms, caught in the fluid of an evolutionary life force. That Gregor slides down the evolutionary ladder in his quest for artistic self-realization is only one of the ironies behind his bizarre transformation.

III

To describe Gregor's animal form as it manifests itself in the narrative, one can best begin by noting what it is not: clothing. In Kafka's novel fragment of 1907, *Wedding Preparations in the Country*, we find an anticipation of Gregor Samsa's transformation. There Eduard Raban imagines himself split into two distinct selves: a giant beetle who stays in bed while his 'clothed' human body is sent into the *Verkehr* of the world, 'travelling' to the country to get married:

> I don't even need to go to the country myself, it isn't necessary. I'll send my *clothed body* . . . For I myself am meanwhile lying in my bed, smoothly covered over with the yellow-brown blanket . . . As I lie in bed I assume the shape of a big beetle, a stag beetle or a cockchafer, I think. (*CS* 55–6, my emphasis)

What is surprising here is that Raban's grotesque form as a beetle connotes protection and warmth. He feels no horror, surprise, or shame at his metamorphosis, but rather an odd kind of satisfaction, as if his hard beetle shell were simply one additional layer of protection from whatever menaces him in the outside world. On the other hand his 'clothed body' is sent like a messenger to take part in the 'traffic of clothes', travelling to the country where he will perform the social rituals necessary for his impending marriage. This clothed body is clearly the unessential self: it 'staggers out of the door', a movement that indicates not the body's fear but 'its nothingness' (*CS* 55). And if it is not certain, as Walter Sokel maintains, that what remains behind in bed is Raban's 'essential', 'naked' self (protected by blanket, beetle shell, and the fetal position of his legs, Raban is everything but naked), it has been removed from the *Verkehr* of society. Raban's beetle self is unclothed and yet covered—'naked' in the sense than an animal is considered naked.

The fiction of *The Metamorphosis*, of course, is to turn Raban's dream into reality. 'It was no dream', a disembodied narrative voice announces at the text's beginning. Here too clothing and *Verkehr* are intertwined. Previously Gregor worked as a travelling salesman, selling 'cloth samples' for a large company; his collection of clothing lies open, like a suitcase, ready to be packed up for another day's journey. His metamorphosis signals first of all a break with this order of reality, with the order of work, travel, clothing, and mortality, as is made clear in Gregor's first extended monologue:

> Oh God, he thought, what an exhausting job I've picked on! Traveling about day in, day out. It's much more irritating work than doing the actual business in the office, and on top of that there's the trouble of constant traveling, of worrying about train connections, the bad and irregular meals, casual acquaintances that are always new and never become intimate friends [*ein immer wechselnder, nie andauernder, nie herzlich werdender menschlicher Verkehr*]. (*CS* 89–90)

Gregor's lament is directed not against work but against the 'travelling' nature of his work, the movement that prevents him from realizing a truly 'affectionate' relation to society, a 'human' *Verkehr*. The irony of this phrase is the rhetorical reversal underlying the entire story, that of an 'animal' who is more human than his human co-protagonists. 'The devil take it all!', Gregor exclaims in a Faustian invocation, and immediately he senses the strangeness of his reptile body—an 'itching up on his belly' which is now covered with small white spots, 'the nature of which he could not understand' (*CS* 90). This 'pact' with the devil seals Gregor's break with his human past, removes him from the 'traffic of clothes', and prepares him for his existence as a radically singular, 'animal' being, whose foreign body he must first learn to master.

The most striking counterexample to Gregor's grotesque form is the photograph that hangs in the Samsas' living room, depicting him during his military service as 'a lieutenant, hand on sword, a carefree smile on his face, inviting one to respect his uniform and military bearing' (*CS* 101). This image of military authority, virility, and happiness depends on the effacement of individual singularity. Gregor wears the uniform that literally and symbolically establishes his participation in a social order whose identity is maintained by a common form of clothing. The 'uniformity' of his military appearance coincides with the nature of his employment as a salesman who shows cloth 'samples' (*Muster*) to his clients. Critics have often taken this word as a pun on *Musterknabe*, as if the text meant to say that Gregor was a 'model child'. He was, but only in the sense of being without any particular identity that would set him above or apart from the others—equivalent and interchangeable, like the cloth samples in his travelling kit. (Or, in an image whose uncanniness gives us a measure of Kafka's ambivalence toward the effacement of individual difference, like the three unnamed, indistinguishable men who later take lodging in the Samsa household.)

Kafka develops further the notion of the uniformization of work and social *Verkehr* through the father, who is forced to take a position as a bank messenger for which he wears a uniform with gold buttons and monogrammed cap. Herr Samsa thus enters the world of commerce as the transmitter of financial messages, a scarcely human vehicle in the circulation of commercial meanings. His uniform secures his identifiability in this network at the same time that it marks him as a prisoner and underling who has sacrificed his personal identity to an abstract order. Branded with the bank's mono-gram and uni-form, Herr Samsa's body functions only as a sign, a bearer of information in the *Verkehr* of the world's meaning; he even eats and sleeps in his uniform, 'as if he were ready for service at any moment and even here only at the beck and call of his superior' (*CS* 123). As always in Kafka, this traffic signifies something irremediably base and unclean: 'his uniform, which was not brand-new to start with, began to look dirty, despite all the loving care of the mother and sister to keep it clean, and Gregor often spent whole evenings gazing at the many greasy spots on the garment.'

Mother and sister also enter the world of *Verkehr*. Grete takes a job as a salesgirl and is learning shorthand to work as a secretary, thus serving as the transmitter of money, letters, information—a 'vehicle' in social and economic traffic. Frau Samsa helps out by sewing 'elegant underwear' for a fashion boutique, working late into the night (*CS* 123). With this covert reference to the fancy goods sold in his father's shop, Kafka depicts Gregor's mother as an unwitting madam *à distance*, mediating the *Verkehr* of elegant clothing, social ritual, and sexual couplings. At the end of the text the notion of traffic is literalized when the Samsas ride a streetcar to the country and envision their daughter's entrance into the sexual *Verkehr* of marriage: 'It struck both Mr. and Mrs. Samsa [that their daughter] had bloomed into a pretty girl with a good figure. They grew quieter and half unconsciously exchanged glances of complete agreement, having come to the conclusion that it would soon be time to find a good husband for her' (*CS* 139).[15]

IV

Gregor's metamorphosis, then, makes a cut in his life, isolating him from the paternal and social order of work, clothing, business, 'traffic'. It defines him negatively: against the family's names he is nameless; against its human uniforms he has his singular animal covering; against its participation in the circulation of social or economic meaning, he remains cloistered in his room, cut off

[15] Kafka's depiction of the counter-metamorphosis that takes hold of the Samsa family reveals the extent of his ambivalence not only toward bourgeois sexuality and marriage but also toward the bourgeois notion of work. Since the Enlightenment, work in the public sphere had been seen as the key to individual self-definition; for liberal and Marxist philosophers alike, personal autonomy and freedom are guaranteed by one's profession or trade, through which individuals realize their identities and participate in the social collectivity. Kafka is closer to Max Stirner and other anarchist philosophers who see work and any participation in the *Verkehr* of the socio-economic sphere as a threat to individual identity. See especially the chapter entitled 'Mein Verkehr' in Stirner's *Der Einzige und sein Eigentum* (1845), in which he emphasizes the individual's need to withdraw from the 'traffic' of familial responsibilities.

from human discourse. And yet the narrative does not limit itself to a merely negative definition of Gregor's identity. In opposition to this family 'traffic' of clothing, it delineates an alternative, Utopian space of play, distraction, and childlike innocence that is curiously consistent with late nineteenth-century definitions of aesthetic experience. In fact, Gregor's metamorphosis fulfils the dream of every serious *fin-de-siècle* aesthete: to become not just an artist, but the artwork, the visual icon, itself.

The second paragraph of *The Metamorphosis*, immediately following the account of Gregor's transformation, describes a picture of a lady dressed in fur that, hanging on the wall opposite him, seems to mirror his newly transformed, animal self:

> Above the table . . . hung the picture which he had recently cut out of an illustrated magazine and put into a pretty gilt frame. It showed a lady, with a fur cap on and a fur stole, sitting upright and holding out to the spectator a huge fur muff into which the whole of her forearm had vanished! (*CS* 89)

The picture clearly constitutes an aesthetic moment within the Samsa's petty bourgeois world. As we learn later, Gregor has himself fashioned the 'pretty gilt frame' with his fretwork, a pastime or 'amusement' that is explicitly contrasted with his work as a travelling salesman. 'The boy thinks about nothing but his work', Frau Samsa explains to the chief clerk. 'He just sits there quietly at the table reading a newspaper or looking through railway timetables. The only amusement he gets is doing fretwork. For instance, he spent two or three evenings cutting out a little picture frame; you would be surprised to see how pretty it is; it's hanging in his room' (*CS* 95–6). Here the mortality of *Verkehr*, evoked through the railway *time*tables and newspapers (*Zeitungen*), is contrasted with Gregor's 'amusement' or distraction (*Zerstreuung*) in making the picture; alienated labour is contrasted with a form of play that results in art, a framed image that is 'beautiful' (*schön*).

Of course, one should be wary of idealizing what is after all a kind of pin-up—an erotic photograph cut out of a magazine that a lonely salesman hangs in his room. And what about the woman's fur clothing? Isn't it part of the same *Verkehr* of clothing, social intercourse, and mortality that defines the Samsa household?

Fur was after all the clothing that Adam and Eve put on after being expelled from the Garden, as Kafka noted when he copied this passage from Genesis into his diary.[16] In fact, these furs function as emblems not so much of wealth and social status as of animality, which in this story symbolizes a liberation from specifically human problems of sin, guilt, mortality, even from pain and self-consciousness. This is the basic narrative movement to *The Metamorphosis*: after his initial transformation, Gregor will attempt to realize the promise implicit in this photograph, to merge with his mirror-image, to descend the evolutionary ladder into an animal state, to become the animal-artwork.

As several studies have pointed out, Kafka borrowed the image of the fur-clad lady as well as the basic plot structure for his story from a classic novel of *fin-de-siècle* eroticism, Leopold von Sacher-Masoch's *Venus in Furs* (1880).[17] The picture Gregor has cut out of a magazine thus functions as a coded reference to Kafka's own appropriation of Sacher-Masoch's narrative. This is not the place to rehearse the numerous and surprising similarities between the two texts, which include not only the fur clothing, but also uniforms, the name Gregor, and analogous 'punishment fantasies', which, in Sacher-Masoch's text, turn the protagonist metaphorically into a 'dog' or 'worm' grovelling at his mistress' feet. Two points of contact between these texts are however worth stressing. The first is that in both works fur functions as a metonymy for sexual desire, either in the Freudian sense as a fetish recalling the mother's genitalia and pubic hair, or in the popular sense of 'animal' passion and corporeality.[18] Secondly, in both texts

[16] 'And the Lord God made for Adam and for his wife garments of skins [*Röcke von Fellen*], and clothed them.' (Diary entry for 19 June 1916.)

[17] Sacher-Masoch's book has recently been reprinted in English with an extensive introduction by Gilles Deleuze (New York: Zone Books, 1989). On the relationship between Sacher-Masoch and Kafka see Ruth Angress, 'Kafka and Sacher-Masoch: A Note on *The Metamorphosis*', *Modern Language Notes* 85 (1970), 745–6; F. Kuna, 'Art as Direct Vision: Kafka and Sacher-Masoch', *Journal of European Studies* (1972), 237–46; and my own 'Kafka and Sacher-Masoch', *Journal of the Kafka Society of America*, 2 (Dec. 1983), 4–19 (repr. in Harold Bloom (ed.), *Franz Kafka's the Metamorphosis*, Modern Critical Interpretations (New York: Chelsea House, 1988)).

[18] Freud writes: 'fur and velvet—as has long been suspected—are a fixation of the sight of the pubic hair, which should have been followed by the longed-for sight of the female member.' Cf. 'Fetishism' (1927), in *The Standard Edition of the Complete Psychological Works of Sigmund Freud* (London: The Hogarth Press, 1961), xxi. 147–58.

desire is a product of images—paintings, sculptures, photographs, staged erotic encounters—in other words, art. One paradigmatic moment in *Venus in Furs* describes for instance the narrator's desire for a white marble copy of the Venus de Milo, which is draped in fur. The novel also opens with the description of a painting of Venus to which it returns in the closing scene.

From Sacher-Masoch's novel one may hypothesize that masochistic desire is dependent on images because by definition the images preclude fulfilment. In between the opening and closing description of the painting, we witness the main protagonist orchestrate his desire in the guise of masochistic self-abasement, dressing his female partner in a variety of fur costumes, engaging her to act out pre-established scenarios of punishment and humiliation with him and other men, while all the time setting up formal obstacles to the consummation of his desire. In effect, the masochist turns his mistress into an actress, himself into her public. He 'frames' her as art, establishing an inviolable line between his reality and material bondage on the one hand and her aesthetic freedom and power over him on the other. The image is merely a more radical form of this same inviolability, its inaccessibility as image guaranteeing the frustration of desire. The frame is so to speak the masochist's rope and chains.

This same dialectic of image, power, and desire is implicit in Gregor Samsa's unspoken relationship with his 'pretty' picture. Unlike, say, Georg Bendemann in 'The Judgment', Gregor has no mistress or fiancée, only the photograph, which through his own efforts he has inscribed as art, framing it and putting it behind glass. Already 'only' an image, the woman is thus raised to the level of art, put into an ideal space that Gregor can aspire to but never truly enter. And this seems to be the source of its

The fetish allows the subject to maintain his fantasy of a female penis, thus sidestepping the threat of castration. This interpretation seems to have validity for Sacher-Masoch's hero, who frequently fantasizes that the furs enclose some hard, erect object (such as a marble statue of Venus) or a source of violent energy. Masoch's emphasis on electricity, his image of the woman in furs as an 'augmented electric battery', seems to suggest that the impersonality of the punishment is a key element in the masochistic experience of pleasure. (The apples that the father bombards Gregor with at the end of the second section roll about as if 'electrisiert'; the machine in 'In the Penal Colony' runs on electric power.) The image of the woman's forearm and fist in the fur muff also corresponds to Freud's notion of the (male) child's fantasy of the female member.

attraction and power. In the story's second section, Gregor's identity is threatened when his sister and mother begin cleaning out his room. He asks himself which object he should choose to rescue, considers (but rejects) his desk, then settles on the image of the woman in fur hanging on the wall. The encounter with art is explicitly erotic, the 'cool' glass which separates Gregor from the image providing the actual 'comfort':

> [H]e was struck by the picture of the lady muffled in so much fur and quickly crawled up to it and pressed himself to the glass, which was a good surface to hold on to and comforted his hot belly. This picture at least, which was entirely hidden beneath him, was going to be removed by nobody. (*CS* 118)

What is unusual about Kafka's text and distinguishes it from Sacher-Masoch's racier but ultimately more conventional narrative, is that the movement toward 'animality' and masochistic desire does not result in sin and guilt, but in a cleansing of these 'human' remnants from Gregor's past. The animal is innocent. Thus his metamorphosis is akin to a rebirth, to a childlike awakening, to self-absorbed games and play. We are told for instance that Gregor's insect legs 'dance . . . as if set free', that he learns to get out of bed by rocking himself to and fro—'the new method was more a game [*Spiel*] than an effort' (94)—and that, despite his grotesque form, he shows no hesitation in offering himself for public viewing. 'He was eager to find out what the others, after all their insistence, would say at the sight of him' (98).[19] The sentiment voiced here is more than a comic device: Gregor is in the process of losing his capacity for self-judgement through the eyes of the world, of becoming an unselfconscious child-animal.

This reacquisition of an originary freedom and innocence coincides with Gregor's *Kunsttrieb*, his impulse toward art and self-display. Two moments stand out in this process. The first is

[19] This itinerary is essentially the opposite of that travelled by Red Peter in Kafka's later story 'A Report to an Academy', an ape living in blissfully unselfconscious freedom on the 'Gold Coast' who is captured and introduced into the *Verkehr* of human society: he learns to talk, wear trousers, drink schnapps, and fornicate with a trained (i.e. half-human) chimpanzee. By contrast *The Metamorphosis* describes Gregor's progressive acquisition of the freedom in his animal body, thereby returning to the 'Gold Coast' of a childlike, prelapsarian innocence.

the delightful interlude of unselfconscious play that takes place in the novella's second section. Despite the damage inflicted to his body by his father, Gregor enjoys a beatific state of distraction (*Zerstreuung*), innocent of memory, swinging like a gymnast from the ceiling, walking the walls, defying the material constraint of gravity much like the trapeze artists, circus riders, and floating dogs figured in Kafka's other writings. High above the furniture in his room, Gregor can breathe more 'freely':

> He especially enjoyed hanging suspended from the ceiling; it was much better than lying on the floor; one could breathe more freely; one's body swung and rocked lightly; and in the almost blissful absorption induced by this suspension it could happen to his own surprise that he let go and fell plump on the floor. Yet he now had his body much better under control than formerly, and even such a big fall did him no harm. (*CS* 115)

A happy state of distraction, easy breathing, the almost musical rhythm rocking his body—these are all privileged terms in Kafka's vocabulary. Capable of 'falling' from a great height without harming himself, Gregor has achieved a state of innocent grace untroubled by his father's *Schulden*, the financial 'debts' that are also, in German, the result of moral transgressions. But this 'immortality' is achieved by the 'artist' who has made his body into the vehicle of his art, a vehicle which performs, in these moments of unselfconscious play, as gracefully as the marionettes in Kleist's essay 'Über das Marionettentheater.' If *Luftmensch*, as Günther Anders points out, connotes in German the artist who has no solid footing beneath his feet, Gregor is the *Lufttier*, much like the floating dogs in the later story 'Investigations of a Dog' who are animated by an uncanny, silent music, or the Japanese tumblers Kafka drew in his diary as an image of artistic freedom (*D1* 12). Gregor literally floats above the traffic of human time, his consciousness absorbed by his dancing, though hardly *Jugendstilian*, body.

The second moment occurs in the third section of the novella and brings out the musical implications of Gregor's artistic self-realization. Gregor's sister Grete begins playing the violin for her parents and the lodgers while Gregor lies in his dirty, dark room. Animated by a corporeal *Kunsttrieb* or will to art, oblivious to the material consequences of his action, he creeps toward his sister or rather her 'playing', her *Spiel*:

Gregor's sister began to play; the father and mother, from either side, intently watched the movements of her hands. Gregor, attracted by the playing, ventured to move forward a little until his head was actually inside the living room. . . . [I]n spite of his condition, no shame deterred him from advancing a little over the spotless floor . . . Gregor crawled a little farther forward and lowered his head to the ground so that it might be possible for his eyes to meet hers. Was he an animal, that music moved him so? He felt as if the way were opening before him to the unknown nourishment he craved. (*CS* 130–1)

Again Kafka's text insists on the ludic, innocent character of this encounter. Despite his animal condition, the filth that his body has accumulated, or even the evidently incestuous nature of his attraction to his sister, 'no shame deter[s] him' on his path toward the 'unknown nourishment' evoked by the music. We should note too the text's insistence on a lived, corporeal experience of the music: the boarders who read the musical notes over Grete's shoulder rather than experience music physically like Gregor are clearly portrayed as philistines. Gregor, the innocent 'child-animal' who wants to 'play' with his sister, has access to the secret of art because his body is itself striving for a weightless, ethereal, musical condition. And this artistic impulse results, for the third and last time, in the body's self-display in a context of aesthetic performance.

Even the process of dying has an aesthetic, spiritual dimension. Like the initial rejection of clothing, cloth 'samples', and the *Verkehr* of his employment, Gregor's progressive rejection of organic nourishment initiates a movement back to the innocence of childhood or, in biblical terms, to the moment in Eden before the eating of the apple. (The apple that Gregor's father throws at him interrupts this movement and ultimately seems responsible for the son's Christ-like death. But the apple originates with the father, not the innocent child, and as such represents the violent intrusion of the 'traffic' of Gregor's previous life into his aesthetic paradise.) As the memory of his human past fades away, Gregor begins to 'play' with his food like an infant, eventually renouncing it altogether for the pleasures of his home gymnastics: 'he was fast losing any interest he had ever taken in food, so that for mere recreation he had formed the habit of crawling crisscross over the walls and ceiling' (*CS* 115). This fasting flattens and lightens Gregor's form, removing it from the circulation of human, organic life, 'spiritualizing' it until it is completely empty. Grete, who shows a particular fascination for the corpse, remarks: '"Just see how thin he was. It's such a long time since he's eaten anything. The food came out again just as it went in." Indeed, Gregor's body was completely flat and dry.' (*CS* 136–7).

The Christian overtones of this death are clear and support the basic narrative of conflict between father and son. Herr Samsa makes the sign of the cross, for example, and Gregor is described as being 'festgenagelt', 'nailed fast' to the floor by the paternal apple bombardment. Yet Gregor is not only a fasting Christ or monk who has withdrawn from the world, but first of all the *fin-de-siècle* aesthete who 'hungers' for music, the highest of the arts in Romantic and Symbolist poetics.[20] Within the corpus of Kafka's own writings, Gregor bears an unmistakable affinity with other artist figures. One thinks for instance of Georg Bendemann in 'The Judgment' who performs his gymnastic 'turn' over the bridge but then hangs to the railing 'as a starving man clutches for food'. Or of the famished musical dogs in 'Investigations of a Dog', or the disappearing artist figures of the last stories, 'A Hunger Artist' and 'Josephine the Singer'. But Gregor's metamorphosis into a dancing musical bug is the most astonishing of all Kafka's self-referential literary figures. Emptied of all organic substance, perfectly isolated from the paternal 'traffic of clothes', he dies as a two-dimensional object, as 'flat' and 'dry' as the pages of printed characters on which he is now immortalized.

V

In the above remarks I have deliberately read Kafka's text against the majority of its critical interpretations, which see in Gregor's

[20] Walter Pater's claim in *The Renaissance* that all the arts strive for the 'condition of music' best sums up this tradition. Knut Hamsun's novel *Hunger* (1890) established the connection between fasting and the dedication to writing for an entire generation of German writers at the turn of the century, including Thomas Mann and Kafka. Mann used the trope in his early story 'Die Hungernden', Kafka most notably in 'A Hunger Artist' and 'Investigations of a Dog', where it is also related to music.

metamorphosis a tragedy visited upon an unsuspecting victim that ends with the 'liberation' of the family through his ritualistic sacrifice. On the contrary, I see the family as enslaved and deindividualized by its re-entrance into the *Verkehr* of work, sexuality, and commerce (the realm of 'clothing'), whereas Gregor carries out the project of self-definition, individual autonomy, and freedom implicit in his transformation into a 'giant vermin'. He takes off the 'clothes of the world', to put it in the terms of this study, not to reveal an 'essential self' or to retreat into religious seclusion, but, in line with the *fin-de-siècle* substitution of aesthetics for religion, to put on the grotesque mask of art, to retreat into the self-enclosed world of aesthetic play and freedom symbolized by his animal shell. Whether self-willed or not, a consciously Faustian transgression of human limits or a sudden eruption of repressed desire, Gregor's behaviour in his new form is sustained by a constant *Kunsttrieb*, an unconscious artistic will that prevents him from ever questioning the necessity of his metamorphosis or attempting to reverse it. Indeed, this consistent volition to *display* himself goes hand in hand with his 'monstrosity' (etymologically related to *monstrare*, 'to show'), which chases the chief clerk from the scene, puts the formerly parasitic Samsas to work, and dislodges the boarders, allowing Gregor to devote himself to narcissistic play, distraction, and innocent desire. Whatever the cause of his transformation, its implicit, unspoken *telos* is finally aesthetic: to turn the clothed, human body into a pure, autonomous artwork.

This is the place to stress Peter Cersowsky's insightful remark in his study of Kafka's relations to literary decadence that Gregor's metamorphosis into an animal can be seen as part of the traditional 'melancholic disposition' and thereby linked to the melancholy of the *fin-de-siècle* decadent aesthete. Noting that Bourget had already defined the decadent as the isolated individual 'unfit for the common labor of society', Cersowsky rightly stresses the parallel with Gregor's exclusion from family and society as an 'unproductive' bug. In this sense Gregor is a decadent 'type' like Kafka's other bachelor figures—isolated, self-absorbed, ill adapted to work, melancholy, sexually impotent by definition (as the single example of his 'species'), and therefore the endpoint of the

Samsa family line. In essence Gregor's metamorphosis establishes the same opposition between aesthete self and bourgeois family that characterizes Thomas Mann's early novellas (which Kafka greatly admired), with all their connotations of health and vitality on one side, parasitism, decadence and death on the other. Gregor represents the bizarre end of his 'race', the tired, melancholy decadent who willingly departs from this life to make way for his 'healthy' family.[21]

What this interpretation leaves out, however, is the positive, even aggressive countertendency in Kafka's text that insists on Gregor's form as the autonomous artwork. *The Metamorphosis* displays none of Mann's nostalgia for blond and blue-eyed *Bürgerlichkeit*. Indeed, the petty bourgeois environment of the Samsa household—dirty, constricted, animated by a mean will for profit and social conformity—finally provokes the reader's disgust, perhaps the very disgust initially associated with the grotesque bug but which fades away as the story progresses and Gregor's 'humanity' comes to the fore. As we have seen, the text's positive affirmations concern Gregor's form: its childlike aptitude for games, dance, music, and spiritual nourishment. And whereas Gregor's consciousness lags behind the radicality of his aesthetic form (even in death he seems tolerant and forgiving of his family), the body itself proclaims all the aggressive, even jubilant qualities of the avant-garde or modernist artwork: Art as an attack on Life, not just its impotent and nostalgic opponent; Art as the grotesque, abstract, ultimately incomprehensible object that has removed itself from the bourgeois social order.

But not outside the biological order of decay and death. Gregor's blissful state of 'free breathing' and self-absorbed *Zerstreuung* while hanging from the ceiling in his room lasts only a brief while, eventually giving way to a melancholy yearning for an 'unknown nourishment' he has never tasted. And the very refusal of organic nourishment that excludes him from the human, social realm and that augments his ethereal, *Lufttier* nature ultimately leads to his death and disappearance. The animal-artwork is not granted an unnatural physical permanence, but is effaced by the

[21] See Cersowsky, 'Mein ganzes Wesen', 74–6.

same cycle of life forces that is presumably responsible for its original transformation. On 9 December 1912, two days after finishing what would become his most famous story, Kafka sent Felice Bauer a postcard of Strindberg asking her if she knew his story 'Alone', thus secretly revealing the meaning and aestheticist origins of his own text. 'That is finally what it means to be alone', Strindberg says at the end of his autobiographical narrative in reference to his isolation as an artist. 'To spin oneself into the silk of one's own soul, to mask oneself in one's own cocoon, and wait for the metamorphosis, which never fails to come about.' Kafka spun himself into his own literary cocoon and waited. Yet the metamorphosis that took place in Prague in November 1912 did not produce the strange, beautiful butterfly of Strindberg's *fin-de-siècle* imagination, but a grotesque, primitive ornament of modernity: the 'monstrous vermin'.

6

The Physiognomy of Guilt: The Trial

> You're supposed to tell from a man's face, especially the line of his lips, how his case is going to turn out. Well, people declared that judging from the expression of your lips you would be found guilty.
>
> (The Tradesman Block to Joseph K.)

I

FEW readers of *The Trial* would disagree that the central enigma of the novel is posed by its first sentence announcing Joseph K.'s arrest although apparently he has not done anything 'wrong' or 'evil': 'Someone must have been telling lies about Joseph K., for without having done anything wrong he was arrested one fine morning.' This same idea is repeated later in the first chapter when one of the arresting warders explains to K. that the Court officials 'never go hunting for crime in the populace, but, as the Law decrees, are drawn toward the guilty' (*T* 6).[1] In other words, this particular Court does not prosecute a criminal act that has already taken place, but is 'attracted' (*angezogen*) by a condition of guilt that either precedes or in some sense is independent of an actual crime. Confronted with this enigma, commentators have often turned to the biblical notion of original sin to explain K.'s 'trial', which the novel's Christian symbolism admittedly seems to corroborate. Joseph K. eats an apple on the morning of his arrest, and shortly before his execution visits a cathedral where he discovers a painting of Christ's burial.

[1] The German text is 'wird . . . von der Schuld angezogen'. Kafka's formulation is a good deal more abstract than the Muirs's English translation. They avoid the biblical connotations of the key opening adjective *Böse* (evil) by translating it as 'wrong'; and here they personalize the singular, abstract noun *Behörde* (authority) into 'officials' and the equally abstract *Schuld* (guilt or debt) into 'the guilty'.

Without contradicting this line of interpretation, it is worth pointing out that the European legal system of Kafka's day had developed a selective version of original sin with the concept of the 'born criminal'. One of the leading figures in this development was the Italian criminologist and medical anthropologist Cesare Lombroso, whose main work *L'uomo delinquente* (*Criminal Man*, 1875) was based on the thesis that a 'criminal type' existed as an actual species or subspecies of *Homo sapiens*. H. G. Kurella, one of Lombroso's most influential supporters in Germany at the turn of the century, sums up Lombroso's contribution thus:

> According to this doctrine all true criminals possess a continuous series . . . of physical characteristics, the existence of which is proved by anthropology, and of moral characteristics, the existence of which is proved by psychophysiology; these characteristics constitute criminals of a particular variety, an anthropological type of the human race, and those who possess them are criminals by the stern decree of fate—even if they are never found out,—and that too independently of all social and individual conditions. Such a man is born to be a criminal, he is as *Lombroso* puts it, *delinquente nato*, the genuine original sinner.[2]

A salient and controversial aspect of Lombroso's doctrine was the idea that such 'born criminals' invariably displayed physical characteristics of their inner nature; like a life of crime, these corporeal 'stigmata' were merely an outer symptom of this biological nature. Kurella writes, for instance, that the 'indications of this [criminal] disposition are certain physical peculiarities not the result of bodily disease . . . the knowledge of which enables the psychologist to declare that those possessing them cannot help becoming criminals' (quoted in Gross, *Criminal Investigation*, 80). An 'abnormally' small cranium or low forehead, a twisted nose, an 'unsteady' or 'wild' look, facial asymmetries, and other corporeal marks were cited as evidence that could be

[2] Kurella as quoted by Hanns Gross, *Criminal Investigation: A Practical Textbook for Magistrates, Police Officers and Lawyers*, adapted from *System der Kriminalistik* by J. Collyer Adam (London: Sweet & Maxwell, 1924), 80. The number of criminological studies carried out at the turn of the century according to this principle exceeds the scope of the present work. A representative sample would include Kurella, *Naturgeschichte des Verbrechers* (1893); Havelock Ellis, *The Criminal* (1890); Kraus, *Die Psychologie des Verbrechens* (1884); Bonfigli, *Die Naturgeschichte des Verbrechers* (1892); Koch, *Die Frage nach dem geborenen Verbrecher* (1894).

used to identify criminals reliably—whether or not they had committed a crime.

The study of human physiognomy existed earlier of course. One finds scattered observations on the physical signs of character in Aristotle, La Bruyère, and, more systematically, the Swiss writer Johann Caspar Lavater, whose *Essays on Physiognomy* (1775–8) were popular throughout Europe.[3] But in the nineteenth century the study of physiognomy became increasingly quantitative and diagnostic as researchers attempted to derive natural laws with which to predict human behaviour. Franz Joseph Gall, a Viennese anatomist who later settled in Paris, claimed that human character and talent were dependent on the functions of the brain and thus could be inferred with precision by measuring the skull. Lombroso, a positivist, used Gall's phrenology to measure the skulls of countless convicted criminals in Italian jails and morgues. He also extended his analysis to facial features, corporeal stigmata, tattoos, handwriting, and prison graffiti as signs of an 'innate' criminal disposition. The growth of criminal anthropology as a scientific field in the 1870s was in no small part due to Lombroso, whose wide-ranging theories influenced research in medicine, biology, anthropology, and law.[4]

One of the men who did most to apply Lombroso's method in German-speaking countries was none other than Hanns Gross, a magistrate and law professor from Graz who taught Kafka criminal law at the University of Prague from 1902 to 1905.[5] It is

[3] Reference here is to the original publication of *Physiognomische Fragmente zur Beförderung der Menschenkenntnis und Menschenliebe*; an English translation appeared between 1789 and 1798.

[4] Lombroso founded a journal called the *Archivio di psichiatria* for this type of research and directed it for over 29 years; similar journals were established in France, England, and Germany. Lombroso also published widely for a lay audience, including his popular essay on the relations between madness and genius, *Genio e follia* (1864; German translation 1887). His *Grafologia* appeared in 1895 (German edn. 1896), his *Palinsesti del carcere*, on criminal 'graphomania', in 1891 (German edn. 1899).

[5] According to Wagenbach and Binder, Kafka heard Gross lecture up to 16 hours per week on criminal law and Austrian criminal process in his 5th, 6th, and 7th semesters. See K. Wagenbach, *Franz Kafka: Eine Biographie seiner Jugend* (Berne: Francke, 1958), 244; H. Binder (ed.), *Kafka-Handbuch* (Stuttgart: Alfred Kröner, 1979), i. 291. Recently, W. Müller-Seidel has interpreted 'In the Penal Colony' in terms of Gross's published arguments in favour of deporting criminals to penal colonies; see his *Die Deportation des Menschen* (Stuttgart: Metzler, 1986).

through Gross that Kafka undoubtedly came into contact with this school of thinking, which had already attracted considerable professional and lay interest by the turn of the century. Although Gross took issue with Lombroso's tendency toward sweeping generalization, arguing that the anatomical variations discovered by the Italian criminologist were not sufficient 'to establish a determinate type of criminal' (*Criminal Investigation*, 80), he none the less believed in the notion of an inner 'criminal' nature or disposition. He founded and edited the German equivalent to Lombroso's journal, the *Archiv für Kriminologie*, in 1899. He also wrote several widely disseminated handbooks for magistrates, policemen, and lawyers which gave practical advice in identifying criminal 'types' before or after they actually committed a crime.[6] Unlike Lombroso, who applied his theories in popular essays to literature and art, Gross confined himself to criminalistic study and wrote for a professional audience. But his definition of the field was remarkably large and betrays the social and political bias of the late nineteenth century: prostitutes, homosexuals, gypsies, anarchists, the mentally insane, and to a certain extent Jews and women, all exhibited in his view physiological and moral traits resembling those of the 'born' criminal.[7]

A selection of representative quotes from Gross's *Criminal Psychology* (1898) will help make clear the legal method that, as we shall see, was not without importance for the author of *The Trial*. Claiming that physiognomics has the right to be considered 'an independent science', Gross cites approvingly the assertion by a French psychophysiologist that a person will invariably shut his eyes when energetically denying a point and will keep them wide

[6] *Handbuch für Untersuchungsrichter als System der Kriminalistik* (*Handbook for Examining Magistrates as Criminalistic System*, 1893) and *Criminalpsychologie* (*Criminal Psychology*, 1898). Like Lombroso's writings, these works went through multiple editions and were widely translated in Europe and the United States.

[7] Lombroso, although himself a Jew, had paved the way for this kind of analogy, which merges with the developing racial and degeneration theories of Gobineau, Morel, Chamberlain, Nordau, and, not much later, the National Socialists. See S. Gilman, *Jewish Self-Hatred: Anti-Semitism and the Hidden Language of the Jews* (Baltimore: Johns Hopkins University Press, 1985) and *Difference and Pathology: Stereotypes of Sexuality, Race and Madness* (Ithaca, NY: Cornell University Press, 1985).

open when assenting.[8] Such phenomena, Gross notes, 'are significant during examinations, as when we show the accused a very effective piece of evidence (e.g.: a comparison of hand-writings which is evidential), and he closes his eyes. . . . The contradiction between the movement of his eyes and his words is then suggestive enough' (89). Similarly, he uses Darwin's law of 'purposeful associated habits' to claim that 'there is significance in the sudden closing of the mouth by either the accused or the witness. Resolution and the shutting of the mouth are inseparable.' This observation allows the conclusion that if an accused person shows these signs 'he has certainly resolved to pass from denial to confession, or to stick to his denial, or to confess or keep track of the names of his accomplices, the rendezvous, etc.' (91). Similarly, Gross relates Darwin's claim that the 'conviction of one's own guilt is from time to time expressed through a sparkling [*Glänzen*] of the eyes'. Hence the conclusion for the criminologist: 'There is something in the guilty sparkle of the eye. The sparkle in the eyes (however seemingly poetical) is no more than the intensified secretion of tears. The latter gets its increase through nervous excitation, so that the guilty sparkle should also be of the same nature' (96).

Not surprisingly, clothing occupies much of Gross's criminalistic acumen. Like the criminal's characteristic gestures or corporeal traits, clothing is also deemed to be expressive of an inner disposition that can never be fully disguised. The passage deserves extended citation:

It is easy to write a book on the significance of a man's clothes as the expression of his inner state. It is said that the character of a woman is to be known from her shoes, but actually the matter reaches far beyond the shoe, to every bit of clothing, whether of one sex or the other. . . . If we see a man whose coat is so patched that the original material is no longer visible but the coat nowhere shows a hole; if his shirt is made of the very coarsest and equally patched material but is clean; and if his shoes are very bad but are whole and well polished, we should consider him and his wife as honest people, without ever making an error. We certainly see very little wisdom in

[8] *Criminalpsychologie* (Graz: Leuschner & Lubensky's, 1898); English edn., *Criminal Psychology: A Manual for Judges, Practitioners, and Students* (Boston: Little, Brown & Co., 1911), 86.

our modern, painstakingly attired dandies [*Stutzer*], we suspect the provocatively dressed woman of some little disloyalty to her husband, and we certainly expect no low inclinations from the lady dressed with intelligent, simple respectability. (82)

What is striking here is Gross's self-assured tone of voice, his certainty that the choice of clothing is 'always' an expression of a person's character, that the observer can judge character 'without ever making an error'. Later he rejects factors such as caprice, mood, or economic conditions as 'not particularly deep' influences on clothing (83). 'Who has ever seen an honest peasant wearing a worn-out evening coat?' he asks rhetorically. '[The peasant] leaves such clothes to others whose shabby elegance shows at a glance what they are.' He concludes:

Conceit, carelessness, cleanliness, greasiness, anxiety, indifference, respectability, the desire to attract attention and to be original, all these and innumerable similar and related qualities express themselves nowhere so powerfully and indubitably as in the way people wear their clothes. And not all the clothes together; many a time a single item of dress betrays a character. (83)

Gross's impulse to 'type' individuals on the basis of their external appearance is by no means an isolated phenomenon of late nineteenth-century science. We see it in such diverse fields as art history, psychology, anthropology, the developing 'science' of racial characteristics, and to a certain extent psychoanalysis.[9] But our focus here is on Kafka and specifically *The Trial*, where every physiognomical detail, every gesture and piece of clothing, is subjected to the same type of intensive scrutiny that Hanns Gross demanded of legal experts. Indeed, Lombroso's theory of the physiognomy of the born criminal seems to be part of Joseph K.'s

[9] As Carlo Ginzburg has recently pointed out, the interest in seemingly insignificant anatomical details links the investigation methods of figures as diverse as Morelli (in the attribution of Renaissance paintings), Freud, and Conan Doyle's Sherlock Holmes (in identifying criminal 'types'). Ginzburg quotes the following passage from 'The Cardboard Box' (1892) in which Holmes refers to the English equivalent of Lombroso's journal: 'As a medical man, you are aware, Watson, that there is no part of the human body which varies so much as the human ear. Each ear is as a rule quite distinctive, and differs from all other ones. In last year's *Anthropological Journal* you will find two short monographs from my pen upon the subject.' 'Clues: Morelli, Freud, and Sherlock Holmes', in U. Eco and T. Sebeok (eds.), *The Sign of Three: Dupin, Holmes, Peirce* (Bloomington, Ind.: Indiana University Press, 1984), 84.

legal battle. Semi-official claims are made that he and other accused individuals display physical characteristics distinguishing them from the rest of the population. Huld the lawyer explains to K. for instance that 'if you have the right eye for these things, you can see that accused men are often attractive. It's a remarkable phenomenon, almost a natural law' (*T* 183).[10] This 'natural law' allows a trained observer infallible powers of judgement: 'those who are experienced in such matters can pick out one after another all the accused men in the largest of crowds' (*T* 184). Block, a defendant with years of experience in Court matters, tells K. about a widespread 'superstition': 'you're supposed to tell from a man's face, especially the line of his lips, how his case is going to turn out. Well, people declared that judging from the expression of your lips you would be found guilty' (*T* 174).[11] K.'s landlady Frau Grubach, who has talked to the warders and learned something about the Court's unusual methods, also explains to K. the difference between his guilt and that of an actual criminal: 'If one's arrested as a thief, that's a bad business, but as for this arrest—. It gives me the feeling of something very learned [*etwas Gelehrtes*], forgive me if what I say is stupid, it gives me the feeling of something learned which I don't understand' (*T* 19).

This emphasis on 'natural law', expert observation and 'learned' accusations of guilt suggests that Kafka may have drawn on his academic training in depicting the unusual legal criteria by which Joseph K. is arrested and executed. We should note, however, that *The Trial* posits only a relation between physical appearance and accusation, not guilt. The line of K.'s lips indicates that he will be *found* guilty, not that he actually is guilty; experienced observers can pick out the 'accused' from a crowd, but their guilt (like K.'s) is still to be determined. In other words, Kafka's novel maintains the opening discrepancy between K.'s arrest and the

[10] The German text makes clear here the relation betwen guilt and accusation, since the word for 'attractive', *anziehend*, points back to the notion of the Court authorities being 'attracted' (*angezogen*) by guilt. Leni seduces K. because, according to Huld, she finds 'nearly all accused men attractive' (*T* 183). The key to this relation betwen guilt and sexual attraction lies in Kafka's concept of clothing, which will be discussed below.

[11] This may explain retroactively why Fräulein Montag keeps 'staring so fixedly at [K.'s] lips' (79), an interest he notes but cannot explain to himself at the time.

lack of a motivating criminal action to the very last page, when K. is executed without ever having been formally accused, tried, or found guilty. Whereas Lombroso and Gross posit a relation between a criminal's appearance and his inner nature, Kafka shifts the question back on to the Court. If the accused display unique physical signs (which itself is presented only as 'superstition' or the opinion of a lawyer K. eventually comes to distrust), these signs derive from their treatment at the hands of the Court, which at one point is described as *hetzen*, 'harassment' or 'persecution' (*T* 203).

To state our opinion straight out: Kafka does not believe in the validity of 'typing' individuals according to external marks. Again and again *The Trial* demonstrates the fallaciousness and devastating consequences of Hanns Gross's claim that 'the inner condition of men implies some outer expression' (*Criminal Psychology*, 69). The lawyer Huld admits this crucial distinction between guilt and accusation:

> It cannot be guilt that makes [the accused] attractive, for—it behooves me to say this as a lawyer, at least—they aren't all guilty . . . *so it must be the mere charge preferred against them that in some way enhances their attraction*. Of course some are much more attractive than others. But they are all attractive, even that wretched creature Block. (*T* 184, my emphasis)

Kafka also opposed Hanns Gross and his legal views for another reason. We know for instance that he sided with Gross's son Otto in the *cause célèbre* that rocked German artists and intellectuals in 1913 when Hanns Gross used his considerable legal influence to have his son arrested in Berlin, brought back to Austria, and confined to a mental institution on the grounds that, although not formally charged of any crime, he was behaving irresponsibly and could be a danger to others. Part of the problem was Otto Gross's outspoken opposition to patriarchal capitalism and its sexual ethic. A doctor and psychoanalyst who had trained with Freud and Jung, Gross had already published a number of articles in avant-garde cultural journals advocating a Nietzschean and Bachofenian version of psychoanalysis: psychotherapy as the tool for a social and sexual liberation from patriarchy. His call for the overthrow of the bourgeois state in favour of a socialist and matriarchal Utopia went against the very order his father sought to defend from 'criminal' elements, which included anarchists, revolutionaries, the insane, and the *Lumpenproletariat*. The deeply personal conflict between father and son thus turned on contemporary political as well as social values, and Otto Gross's supporters denounced his arrest as an exemplary instance of the arbitrary violence inherent in patriarchal capitalism.[12]

Through his friends Max Brod and Franz Werfel, Kafka followed closely the Berlin avant-garde journals *Sturm*, *Aktion*, and *Zukunft* which took up Gross's defence. Critics have even suggested that Gross's illegal imprisonment by his father may have been a historical 'source' for Joseph K.'s arrest in *The Trial*.[13] In any case Kafka found himself in a similar if less public battle with his own father and, one year after Gross's arrest, characterized his trip to Berlin with his father to celebrate his engagement as a criminal arrest: 'June 6. Back from Berlin. Was tied hand and foot like a criminal. Had they sat me down in a corner bound in real chains, placed policemen in front of me and let me look on simply like that, it could not have been worse. And that was my engagement.' Kafka met Otto Gross several years later in Prague with Brod and Werfel, and agreed to participate in Gross's project to publish a journal against the 'patriarchal will to power'.[14] In mid-November 1917 he wrote to Max Brod: 'If any magazine seemed tempting to

[12] Martin Green notes in *The von Richthofen Sisters: The Triumphant and the Tragic Modes of Love* (Albuquerque, NM: University of New Mexico Press, 1974) 'Otto explained his father's action as a retaliation for an essay on the social functions of sadism Otto had just written for a psychoanalytic journal, in which he used his father's life, public and domestic, as his prime example' (37). More generally, Green writes that 'Otto Gross made himself a living antithesis to his father. He came to stand for total freedom and for the repudiation of patriarchal authority in every possible way' (38). See also Imanuel Hurwitz's biography of Otto Gross, *Paradiessucher zwischen Freud und Jung* (Frankfurt: Suhrkamp, 1982), and Müller-Seidel's *Deporttion des Menschen*.

[13] Hartmut Binder was the first to point out the possible connection between Kafka's novel and this incident, although only in general terms and without any sense for Kafka's critical distance from Hanns Gross's theories. See his *Motiv and Gestaltung bei Franz Kafka* (Bonn: Bouvier, 1966), 106 and the *Kafka-Handbuch*, i. 292. Thomas Anz argues the same point in greater detail in '"Jemand mußte Otto G. verleumdet haben . . . " Kafka, Werfel, Otto Gross und eine 'psychiatrische Geschichte"', *Akzente*, 2 (1984), 184–91. Neither Binder nor Anz discusses Lombroso's theory of criminal types in relation to *The Trial*.

[14] Titled in German the *Blätter zur Bekämpfung des patriarchalischen Machtwillens*, the journal was never published.

me for any length of time . . . it was Dr. Gross's—perhaps because I felt the warmth of a certain personal connection glowing from it.' As critics have pointed out, the 'Letter to His Father' written in 1919 bears the imprint of Gross's theories.

Given this nexus of relations—Kafka's conflict with his father and his 'personal' connection with Hanns Gross's son Otto—it seems possible that in conceiving the narrative structure for *The Trial* he merged two fathers into one overarching patriarchal figure: Hermann Kafka, who had taught his son the capricious laws of paternal domination at home; but also Hanns Gross, who had taught his student the professional methods by which a patriarchal society could identify and hunt down those members it judged undesirable.[15] His first use of the name Joseph K. comes in a literary sketch in his diary on 29 July 1914 that clearly anticipates the novel:

> Joseph K., the son of a rich merchant, one evening after a violent quarrel with his father—his father had reproached him for his dissipated life and demanded that he put an immediate stop to it—went, with no definite purpose but only because he was tired and completely at a loss, to the house of the corporation of merchants which stood all by itself near the harbor. The doorkeeper made a deep bow.

Instead of continuing this narrative, however, which apparently would have taken the course of his earlier 'Son' stories of 1912, Kafka shifted Joseph K.'s personal struggle with his father to the criminological, bureaucratic, abstract structures of the Court. In the version that has come down to us, K. lives alone, his father has long been dead, and the immediate family is largely absent. None the less, the patriarchal nature of the Court that arrests K. is unmistakable: all the Court officials are adult men who brutally subject women to their lust for power, their *Machtwillen*. As K.

[15] Martin Green paraphrases the main idea of Gross's 1905 essay 'Degeneration and Deportation' (*Politisch-Anthropologische Revue*, 4) thus: 'We must deport degenerates in order to save society, he argues. Degenerates are more dangerous than criminals, for some of the latter at least are not lacking in Life-Force. Moreover, there are many degenerates who escape prosecution as criminals—tramps, imposters, the idle, the perverse, revolutionaries—but all are dangerous to the state. . . . Send them to the colonies for life.' In 1913 Gross published an essay on 'Castration and Sterilization'. See Walter Müller-Seidel's illuminating interpretation of 'In the Penal Colony' as a reaction to Gross's theories in *Deportation des Menschen*.

explains to the priest after a year's experience with its legal methods, the Court consists 'almost entirely of petticoat-hunters. Let the Examining Magistrate see a woman in the distance and he knocks down his desk and the defendant in his eagerness to get at her' (*T* 211).

In the following pages I will read *The Trial* as a denunciation of patriarchal authority in the family and the state—as a protest against the teachings of both Hermann Kafka and Hanns Gross. Rather than depicting Joseph K. as a 'born criminal', Kafka demonstrates how his guilt and its physical 'stigmata' are produced by accusation and the attendant persecution. Joseph K. *is made* guilty—but only when he agrees (and he is given little choice) to 'play along' with the 'comedy' staged by the Court, to enter its patriarchal world. The link between the Court's bureaucratic and patriarchal/sexual nature is provided by Kafka's notion of *Verkehr*, which in *The Trial* refers both to the bureaucratic 'traffic' of clients and documents (*Parteienverkehr*) and to sexual intercourse (*Geschlechtsverkehr*).[16] As we shall see, Joseph K.'s trial begins when he enters the 'traffic of clothes', the paternal realm of fancy goods. And it ends when he is undressed by two representatives of this realm who execute him 'like a dog', with the question of his guilt still unresolved.

II

Kafka had literary as well as legal reasons for being opposed to the notion of human 'types'. The relation between a protagonist's character and his or her external appearance was a crucial aspect of European literature throughout the nineteenth century, especially in those works I have described as 'property narratives' in Chapter 4. Novels by Jane Austen, Honoré de Balzac, Charles Dickens, Theodor Fontane, and other realists relied on the same processes

[16] Indeed, as Rainer Stach has recently pointed out, the legal and sexual meanings of *Verkehr* are interchangeable: 'Eros and Justice are actually *not* separate. The pornographic kitsch [the obscene law books in the Court] does not stand in place of the law; rather . . . the law itself is pornographic, it defines the work of the Court as erotic consummation . . . *Verkehr* rules' (148). See 'Eros, Macht und Gesetz: Der Verkehr der Behörden', in *Kafkas erotischer Mythos: Eine ästhetische Konstruktion des Weiblichen* (Frankfurt: Fischer Taschenbuch, 1987), 145–57.

of observation and characterization that went into the scientific studies of Lavater, Gall, Lombroso, Morel, Hanns Gross, and many others. Indeed, there was often a relation of mutual dependence, Balzac quoting, say, the phrenological studies of Gall as often as Lombroso turned to Dostoevsky or Leopardi for poetic corroboration of his theories. Realist novels sought to depict individual lives in terms of social class, milieu, geography, historical epoch; they offered their portrait of society as a form of knowledge and hence as part of the same epistemological description of the human world undertaken by the social sciences.

Balzac is a representative example. In his *Comédie humaine* every surface—a piece of clothing, a building façade, a protagonist's facial features or gait—ultimately turns out to bear a direct relationship to some inner essence or identity. Surfaces are always 'readable' because they are inscribed in a closed system of causal relations that is as regular and predictable as that of the natural world. Consider for instance his minute physical description of the avaricious Grandet in the opening chapter of *Eugénie Grandet*, significantly entitled 'Bourgeois Physiognomies':

> Physically, Grandet was five feet tall, stocky, almost square, the calves of his legs measuring twelve inches around, with fleshy knee-caps and broad shoulders. His face was round, tanned, marked by smallpox . . . his eyes had the calm, voracious expression that peasants attribute to basil, his forehead, full of horizontal creases, was not lacking in significant protuberances.[17]

This passage has a realist rigour and care for physical detail that make it appear objective. And yet no detail is innocent. The portrait constitutes what might be called a 'signifying surface' in which every fact is already coded in terms of Grandet's past history, character, or imminent fate. The pockmarks on his face indicating a past disease, the 'basil' expression signifying avarice according to popular wisdom, the 'protubérances significatives' in his forehead whose meaning Balzac has learned from Gall's lectures on phrenology and will eventually disclose to the reader—each physical detail is presented in such a way that Grandet's inner character can be deciphered by attentive observation. Balzac's protagonists are almost always legible in this way, and even those

[17] *Eugénie Grandet* (Paris: Gallimard, 1972), 29, my translation.

who attempt to disguise their true character (like the criminal Vautrin) are given away by external markings or corporeal 'stigmata'.[18]

The process of 'typing' fictional characters continued throughout the nineteenth and early twentieth centuries and is clearly evident in Thomas Mann's early works. His two main types, the artist and the *Bürger*, are invariably recognizable through a specific set of corporeal marks such as blue eyes, a ruddy complexion and vigorous constitution or, in the case of the 'decadent' artist, bad teeth, blue shadows under the eyes, and a nervous sensibility. Although fascinated by Mann's early novellas, Kafka took exception to this kind of literary typing and particularly objected to Balzac's excessive generalizations. Willy Haas relates that Kafka once composed for him the following parody of a sentence by Balzac: 'At five in the afternoon the duchess left her hotel, slipping on her gloves with the same smooth gestures that all Parisian duchesses use at five in the afternoon.' 'You see', he explained to Haas, 'this generalization is effective but false. You can't narrate anything that way.'[19] Max Brod relates a similar anecdote, noting that Kafka's style is the exact opposite of Balzac's, although he admits that his friend admired the French novelist's narrative 'line' and 'sweep of life'.[20]

Opposites often have much in common, however, and one might describe Kafka's prose style, particularly that of *The Trial*, as the negative version of characterological typing used by Balzac and other realists, as well as by Gross and the Lombroso school of legal anthropology. Kafka constructs the same system of 'signifying surfaces' in which physiognomy, gestures, clothing, and other

[18] The ex-convict Vautrin, a key protagonist in *Illusions perdues* and *Splendeurs et misères des courtisanes*, has a tattoo from his stay in prison that reveals his criminal past; he also has a limp from working there with a ball and chain attached to his leg and which he must consciously suppress in his new identity as . . . chief of police. See the following chapter for the significance of tattoos and criminality.

[19] 'Um 1910 in Prag', *Forum*, 4 (1957), 225, my translation. Note also Kafka's rejection of Dickens's 'rude characterizations which are artificially stamped on everyone and without which Dickens would not be able to get on with his story even for a moment' (diary, 8 Oct. 1917).

[20] Kafka's identification with Balzac was self-consciously negative: whereas Balzac inscribed on his walking stick the motto 'I overcome every obstacle', Kafka said his would be: 'every obstacle overcomes me.' *Franz Kafka: A Biography*, (New York: Schocken Books, 1947; enlarged edn. 1960), 52.

visible details seem imbued with meaning which Joseph K. and the reader are called upon to decipher. But unlike Balzac he never discloses the mechanism of this system; he leaves K. outside the 'great organization' that pursues him, outside the signifying system that claims it can read his guilt by external marks.[21] The world has become inscrutable, conspiratorial, and K. and the reader are caught at the surface of things, anxiously trying to restore the lost relation between a sign's physical appearance and its meaning.[22]

III

When Joseph K. is arrested, he is dressed only in his nightshirt. By contrast, the stranger who arrests him is outfitted with a black suit whose ornate details K. studies carefully:

> He was slim and yet well knit, he wore a closely fitting black suit furnished with all sorts of pleats, pockets, buckles, and buttons, as well as a belt, like a tourist's outfit, and in consequence looked eminently practical, though one could not quite tell what actual purpose it served. 'Who are you?' asked K., half raising himself in bed. But the man ignored the question. (*T* 1)

This scene provides a proleptic instance of K.'s entire relation to the Court: a scene of reading in which he is confronted with a signifying clothing surface ('furnished with *all sorts* of pleats, pockets, buckles, and buttons, [the coat] *looked* eminently practical')

[21] It is important to note that the Court does not appear random to Joseph K. Whether or not it is the 'great organization' he takes it to be, the Court is terrifying precisely because it seems governed by a coherent system of specific rules that he repeatedly attempts to divine. Indeed, he even accepts the argument that the Court is attracted by his guilt, that it corresponds to his own internal disposition. Hence his assumption when looking for the Court during his first interrogation that he will find it with a 'random' choice: 'Finally, however, he climbed the first stairs and his mind played in retrospect with the saying of the warder Willem that an attraction existed between the Law and guilt, *from which it should really follow that the Court of Inquiry must abut on the particular flight of stairs which K. happened to choose*' (*T* 35, my emphasis).

[22] By contrast, the relation between surface detail and inner character in *The Metamorphosis* is relatively unproblematic: the chief clerk is identified as a 'skirt-chaser' merely on the basis of his patent leather shoes; the father's bank uniform signals his inner obedience, etc. Apart from Gregor (whose monstrous, singular form resists such transparent reductions), the characters are all 'readable'. Joseph K. is not equipped with Gregor's monstrous covering; his tragedy is to wake one morning and find himself undressed and exposed to the Court's all-seeing eyes.

but which he just fails to decipher ('one could not *quite* tell what actual purpose it served'). The surface of the man's suit is like the 'long, apparently significant, yet incomprehensible look' (*T* 6) he gives K. a few minutes later. Nothing will ever deviate from this pattern. K. will never see anything more of the Court than this man's impenetrable clothing and facial expressions, will never receive a response to his most basic and legitimate question: Who are you?

None the less, Kafka has included several signs that, although K. is unable to read them, will turn out to be part of a system of signification. The stranger is said to be wearing something like a 'tourist's outfit', a *Reiseanzug*. He is thus designated as a representative of *Verkehr* in the complex, multivalent sense that that word bears in Kafka's writing and which in this novel will take the primary sense of bureaucratic 'traffic'—the circulation of legal documents, clients, lawyers, and officials through the labyrinthine hallways of the Court. In a way, this 'traveling clothing' functions as a uniform for the Court officials. 'What authority is conducting these proceedings?' K. asks the warders. 'Are you officers of the law? None of you has a uniform, unless your suit . . . is to be considered a uniform, but it's more like a tourist's outfit' (*T* 11). At this point the Inspector becomes angry and seems to deny the notion of a uniform. 'We might wear the most official uniforms and your case would not be a penny the worse' (*T* 12).

In fact, the representatives of the Court do wear a sort of uniform, as K. discovers to his horror during his first public interrogation. At first he thinks the men in black beards and coats in the audience represent two different groups whose favour he can win by trying different defence strategies.

But under [their] beards—and this was K.'s real discovery—badges of various sizes and colors gleamed on their coat-collars. They all wore these badges, so far as he could see. They were all colleagues, these ostensible parties of the right and the left, and as he turned round suddenly he saw the same badges on the coat-collar of the Examining Magistrate, who was sitting quietly watching the scene with his hands on his knees. 'So!' cried K., flinging his arms in the air, his sudden enlightenment had to break out, 'every man jack of you is an official, I see, you are yourselves the corrupt agents of whom I have been speaking. (*T* 47)

When K. returns to this room the following Sunday, he notices that the usher's civilian clothes display, in addition to the ordinary buttons, 'two gilt buttons that looked as if they had been stripped from an old army coat' and that serve as the 'emblem of his office' (*T* 61).

In the above passages the notion of a uniform is subtly proffered but then retracted. Joseph K. has discovered signs of consistency and coherence in the Court's appearance, but they are of little use to him. The badges are of 'various sizes and colors' and thus seem to refer to different authorities; their origin is never revealed.[23] Similarly, the gilt buttons on the usher's clothing have literally been cut off from their previous signifying context. The uniform emblems thus establish the men's affiliation with what K. surmises is a 'great organization' (*T* 45), that is, a coherent sign system, but not one he can understand, since the content of this system—the Court or supreme judge or authority represented by the uniform and guaranteeing its legitimacy—remains inaccessible to him. The uniform is not mere surface (the badges and gilt buttons are 'apparently significant'), but neither is it connected to an underlying 'body' or source of deeper meaning.

Caught within the double bind of this apparently coherent yet indecipherable sign system, Joseph K. will allow himself to be marked by the Court's signs, to put on the clothes of guilt. After his arrest he attempts to enter Fräulein Bürstner's room for his interrogation with the Inspector, dressed only in his nightshirt. But the warders hold him back: 'What are you thinking of?' they cried. 'Do you imagine you can appear before the Inspector in your shirt? He'll have you well thrashed, and us too' (*T* 9). K. does not take their objections seriously, calling them 'silly formalities'. None the less he lifts up his coat from the chair and displays it to them for their 'judgment', which is negative. 'It must be a black coat.' K. then opens his wardrobe, searches among his suits, chooses a formal black suit which 'had caused almost a sensation

[23] Note also that the scene is set up so that K. cannot see distinctly: 'The fuggy atmosphere in the room was unbearable, it actually prevented one from seeing the people at the other end' (44–5); [K.] peered from beneath his hand to see what was happening, for the reek of the room and the dim light together made a whitish dazzle of fog' (46).

among his acquaintances because of its elegance', and begins to dress 'with great care'. Here is the beginning of K.'s trial, his entrance into the *Verkehr* of the Court.[24]

The sexual dimension of this traffic is immediately established by the discrepancy between K.'s undressed state and the fully clad stranger who enters his room; the arrest is an intrusion into his intimate life, almost a rape.[25] This impression is reinforced by the prurient interest both warders take in K.'s 'fancy underwear', his *Wäsche*. 'They both examined his nightshirt and said that he would have to wear a less fancy shirt now, but that they would take charge of this one and the rest of his underwear and, if his case turned out well, restore them to him later' (*T* 3). The warders are later punished for having stolen K.'s underwear, but as K. will soon discover, their interest is characteristic of the Court generally, which is made up of 'petticoat-hunters', silk and leather fetishists, voyeurs, sadists, and other elegantly dressed, lascivious, and brutal men.[26] In fact, the sado-masochistic nature of the warders' punishment—they are flogged in an abandoned lumber room in K.'s bank by a man dressed in black leather and naked to the waist—seems a logical extension of the sexual violence implicit in K.'s arrest.

Part of the Christian symbolism behind K.'s trial involves his eating of an apple on the morning of his arrest. This biblical motif, coupled with the equally symbolic act of dressing, suggests the beginning of K.'s 'sinful' or 'guilty' existence. However, K. eats the apple only because his usual breakfast has been consumed by the Court officials, and he puts on his elegant black suit only at their insistence. Later he will behave in guilty fashion, sexually assaulting his neighbour Fräulein Bürstner 'like some thirsty

[24] Note the pun on the word *angezogen* ('attracted' but also 'dressed') in the key sentence revealing that the Court is 'attracted' by guilt. It is as if Joseph K. were acting out the literal meaning of the sentence, 'putting on' or 'dressing' himself with the garments of the Court.

[25] The manuscript of *The Trial* reveals that Kafka initially wrote 'gefangen' (seized) in place of 'verhaftet' (arrested) in the opening sentence. The first term is used later in the chapter and in K.'s description of his visit to Fräulein Bürstner's room.

[26] The warder named Franz cites Court 'tradition' for his theft: 'Your fine shirts were a temptation, of course that kind of thing is forbidden to warders, it was wrong, but it's a tradition that body-linen is the warders' perquisite, it has always been the case, believe me' (*T* 84).

animal lapping greedily at the spring of long-sought fresh water' (*T* 29). But if K. behaves 'like a dog' it is because he has been treated like a dog by the Court, because he has entered their 'traffic' and unwittingly begun to imitate them. 'What kind of man are you?' K. asks the Inspector. 'You ask me to be sensible and you carry on in the most senseless way imaginable yourself! It's enough to sicken the dogs. People first fall upon me in my own house and then lounge about the room and put me through my paces for your benefit' (*T* 13). Like the soldier in 'In the Penal Colony' who is whipped in the face and who then responds with the language of an animal,[27] K. is 'put through his paces' by an inhuman Court, systematically 'persecuted' and degraded until he is finally executed 'like a dog' (*T* 229) in an abandoned quarry at the edge of the city.[28] His fate is to become like the merchant Block, whom K. derisively calls Huld's 'dog'.

Throughout his trial, however, K. attempts to forge a human relationship to the Court, which he sees embodied in the handshake—the non-sexual, physical sign of trust and agreement between two individuals—and which the text systematically contrasts with clothing. When K. offers to shake the Inspector's hand in the opening scene, the latter hesitates but then returns to the 'traffic of clothes':

> The Inspector raised his eyes, bit his lips, and looked at K.'s hand stretched out to him; K. still believed he was going to close with the offer. But instead he got up, seized a hard round hat lying on Fräulein Bürstner's bed, and with both hands put it carefully on his head. . . . 'How simple it all seems to you!' he said to K. . . . 'No, no, that really can't be done' (*T* 14).

The same scene is repeated with Frau Grubach, whom K. finds later that night darning a 'heap of old stockings' (*T* 18). When he seeks her agreement with his assessment of what has happened to him and asks her to shake his hand, she too evades this human contact (*T* 20).

[27] 'Throw that whip away or I'll eat you alive' (*Wirf die Peitsche weg, oder ich fresse dich*, *CS* 146).

[28] This dog motif recurs throughout the novel to characterize the Court's treatment of the accused. When K. discovers the two warders being whipped like animals in the lumber room, he explains their 'inhuman' shrieks to the bank clerks as the howling of a dog (*T* 87).

K.'s desire for Fräulein Bürstner, a woman 'with whom he had exchanged little more than a few words in passing' (*T* 10), is also kindled by an article of clothing—the white blouse that the Court officials have taken from her wardrobe and that K. sees dangling from the latch of an open window when he first enters her room for his interrogation. Like the photographs on her desk which the three bank clerks have 'fingered', the blouse clearly signals the illicit intrusion of the Court officials into her bedroom; she and K. are thus in similar positions. But the empty blouse, a sexual metonymy for the woman who took it off, also triggers his 'animal' interest in her and makes him into her persecutor. When she returns late that night he insists on acting out the events that took place in her room that morning, taking the role of the Inspector for himself:

> 'You must picture to yourself exactly where the various people are, it's very interesting. I am the Inspector, over there on the chest two warders are sitting, beside the photographs three young men are standing. At the latch of the window—just to mention it in passing—a white blouse is dangling. And now we can begin.' (*T* 27)

With this theatrical game (an extension of the 'comedy' he agreed to 'play along with' that morning), K. *becomes* the Inspector to Fräulein Bürstner's K.—to the point where she accuses him of 'tormenting' her and he himself calls his late-night visit an 'assault' (*T* 28), the same word that Kafka originally used in the manuscript to designate K.'s 'arrest'. When he finally attacks her sexually, lapping at her face and neck 'like some thirsty animal', he behaves like the lascivious Court officials, not the peaceful neighbour he was before his arrest.

IV

From this point on, K.'s 'criminal' itinerary in the *Verkehr* of the Law is set. He goes to his first interrogation expecting to find legal offices and the appropriate personnel. Instead, he finds a working-class tenement building that is thriving with an animal-like, indiscriminate sexuality that is repeatedly symbolized by clothing. His first glimpse of the building reveals windows that are 'piled high with bedding' (*T* 34); in the courtyard he sees a clothes-line hung with wet washing; two children with the faces of 'adult rogues' hold him by his trousers; half-grown girls are dressed in 'nothing but an apron'. On a later visit, he grows faint because of the poor air in the Court offices, which is attributed to the tenants' 'dirty linen' (*T* 68).

Appropriately enough, K.'s first direct contact in this scene is with the unnamed 'washerwoman' (*Wäscherin*), whose designation establishes a link with the warders' theft of K's underwear (*Wäsche*) in the previous chapter. Later the woman enters the assembly hall, is undressed by a law student, and engages in sexual intercourse with him on the floor in full view and to the great delight of the male spectators. Still later she will be physically abducted by this same student and delivered to the Examining Magistrate, who is also her lover and has given her 'beautiful' silk stockings (*T* 55). This is the Law of *Verkehr*, where women are subjected to sexual 'persecution' by even the most insignificant male officials: 'The man you saw embracing me has been persecuting me for a long time', the woman explains to K. 'There's no way of keeping him off, even my husband has grown reconciled to it now . . . that man . . . is one of the students and will probably rise to great power yet. He's always after me' (*T* 5–1).

No matter how hard K. tries to enter the legal realm of the Court proper, he will never get past this obscene traffic of elegant 'clothing' and 'animal' desire. When finally allowed to inspect the law books that the Examining Magistrate uses in the initial interrogation, he discovers only obscenities—a crude drawing of a naked man and woman engaged in a sexual act, and a novel with the engaging title *How Grete was Plagued by her Husband Hans*. 'These are the law books that are studied here', K. exclaims furiously. 'These are the men who are supposed to sit in judgment on me' (*T* 52). This does not prevent him, however, from responding to the woman's sexual advances in the hope of gaining information about the Court; he pulls back only when challenged by the student Berthold, who physically carries her off.

Throughout the novel, the Court is repeatedly depicted through the signifying device of elegant clothing, but in such a way that

K. can never divine the relationship between surface and essence. Thus the man representing the Court's 'Information Bureau' is 'stylishly dressed' and wears a 'conspicuously smart gray waistcoat ending in two long sharp points' (*T* 68–9). This appearance is false, since working-class conditions lead most of the other clerks to be 'badly and old-fashionedly dressed', yet important enough for the staff to have taken up a collection to finance his wardrobe. As a female companion explains, 'We—that's to say the staff—made up our minds that the Clerk of Inquiries, since he's always dealing with clients and is the first to see them, must be smartly dressed.' The Clerk answers: 'That's how it is . . . yet I don't understand, Fräulein, why you should tell this gentleman all our intimate secrets' (70). In fact, little of essence has been revealed, since the clothing represents the staff's initiative, not the will of the higher authorities: 'And as the management, which in this respect is somewhat peculiar, refused to provide these clothes, we opened a subscription.' The relation between clothing and 'management', between the Court's appearance and the source of its authority, has thus been disrupted, and Joseph K. will never be able to uncover the truth of the management's identity. The Court remains clothed because it is—or at least seems to be—nothing but ornate, false clothes.

Clothing in *The Trial* thus poses the problem of aesthetic representation, which Kafka explicitly thematizes in a chapter dedicated to art. Titorelli—the first artistic figure to appear as such in Kafka's work—works for the Court, painting official portraits of the judges and lower officials. When K. visits his studio, he is immediately struck by an odd detail: 'In the middle of the room an easel supported a canvas covered by a shirt whose sleeves dangled on the floor' (*T* 144–5).[29] On an immediate level, this incongruous juxtaposition establishes a relation between Titorelli's portrait and the *Verkehr* of Court clothing. But more importantly it points to the absence of origin or referent characterizing the Court generally. Like the shirt, Titorelli's paintings

[29] Like the white blouse in Fräulein Bürstner's room, this shirt has several functions. It triggers the erotic dimension of *Verkehr*: Titorelli is half-dressed, will later invite K. to undress and lie in his bed, and the entire encounter is witnessed by a horde of debauched girls in an attic that turns out to abut on the Court offices.

are merely another layer of clothing that cover rather than reveal the Court's true identity.

'Titorelli', we should point out, is only an artist's pseudonym; the painter's real name (like his past, his origin, or his 'true' character) is never disclosed. So too his portraits, which are not executed mimetically but according to the capricious dictates of the officials. As he tells K. when asked about a figure in his painting of Justice, 'I have neither seen the figure nor the high seat, that is all invention, but I am told what to paint and I paint it.' Here we find the same mixture of order and arbitrariness that informs the Court in other instances. Titorelli is given instructions how to paint; there is (or might be) some coherence to these instructions. But because there is no model, no referent, and because the officials' vanity precludes a realistic portrait, the actual painting reflects the artist's personal 'invention'. The chain of signification is self-enclosed and effectively bars K. from any insight into the actual nature of the Court.

The same is true of Titorelli's ostensibly 'personal' paintings, which he sells to K. after explaining to him the unlikelihood of ever being exonerated by the Court. Sombre landscapes of a wild heath with two stunted trees, the three paintings are not merely similar studies, as the artist claims, but pictures identical in every respect. The scene is quite humorous—one of the few in which Kafka's depiction of the Court as the grotesque repetition of the same slides into a comic mode. But it has its chilling aspect, since the paintings' lack of individuality indicates that they, that is, Titorelli's 'private' artwork, have also been usurped by the Court. It thus comes as no surprise to learn that Titorelli's studio 'really belongs to the Law Court offices' (*T* 164). When K. slips out the back door he encounters a 'small traffic' (*Parteienverkehr*) of defendants in the corridor as well as an usher wearing an extra gold button.

Art is thus a form of clothing: both are 'mere' representations without any discernible or reliable relation to that which they represent. Art is part of K.'s problem therefore, and cannot help him with his battle to get beyond the mere representatives of the Law he actually encounters—low officials with no knowledge of the Law in an endless hierarchy of other identical officials.

Titorelli makes clear the connection between artistic representations and the inaccessibility of the Court in a devastating analogy: 'The Court can never be dislodged from that conviction. If I were to paint all the Judges in a row on one canvas and you were to plead your case before it, you would have more hope of success than before the actual Court' (*T* 150).

In the fragmentary chapter entitled 'The House', Joseph K. dreams of an end to his trial that contrasts strikingly with the novel's actual conclusion. He imagines an encounter with Titorelli in the Law Courts, believing that here he will finally 'break through' the mystery surrounding his case. 'Gliding along as easily as a buoyant craft through water', he suddenly experiences a 'metamorphosis' (*Verwandlung*) that is signalled by an abrupt change in the direction and intensity of the light:

> He was in the corridor of the Law Courts again, but everything was quieter and simpler and there were no conspicuous details. He took it all in at a glance, detached himself from Titorelli, and went his way. He was wearing a new long dark suit which comforted him by its warmth and weight. He knew what had happened to him; but he was so happy about it that he could not bring himself to acknowledge it. In the corner of one of the passages he found his other clothes in a heap; the black jacket, the pin-striped trousers, and on the top the shirt stretched out with crumpled sleeves. (*T* 249–50)

Here too the biblical resonance of clothing is audible. Like Christ's linen garments in the tomb after his resurrection, the black formal clothing that K. put on at the beginning of his trial lies on the floor, an image of his former self. In his dream, at least, K. is transfigured: he 'sees' everything calmly and effortlessly, no longer needs Titorelli's help, and wears a warm new suit.

The actual ending to *The Trial* refuses any such transfiguration, but it too ties together the various strands of clothing imagery used throughout the novel to depict the Court's *Verkehr*. On the evening before K.'s thirty-first birthday, two men dressed in black formal clothing, 'with top hats that were apparently irremovable', (*T* 223), appear at his door. This uncanny detail signals the absolute eradication of any difference between clothing and body, surface and interior: the men are in the 'uniform' of the Court and have no interiority other than their function as representatives, as 'clothing' of the Court. This effacement of individual identity is supported by other details—the fact that there are two executioners with identical features and clothing, that they virtually never speak, and that at times their bodies seem to merge into a single undifferentiated mass.

But an important shift in narrative perspective has taken place. K. now knows what clothing the Court requires of him and sits waiting for the executioners in proper formal attire: 'K. was sitting also dressed in black in an armchair near the door, slowly pulling on a pair of new gloves that fitted tightly over the fingers, looking as if he were expecting guests' (*T*223). Dressed like them, K. physically merges with the henchmen in an inhuman 'unity' on his way to the execution: 'K. walked rigidly between them, the three of them were interlocked in a unity which would have brought all three down together had one of them been knocked over. It was a unity such as can hardly be formed except by lifeless matter' (*T*224). The men take K. to a deserted quarry and remove 'his coat, his waistcoat, and finally his shirt' (*T*227). In this state of undress—the same in which his trial began—K. is then executed with a butcher's knife, 'like a dog'. To the very last moment K. tries to see the Court that is masked behind its grotesque representatives. But his eyes fail him and he remains the object, not the subject, of this theatrical vision: 'with failing eyes K. could still see the two of them before him, cheek leaning against cheek, watching the final act' (*T*229).

V

From the above remarks it should have emerged that Kafka's depiction of *Verkehr* in *The Trial* is associated with the paternal order of clothing, sexuality, power, and the loss of individual identity that we have seen in his earlier works. As in *Amerika*, this traffic implies a meaningless circulation of intriguing but elusive surfaces, without origin or center or purpose. This circulation is not random, or at least appears not to be to K., and he interprets its individual signs as evidence of a 'great organization'. But because he ultimately remains outside this traffic, the relation between signifying surface and inner meaning is never established. The Court remains cloaked in the elegant, seductive, but deceptive 'tourist suit' in which it initially appeared. Kafka employs other metaphors in his novel to convey this same problematic of ungrounded or doubled surfaces—an endless series of doors in the parable 'Before the Law', or the Escher-like architecture of interlocking stairways and passageways. But the movement through these passages is part of the general mechanism of *Verkehr*, whose master trope remains that of 'travelling clothing' and which appears in every crucial scene—Joseph K.'s arrest, his encounter with Fräulein Bürstner, his dream of 'metamorphosis', his execution.

On an immediate biographical level Joseph K.'s forced induction into the realm of *Verkehr* no doubt corresponds to Kafka's engagement with Felice Bauer and the prospect of leading a life like his father's—a married life of bourgeois domesticity, sexuality, and children that he feared as a threat to the purity of his vocation as a writer.[30] When the letters to Felice Bauer were published in 1967, Elias Canetti quickly pointed out their relationship to *The Trial*: Joseph K.'s arrest matches Kafka's engagement, his execution the dissolution of the engagement in the Askanischer Hof. Even one of the main literary sources for *The Trial*, Casanova's account of his escape from the Venetian prisons, echoes this biographical predicament: arrested in his bedroom at daybreak, Casanova puts on a 'laced shirt' and his 'holiday suit', as if he were 'going to a wedding.'[31]

But Kafka's depiction of the Court goes far beyond this immediate biographical context. It depicts in nightmarish detail the criminal-justice system and sexual ethics of the patriarchal society embodied in the teachings of Cesare Lombroso and Hanns Gross, and publicly critiqued by Gross's son Otto. With Joseph K. the reader experiences the violence of a legal system that can arrest and execute someone on the basis of a supposedly criminal *nature* (visible in external characteristics) rather than a criminal *act*. *The Trial* has often been read as a prophetic anticipation

[30] See the diary entry for 21 July 1913 in which Kafka sums up the arguments for and against his marriage to Felice Bauer.

[31] See Michael Müller, 'Kafka, Casanova and *The Trial*' in M. Anderson (ed.), *Reading Kafka: Prague, Politics, and the Fin de Siècle* (New York: Schocken Books, 1989), 190.

of the Nazi period when Jews, homosexuals, gypsies, and others were arrested, tortured, and executed according to a similarly specious logic. Such a reading is valid not because Kafka's novel is prophetic, but because the basis of the Nazi criminal-justice system had already been established at the end of the nineteenth century by men like Lombroso, Morel, Chamberlain, Nordau, and Hanns Gross with the notions of biological or racial 'types' and an inherently 'criminal man'. As a Jew in an intensely anti-Semitic culture, Kafka was constantly exposed to such false typological reductions.[32]

Critics have often attacked *The Trial* for what they see as Kafka's justification of the criminal system that executes Joseph K. Kafka himself called his protagonist 'guilty' in a diary entry of September 1915, and numerous passages in the novel indicate Joseph K.'s guilty conscience, despite the absence of any criminal wrongdoing. The most serious indication is the claim that the Court, being 'attracted' by guilt, 'corresponds' to K.'s inner nature, that it comes to him only when he calls, and that in some sense the entire criminal apparatus is a projection of K.'s self-punishing fantasy. This explanation would account for one of the oddest and least verisimilar aspects of Joseph K.'s world in which, no matter where he 'happens' to turn, he will inevitably stumble upon the Court offices. Joseph K. (or Kafka), in this reading, is a paranoid, ego-splintered masochist who has himself arrested by his alter-ego Franz and who distorts reality into one giant conspiracy.[33]

To admit that such indications exist in the novel is not the same as accepting them as a general interpretation of its meaning.

[32] And naturally conscious that non-Jews often sought to determine his Jewishness by external characteristics. E. T. Beck notes that 'the seminal scene of *The Trial*, Joseph K.'s arrest, corresponds to a brief but important sequence in one of the Yiddish plays, the arrest of Don Sebastian in Faynman's *The Vice-King* . . . Two masked servants of the Inquisition come to Don Sebastian's home and announce that they have been sent to arrest him on suspicion of being a secret Jew' (*Kafka and the Yiddish Theater: Its Impact on His Work* (Madison, Wis.: University of Wisconsin Press, 1971), 155).

[33] Although not all interpretations go this far in condemning Joseph K., the majority see him as guilty in a religious or existential sense, and interpret the world of the novel as a *Scheinwelt* or *Denk-Prozess*, a projection. See P. Beicken's summary of the critical literature, *Franz Kafka: Eine kritische Einführung in die Forschung* (Frankfurt: Fischer Taschenbuch, 1974), 273–86.

However willing Kafka may have been to find himself guilty as a son, a fiancé, or even a Jew, his profound ambivalence toward patriarchy, bourgeois sexuality, and the criminal-justice system in his society resulted in their consistently negative portrayal in *The Trial*. The Court horrifies and disgusts K. with its arbitrary, pornographic, inhuman proceedings, and this sentiment, it seems to me, is meant to carry over to the reader. That K. 'plays along' with its rules is no proof of his guilt, only of the powerful reach of a Court system that can corrupt everything, even the accused men it persecutes without reason and will finally execute.

From a literary perspective the novel represents a break with the realist mode of signifying description and characterization, which Kafka saw as tautological and deceptive. The duchess who puts on her gloves at five in the afternoon with the same movements as every other duchess at five in the afternoon reveals nothing about empirical reality, only about a narrator's literary bag of tricks. Unlike Balzac or Thomas Mann, he never allows the external signs of his narrative world to become legible through a signifying system of cause and effect, surface and ground. His characters remain opaque, their past lives, true characters, and deep thoughts covered over by an endless series of deceptive, changing surfaces—by the 'traffic of clothes'. Like *Amerika*, *The Trial* is a 'travelling narrative' whose movement undermines the epistemological certainties of nineteenth-century fiction. Literature no longer asserts itself as a form of knowledge but as the denial of facile, tautological, reductive characterizations. And it no longer sees itself as an extension of the social sciences.

Four years of war and an increasingly nationalistic, anti-Semitic climate only confirmed the warnings Kafka formulated in the novel he began in 1914. Otto Gross's sexual and political Utopia ended in schizophrenia and drugs; Gross was found near starvation on a street in Berlin in March 1920 and died shortly thereafter. Unlike his Prague acquaintances who caricatured Gross in their literary works, Kafka remained faithful to the figure whose private and public trials so closely paralleled his own.[34] When

[34] Max Brod portrayed Gross as the charismatic but half-insane Dr Askonas in his novel *Das große Wagnis* (*The Great Wager*, 1918), and Franz Werfel painted a similarly suspicious portrait in his novel *Barbara* (translated into English as *The Pure in Heart*).

news of Gross's death reached him in Prague, he wrote to Milena Jesenská, perhaps with an eye to Joseph K.'s trial: 'I did notice that there was something essential in [Otto Gross], something which was at least attempting to extend a hand from amid everything so "ridiculous." The bewildered mood of his friends and relatives . . . was somewhat reminiscent of the mood prevailing among Christ's disciples as they stood beneath the Crucified.'[35]

[35] Letter to Milena Jesenská, 25 June 1920.

7

The Ornaments of Writing: 'In the Penal Colony'

Je suis la plaie et le couteau!
Je suis le soufflet et la joue!
Je suis les membres et la roue,
Et la victime et le bourreau!
(Baudelaire, 'L'Héautontimorouménos')

I

IN Kafka's fictions certainty of perception is often undermined by an absence of light. Darkness, shadows, snow, or rain habitually obstruct the main character's vision of the object or scene he must interpret. The evening landscapes of *The Castle*, *The Trial*, the darkness of Gregor Samsa's room in *The Metamorphosis*—these elements distance the characters from truth and make Kafka's fictional topography akin to that of Dante's *Inferno*, which is not only the moral realm of guilt and sin but also an epistemological realm of error and confusion, the realm into which God's light refuses to penetrate.

'In the Penal Colony' is unusual among Kafka's works in that its landscape is marked by an abundance of light. But this light does not illuminate the field of perception, allowing the protagonist to interpret correctly the objects and events before him. Light is an obstacle to perception. The explorer must shield his eyes against the blinding desert sun to gaze at the penal machine. The glare of the sun in the 'shadeless valley' hurts the explorer's eyes, making it difficult for him to collect his thoughts. And the machine itself, with its hard, polished surfaces, doubles the sun's violent radiance: 'The Bed and the Designer were . . . bound at the corners with four rods of brass that almost flashed out rays in the sunlight' (*CS* 146). In Kafka's text sunlight blinds the characters; as in his other writings, they are left without true vision. The explorer leaves the penal colony without an understanding of the execution apparatus; and the officer is left hanging in the machine's jaws without having experienced the promised 'Verklärung', the transfiguration or spiritual 'illumination'.

The first readers of 'In the Penal Colony' were beset by much the same blindness that afflicts the explorer. For the story's vivid, detailed presentation of torture and execution seemed so gruesome that some protection was felt to be needed against its literal meaning. Like *The Metamorphosis* before it, 'In the Penal Colony' provoked a series of allegorical readings which, like a shielding hand over the eyes or an averted gaze, shifted attention away from the first and literal level of the story, away from its troubling surfaces, in an attempt to get behind or beyond this level and understand its 'deeper' significance. Kurt Tucholsky, one of the story's first favourable critics, dramatizes this reading process in the following words:

> After I had read to the point where the naked man is lying under the machine and a wad of felt is shoved into his mouth from below so that he can't scream . . . and then this complicated machinery slowly starts functioning, the needles write, and water from small canals washes the blood away—when I had read this far I swallowed a faint taste of blood and looked for an excuse and thought: allegory . . . military justice.[1]

Subsequent readings of the text have not differed substantially from this procedure. The story's pornological, sado-masochistic elements, its grotesquely playful presentation of torture and death—'das Peinliche', as Kafka himself termed it in a letter to his editor Kurt Wolff—have repeatedly been avoided or treated only obliquely by critics interested in the 'deeper' or 'higher' problems of grace, redemption, justice, and the Law. Commenting on this critical tendency toward the allegorization of pain and sado-masochistic pleasure in the story, Margot Norris points out that this procedure results in grouping 'In the Penal Colony' with Kafka's other 'punishment fantasy' texts like 'The Judgment' and *The Trial*, thereby obscuring an important structural similarity with the later 'performance' texts such as 'A Hunger Artist'. In

[1] *Berliner Weltbühne*, 13 June 1920. Reprinted in Ludwig Dietz, 'Drucke Franz Kafkas bis 1924', in J. Born (ed.), *Kafka-Symposion* (Berlin: Wagenbach, 1965), 155, my translation.

both these works, Norris writes, 'a fanatical believer in meaningful suffering reenacts a spectacle that in an earlier age drew huge, festive crowds, but now results only in sordid death and burial'. She concludes that 'allegorical readings mask this symmetry by giving the stories different ideational contexts derived from the idea that governs the suffering in the work: the Law in "In the Penal Colony" and the Ideal in "A Hunger Artist"'.[2]

This emphasis on the Law has meant that the condemned man in Kafka's text is understood primarily as a criminal, similar to the 'guilty' Georg Bendemann and Josef K., rather than as an artist who has become his own artwork, akin to the performing artists of his last works, 'A Hunger Artist' or 'Josephine the Singer'. A blind spot in such interpretations is their emphasis on the written judgement inscribed into the prisoner's skin and the corresponding failure to account for the other corporeal marks, namely, the ornamental arabesques or 'Verzierungen' covering the entire body: 'The script itself runs around the body only in a narrow girdle', the officer points out. 'The rest of the body is reserved for the embellishments' (149). Allegorical readings focus on the script, the legible markings, thus failing to account for or even mention the purely decorative, abstract, aesthetic context of the judgement, the 'embellishments' or 'Verzierungen'.

And yet this context is what gives the judgement meaning. The twelve hours it takes to inscribe these decorations constitute the actual spectacle which, in an earlier age, drew a festive crowd. Simply writing the judgement on the prisoner's body would kill him; it would not induce the 'transfiguration' which distinguishes this penal invention from other, all too familiar means of execution. The decorative margin to the judgement (which is also the time of 'Spiel', understood as both spectacle and sado-masochistic play) is thus the decisive element in the process of a transfigured death. As the officer explains it to the explorer in his matter-of-fact way: 'Of course the script can't be a simple one; it's not supposed to kill a man straight off, but only after an interval of, on an average, twelve

[2] 'Sadism and Masochism in Two Kafka Stories', *Modern Language Notes*, 93/3 (1978), 430. See also the two chapters dedicated to Kafka in Norris's recent book, *Beasts of the Modern Imagination* (Baltimore: Johns Hopkins University Press, 1985).

hours . . . So there have to be lots and lots of flourishes around the actual script' (149).

II

What are these 'flourishes' or 'embellishments'? And why are they given such importance in the otherwise austere circumstances of the penal colony? The key to these questions lies in Kafka's problematic relationship to *fin-de-siècle* aestheticism and will require a brief historical detour. Critics have long known that the main literary source for 'In the Penal Colony' is Octave Mirbeau's novel of 1899, *Torture Garden*, which tells the story of a French explorer who visits an Oriental island and is at once fascinated and repulsed by the refined torture techniques practised there.[3] What has been consistently overlooked however is that Mirbeau's novel is written entirely in the purple hues of art nouveau aestheticism. Consider for instance the opening description of the Chinese torture garden, whose exotic plants and shrubs provide the setting for the most gruesome 'apparatus' of torture:

> The Chinese are rightfully proud of the Torture Garden, the most thoroughly beautiful perhaps in all China. . . . Here are gathered the rarest species of their flora, the most delicate as well as the hardiest. . . . White water-lilies and nelumbos brighten [a vast pool] with their trailing leaves and floating corollas—yellow, mauve, white, rose and purple.[4]

In the midst of this floral 'magic' arise the instruments of torture, the 'apparatus' (*Apparaturen* in the German text Kafka read) of crucifixion: 'gibbets with violent decorations and black gallows, on whose tops there leered frightful demon masks; high gallows for simple strangulation, lower gibbets mechanically equipped for the tearing of flesh' (184). The man in charge of these torture machines sits at the foot of one of these flower-bedecked gibbets, his instrument-case between his feet, cleaning his 'fine steel implements

[3] See W. Burns, '"In the Penal Colony": Variations on a Theme by Octave Mirbeau', *Accent*, 17 (1957), 45–51.

[4] I quote from the English translation of Mirbeau's novel, entitled *Torture Garden* (New York: Citadel Press, 1948), 165–6.

with silk cloths'. Mirbeau's description again provides the requisite *fin-de-siècle* imagery:

He put the cleansed and gleaming saw into the case and closed it. Its box was lovely and of an excellent lacquer: a flight of wild geese flew over a nocturnal pool, where the moon silvered the lotus and the iris. At that moment the shadow of the gallows threw a violet bar across the body of the executioner (187).

Often written off as pornography or decadent kitsch, Mirbeau's highly sexualized description of Chinese torture is actually a critique of European decadence. The executioner's impassioned defence of his trade serves as the author's tongue-in-cheek parody of his contemporaries: literary aesthetes, anti-Semites, and the supposedly 'cultivated minds' of French politics who condoned, as in the Dreyfus affair, the 'passion for murder and the joy of the man-hunt'.[5] In a passage that recalls the officer's explanation of the embellishments cited above, Mirbeau's executioner describes his trade as a highly refined 'art':

Art does not consist in killing multitudes . . . in slaughtering, massacring, and exterminating men in hordes. Really, it's too easy. Art, milady, consists in knowing how to kill, according to the rites of beauty, whose divine secret we Chinese alone possess. . . . Know how to kill! That is to say, how to *work* the human body like a sculptor works his clay or piece of ivory. [For that] science is required, variety, taste, imagination . . . genius, after all. (189).

Like Kafka's officer, who defends the Old Commandant's methods against the New Commandant's 'modern' and milder procedures, Mirbeau's executioner describes himself as the defender of a noble artistic tradition against the 'filth of progress' that has made death a 'collective, administrative and bureaucratic' affair. By

[5] In the opening dialogue between French *savants*, a philosopher rails against the notion that the 'cultivated minds' of contemporary society have made any moral progress over 'primitive' cultures: 'The Dreyfus affair affords us an excellent example [of the enjoyment of the "cultivated minds"], and never, I believe, was the passion for murder and the joy of the man-hunt so thoroughly and cynically displayed. The pursuit of Monsieur Grimaux [a noted French scientist and supporter of Dreyfus] through the streets of Nantes remains the most characteristic of the startling incidents and monstrous events to which it gave opportunity daily during the past years' (23–4). Kafka owned German editions of two other works by Mirbeau, including *Enthüllungen einer Kammerzof* (*Confessions of a Chambermaid*), which also raises the spectre of anti-Semitic manhunts in contemporary France.

contrast: 'Our trade, just like our lovely vases, our beautiful embroidered silks, and lovely lacquers, is disappearing little by little. Today we no longer know what torture really is, although I try to carry on its real tradition. I am swamped, and I can't stay the rise of decadence all by myself' (187).[6]

Although the *Torture Garden* provided Kafka with the notion of 'working' the human body into an artwork, it contains no reference to the embellishments *per se*, which, in Kafka's text, are inscribed into the prisoner's skin like tattoos with the help of glass needles, an acid fluid, and the electrically-powered 'apparatus'. But for this detail too there is precedent in the *fin de siècle*. Cesare Lombroso, the Italian criminal anthropologist discussed in the previous chapter, popularized the notion that certain human types—'born' criminals, but also prostitutes, the insane, epileptics, and artists—invariably displayed symptoms of 'graphomania', the uncontrollable urge to cover everything at hand with writing and drawings. This explained, according to Lombroso, why criminals had tattoos applied to large parts of their bodies. In a chapter from his widely diffused legal handbook *Criminal Man*, richly illustrated with drawings of actual criminals and their tattoos, Lombroso noted for instance that a certain Malassen, a 'ferocious murderer' who became the executioner of deported convicts in New Caledonia,

> was covered with grotesque and terrifying tattoos from head to foot. Inscribed on his chest was a red and black guillotine with these words in red: *J'ai mal commencé—Je finirai mal—C'est la fin qui m'attend*. On his right arm, which had killed so many men, he had sculpted the horrible motto of his profession: *Mort à la chiourme!*[7]

[6] Compare also the distinction between West and East formulated by Clara, the lascivious *femme fatale* whose senses are inflamed by the spectacle of refined torture: 'In our frightful Europe which, for so long a time has not known what beauty is, they torture in secret, in the depths of their jails, or in public squares, among the vile drunken crowds. [In China] it's among flowers, amid the prodigious enchantment and prodigious silence of all the flowers, that the instruments of torture are erected, the stake, the scaffold and the cross' (170).

[7] *L'uomo delinquente* (Turin: Fratelli Bocca, 4th edn. 1889), 296, my translation. In Lombroso's typological scheme, tattoos were just one more physiognomic trait which the trained observer could use to detect an inherent 'criminal', whether or not he had committed a crime. Other symptoms included the graffiti which prisoners scribbled on prison walls, or the poems, stories, and drawings which their unstable

A controversial point in Lombroso's typological theory was the connection between criminals and artists. Because Lombroso saw any deviation from the norm as the result of a similar regression, he grouped together poets and murderers, visionary artists and epileptics, geniuses and the insane. Dostoevsky was an example for Lombroso of a 'criminal' and 'sick' nature who expressed himself in great literature *about* crime, whereas a murderer who wrote mediocre poetry and covered his body with tattoos 'expressed' himself directly in criminal acts. Both represented an atavistic regression on the evolutionary ladder, a throw-back to man's primitive origins, although admittedly with quite different results.[8]

At the end of the nineteenth century, such typological theories were often used to buttress conservative charges of artistic decadence or, to use the trumped-up scientific term, 'degeneration'.[9] Hanns Gross, Kafka's law teacher at the University of Prague, accepted Lombroso's equation between tattoos and criminal types, although with certain reservations:

> If we mention that such a crude dressing-up of the body [i.e. tattoos] is to be observed only among coarse individuals (Lombroso says: among peoples of Celtic origin), we have everything we need to account for the incidence of tattoos in criminals. We thus find tattoos only among energetic types—murderers, armed robbers, etc.; and among very sensuous individuals—pimps, pederasts, rapists and voyeurs; but not confidence-men, petty thieves, or the like.[10]

Gross also noted the recent fashion among 'young English noblemen' (read: upper-class aesthetes and homosexuals) to have their entire bodies covered with tattoos. The sign of a 'degenerate'

but vigorous 'organisms' could not help but produce. Lombroso analysed these symptoms in a perceptive and not unsympathetic study entitled *Prison Palimpsests* (*Palinsesti del cacere*, 1891).

[8] See Lombroso's *Genio e degenerazione* (*Genius and Degeneration*, 1897).

[9] One of the most visible critics of literary decadence was Max Nordau, author of *Entartung* (*Degeneration*, 1892), a 2-volume polemic against contemporary decadence and 'satanism' from Baudelaire to Nietzsche, Ibsen, and Strindberg. The book was dedicated to Lombroso.

[10] *Handbuch für Untersuchungsrichter als System der Kriminalistik* (Graz: Leuschner & Lubensky's, 1899), 146. Gross also notes that the 'sexual-sensuous nature' of prostitutes explains their tendency to decorate their bodies: 'For this reason one finds tattoos in people of the female sex only among prostitutes; in less civilized cultures tattoos in women are not rare' (145).

sensuality, these tattoos were not applied in the usual fashion with heated needles, 'but rather by specially-employed "artists" with the help of an electric apparatus'.[11]

Kafka need not have come across such claims while studying Gross's legal manuals, for typological theories linking criminal and artistic behaviour had gained wide currency outside the juridical world by the turn of the century. We find them for instance in Adolf Loos's influential polemic against the *Jugendstil*, 'Ornament and Crime' (1908), which Kafka heard as a public lecture in 1911. Loos begins with a deliberately provocative paraphrase of Lombroso, claiming that 'if a tattooed man dies outside of prison, he has merely died a few years before committing a murder'.[12] Like Lombroso, he sees the tattoo as the sign of 'criminal', 'primitive', or 'degenerate' natures:

> The Papuan tattoos his skin, his boat, his rudder, his oars; in short, everything he can get his hands on. He is no criminal . . . But what is natural for a Papuan or a child, is degenerate for modern man. I have discovered the following truth and present it to the world: *cultural evolution is equivalent to the removal of ornament from articles of everyday use.* (78, Loos's emphasis)

Like Mirbeau's novel, Loos's invective was not directed against criminals or Papuan tribe members, but against his contemporaries, the 'degenerate aristocrats', dandies, and cultural aesthetes of the *fin de siècle* who had confused life with art. 'I'm preaching to the aristocrats', he declares at the end of his essay. 'Whoever goes about in a velvet suit nowadays is not an artist but a fool or a house-painter . . . Whoever attends a performance of [Beethoven's] Ninth Symphony and then sits down to draw a wallpaper pattern is either a con man or a degenerate' (88). As Carl Schorske remarks, 'Loos sought to remove "style"—ornamentation or dressing of any sort—from architecture and from use-objects, in order to let their function stand clear to speak its own truth in its own form. Along with his friend and fellow moralist Karl Kraus, he relentlessly condemned the "penetration of life with art" and

[11] The German text reads: 'Allerdings geschieht dies night in ordinärer Weise mit glühenden Stecknadeln, sondern von eigens dazu etablirten "Künstlern" mit Hilfe eines elektrischen Apparates' (146). Kafka's apparatus is also electrically powered.

[12] *Trotzdem: 1900–1930*, ed. A. Opel (Vienna: G. Prachner, 1981 repr. of 1931 edn.), 78, my translation.

the stylization of the house as work of art that reached its apogee in the [Secessionist] Kunstschau.'[13] Loos's attacks on the Wiener Werkstätte were controversial and widely disseminated. Most of them were first published in the *Neue freie Presse*, the leading liberal newspaper of Habsburg Vienna (and available, of course, in all the literary cafés in Prague). Loos also travelled on the lecture circuit, delivering his sermons for an unadorned, functional modernism in major cities throughout Germany and the Austro-Hungarian monarchy. Kafka heard Loos lecture on 'Ornament and Crime' in March 1911, the same month he attended Karl Kraus's reading of 'Heine and the Consequences', an astute if problematic critique of the foreign ornaments 'corrupting' classical High German. Both avant-garde critics from Vienna put forward the same message: ornament, whether a feuilletonistic literary flourish or an arabesque drawn on a building façade, represented the art of a superannuated culture, the 'criminal' and 'degenerate' obstacles to classical modernism.[14]

Kafka had good reason to be interested in this critique of ornament, for, as we have seen in previous chapters, from about 1907, he had sought to purge literary ornament from his writing, fashioning a limpid, sharp-edged prose idiom that would later be recognized as one of the prime examples of German modernism, the literary equivalent to Loos's own unadorned buildings. In all probability Kafka saw himself as Loos's ideological companion in the struggle against the ornate forms of *fin-de-siècle* culture—a struggle he waged with characteristic thoroughness in every aspect of his life, from his clothing and handwriting to his gymnastic regime and literary style.[15]

[13] *Fin-de-Siècle Vienna: Politics and Culture* (New York: Vintage Books, 1981), 339.

[14] See his diary entry for 26 Mar. 1911, which names Kraus and Loos without specifying title or content of their lectures. Loos and Kraus returned to Prague for a repeat visit in March 1913. For details see V. Šlapeta, 'Adolf Loos' Vorträge in Prag', in exhibition catalogue *Adolf Loos* (Vienna: Graphische Sammlung Albertina, 1989), 41–57.

[15] Loos, for his part, saw himself as the ideological companion of the young Expressionist writers published by Kurt Wolff and submitted to him a collection of his essays, which had been rejected by other more established presses because of their polemical content. Wolff too refused to publish them without alterations, and Loos had to wait until 1921 before a French publisher dared to print them. See Loos's note in the foreword to the 1st edition of *Ins Leere Gesprochen: 1887–1900* (Paris: G. Crès, 1921).

An interesting if elusive indication of this progressive stylistic *ascesis* is Kafka's decision in 1907 to change his handwriting from the Gothic script he had learned in school (*Kurrentschrift*) to the simpler, relatively 'clean' and open Latin characters which he used to write all his major works. The first version of *Description of a Struggle*, for example, displays a highly ornate, decorative handwriting that mirrors its Jugendstil style and is strikingly different from his hand in later manuscripts.[16] Psychologically, this shift may have been related to the desire to break with the calligraphy he had been taught at school as a child. But it had clear political and aesthetic significance too. Well before the rise of National Socialism, the 'German' Gothic script implied nationalist conservatism, while Latin characters signified an openness to modernity and change, continuity with the rest of Europe. Loos for instance refused to capitalize German nouns and used large Latin characters for his short-lived journal *Das Andere*, noting in his editorial introduction that they were not Secessionist but 'modern' letters.[17]

However one interprets the change in Kafka's handwriting, it is consistent with his stylistic turn away from the *Jugendstil* and his taste for leaner, more open and modern modes of expression—a taste that included details of typefount, illustration, and design format for his published works. For instance, he was inordinately pleased with the over-large Latin characters used to print *Meditation*, calling them 'altogether beautiful' in a letter to his editor. When Kurt Wolff proposed using them again for 'In the Penal Colony',

[16] Max Brod notes in his biography: '[Kafka's] handwriting went through various stages of development in the course of years. The Gothic flourishes in the beginning accord with the rich, rounded-off, decorated, occasionally precious, style of his prose. . . . The letters to Oskar Pollak, are written in a still more ornamental handwriting. The period of his spacious Latin handwriting is the period of comparatively peaceful maturity and mastery' (*Franz Kafka: A Biography* (New York: Schocken Books, 1947; enlarged edn. 1960), 45).

[17] From the collection of *Trotzdem*, p. 32. The first issue of *Das Andere* appeared in 1903 as an appendix to Peter Altenberg's journal *Die Kunst*. Loos, who lived for several years in the United States and repeatedly contrasted German with Anglo-Saxon culture, insists on the political dimension of his unusual orthography and typeface: 'Besides these german relics . . . should be thrown into the attic. I, a german, protest against the fact that everything that has been abandoned by other peoples is proclaimed to be german. I protest against the barrier between what is german and human.'

Kafka admitted that the offer 'excites me so much that I am ready to drop my defenses' about publication (4 September 1917). Conversely, he objected to the old-fashioned illustration used as the frontispiece for the first edition of *The Stoker* (printed, by the way, in Gothic fount), claiming that his text depicted 'das allermodernste New York', New York at its most modern. Similarly, upon receiving the proofs for *The Metamorphosis*, he complained to Wolff that he was 'sorry that it is not to be in the same typeface as [Carl Sternheim's] *Napoleon*, since when you sent me the latter I assumed that *Metamorphosis* would be printed in the same way. The appearance of the page in *Napoleon* is open and legible, while *Metamorphosis* looks dark and cramped' (15 October 1915).

Kafka's preference for 'legible', open forms was not limited to his handwriting or its translations into print. Because his writing governed every aspect of his life, the same purge of ornament was carried out in his personal life-style as well—in his renunciation of elegant clothing, in his interest in reform clothing, nudism, and Müller's gymnastic system, or even in his vegetarian diet and preference for holistic medicine. Everything in his life was organized in terms of an ascetic life-style, designed to accommodate the needs of his writing 'organism'. As he noted in his diary on 3 January 1912:

> When it became clear in my organism that writing was the most productive direction for my being to take, everything rushed in that direction and left empty all those abilities which were directed toward the joys of sex, eating, drinking, philosophical reflection and above all music. I dieted in all these directions. . . . My development is now complete and, so far as I can see, there is nothing left to sacrifice.

Kafka's 'Loosian' rupture with the *Jugendstil* in the years 1906–12 was thus not an isolated phenomenon and is symbolically evident—to conclude this historical 'embellishment' to 'In the Penal Colony'—in the marginal decorations of the *Neue Rundschau*, a journal Kafka subscribed to and read regularly from 1904 to his death. In 1904 the journal abandoned its unadorned appearance for a highly stylized *Jugendstil* format which made each issue a small artwork in its own right. The Gothic script of the stories and poems is literally invaded by swirling arabesques designed by leading illustrators of the day. But this phase lasted only a few years. In 1908, the year of Loos's essay, the journal trimmed away some of its marginal decorations, and by 1909 it had reassumed its former classical appearance. In 1922, the year Kafka's minimalist text 'A Hunger Artist' appeared in its pages, the Gothic script was exchanged for the modern Latin fount still used by the journal today.

III

From this historical perspective we can now begin to read 'In the Penal Colony' not as a legal meditation on guilt and punishment, but as an ironic, self-reflexive commentary on Kafka's own literary production and its relation to contemporary aesthetic questions. First, one should note that the execution machine *writes* its judgement (the verb *schreiben* is repeated throughout the text), and that the product of its movements is consistently referred to as a text or as 'scripture' (*Schrift*). This writing is an artistic process, as numerous plays on the word for art indicate: the machine inscribes the judgement and embellishments into the prisoner's skin 'like a harrow' working the soil, but 'much more artfully' (*viel kunstgemässer*). Similarly, the master plan drawn by the former Commandant which guides the machine's writing of the arabesques is 'illegible' but 'sehr kunstvoll', literally 'full of art', a nuance obscured by the English translation of 'ingenious':

> [The officer] spread out the first sheet of paper. The explorer would have liked to say something appreciative, but all he could see was a labyrinth of lines crossing and recrossing each other, which covered the paper so thickly that it was difficult to discern the blank spaces between them. 'Read it', said the officer. 'I can't', said the explorer. 'Yet it's clear enough', said the officer. 'It's very artful', said the explorer evasively, 'but I can't make it out.' 'Yes', said the officer with a laugh, putting the paper away again, 'it's no calligraphy for school children.' (*CS* 148–9)

Often interpreted as the 'illegible' Hebrew characters of the Old Testament, these labyrinthine lines correspond to the embellishments which the machine, translating from the drawings, will inscribe as tattoos into the condemned man's body. Like the tattoo embellishments, these lines also evoke the swirling arabesques of *Jugendstil* ornament and, by implication, Kafka's own *Jugendstil* writings. 'Artful' and abstract, they will transform the prisoner's body into a *Jugendstil* 'text', embellished with the appropriate marginalia.

This reading allows us to situate 'In the Penal Colony' not on a tropical island but on an 'island of tropes' (the German term 'Tropen' means both), a hermetic space for the fashioning of linguistic 'turns' of phrase.[18] In German literature at the end of the nineteenth century, the island was a common figure for the autonomy of art. In innumerable writings by Stefan George, Heinrich Mann, Hermann Hesse, and Rilke, it served as a convenient shorthand for the *Insel der Kunst*, or art-for-art's-sake movement. Hesse's novella 'Inseltraum' ('Island Dream', 1899), is typical in this respect and gave the *Jugendstil* movement, as Jürg Mathes observes, 'one of its most significant catchwords'.[19] The same image was adopted by the Insel publishing house as an emblem for the autonomous, hermetic work of literary art.

The events that take place on Kafka's 'tropical' island also have a relation to his own writing. Self-referential clues run through the entire text and, as Axel Witte has pointed out, include Kafka's initials in the name for the 'Former Commandant' (in German, *Früherer Kommandant*) and numerous puns on the word 'judgement'.[20] Variously translated in English as judgement and sentence, the German word for the legible script of the corporeal inscription is consistently *Urteil*, which is also the title of his breakthrough story of 1912, 'Das Urteil', which he dedicated to Felice Bauer. 'The Judgment', we should remember, was written *before* he became engaged to Felice. But the story dramatizes this engagement and the related, deadly conflict with his father. In a prophetic act whose irony he would later have occasion to reflect on, Kafka

[18] The English phrase is paralleled by the German *Redewendungen* and, of course, by Kafka's notion of the 'turning' body of the writer-gymnast. All the works written in August–October 1914, when Kafka had withdrawn into a monk-like isolation after his break with Felice, depict remote insular or abandoned landscapes. See the final chapter of *The Trial*, which takes place in an abandoned quarry, or the fragmentary 'Memories of the Kalda Railway', where the protagonist lives alone in a Russian station described as an 'Einöde', a wilderness.

[19] J. Mathes (ed.), *Prosa des Jugendstils* (Stuttgart: Reclam, 1982), 351.

[20] Unpublished Master's thesis, Free University, Berlin, 1980.

thus wrote his own 'judgement' without understanding its significance. Hence the painfully ironic self-reference in the exchange between officer and traveller about the 'Verurteilte', the condemned man, who has not been informed of the Court 'sentence' (*Urteil*) against him. 'He doesn't know his own judgment?' the traveller asks in horror. 'No', replies the officer matter-of-factly. 'There would be no point in telling him. He'll learn it on his body' (*er wird es auf eigenem Leib erfahren*, *CS* 144–5). Only in July 1914, after he had lived out the story's plot by breaking off the engagement with Felice ('on his own body'), did the story's meaning become clear to him.[21]

But there is more to this biographical subtext. 'The Judgment' occupied a special position in Kafka's estimation of his own works. He saw it as the single instance of successful, inspired writing, carried out 'at one sitting', in one uninterrupted process. Other works, even as masterful a story as *The Metamorphosis*, he judged to be less successful because they had not been written with the same intensity, the same opening out of 'body and soul'. His jubilant diary entry of 23 September, 1912, written immediately after 'The Judgment', testifies to this sentiment and bears an unmistakable relation to 'In the Penal Colony':

> This story, 'The Judgment', I wrote at one sitting during the night of the 22nd–23rd, from ten o'clock at night to six o'clock in the morning . . . The fearful strain and joy, how the story developed before me . . . How everything can be said, how for everything, for the strangest fancies, there waits a great fire in which they perish and rise up again. . . . At two I looked at the clock for the last time. . . . The weariness that disappeared in the middle of the night. . . . Only *in this way* can writing be done, only with such

[21] 'In the Penal Colony' was written in the second week of October 1914 and, in its 'triangular' structure of officer, explorer, and writing machine, resembles the triangle of Kafka, Felice, and his 'work' or 'second self'. Kafka describes this situation in a letter to her of late October in which the fanatical cold-bloodedness of this writing self clearly resembles the officer's dedication to the apparatus: 'The other self, however, thinks of nothing but work . . . the death of his dearest friend would seem to be no more than a hindrance . . . to his work; this meanness is compensated for by the fact that he is also capable of suffering for his work' (*F* 438). If read as a cryptic letter to his ex-fiancée, the 'Explorer' or *Reisender* (literally 'traveller') is Felice, the representative of *Verkehr*, who visits Kafka in his writer's seclusion. The coitus-like act of writing, in which a naked man is put on a 'Bed' and penetrated by 'quivering' needles, is an alternative to the marriage bed and its bourgeois comforts.

coherence, with such a complete opening out of the body and the soul. Morning in bed. The always clear eyes.

The parallel is striking: on the one hand Kafka's description of the writing of 'The Judgment'; on the other, the writing of the 'judgement' and 'embellishments' in 'In the Penal Colony'. The essential elements are almost identical: the duration of the writing (twelve hours in 'In the Penal Colony', an entire night for 'The Judgment'); the passive reception of the text; the disappearance of pain halfway through the process as the body passes from a temporal to a spiritual order; the 'opening' up of body and soul; and finally the luminous eyes as the sign of 'transfiguration'. In both cases an 'artful' execution takes place—Georg Bendemann in the one, the prisoner in the other. The condemned man in 'In the Penal Colony' is punished for transgressing the commandment 'Honor Your Superiors', which recalls the biblical injunction to honour one's parents, precisely Georg Bendemann's 'sin' in 'The Judgment'.

'In the Penal Colony' thus presents us with a play within a play, the story of another story. Or to put it more simply: the judgement is 'The Judgment'. In this sense the embellishments correspond to the literary tropes in Kafka's own story. Simply announcing Georg Bendemann's death would not produce the redemption that Kafka desires; he must submit himself to the 'writing machine', let the text write itself out, inscribe the 'strangest fancies', metaphors, and literary embellishments into his own body. His own body becomes a text, just as the text is seen as a kind of body. As Kafka noted in his diary while reading proofs of 'The Judgment' in February 1913: 'the story came out of me like a real birth . . . and only I have the hand that can reach to the body itself.'

Readers of 'In the Penal Colony' will recall that when the officer puts himself into the machine, he does not experience the 'redemption' he so seductively describes to the explorer. No judgement, no decorative embellishments are written; the machine malfunctions, destroying itself and leaving the officer with an iron spike through his forehead, suspended above the burial pit. This spatial predicament mirrors the existential condition of being caught between death and life. His body is referred to as a corpse, but his face still wears the 'expression' of life: 'It was as it had been in life; no sign was visible of the promised redemption . . . the eyes were open, with the same expression as in life, the look was calm and convinced, through the forehead went the point of the great iron spike' (166). That the officer is not quite dead is also indicated by a variant to the story in which he reappears with the spike protruding from his shattered forehead, announcing to the explorer: 'it was a mistake on your part; I was executed, as you commanded' (diary entry for 9 August 1917).

Here again the analogy of the 'apparatus' with Kafka's own writing 'machine' is instructive. Immediately after breaking off his engagement with Felice Bauer in July 1914, Kafka began *The Trial*. Initially the work went well: 'I have been writing these past few days', he noted in his diary on 15 August, 'may it continue. . . . My monotonous, empty, mad bachelor's life has some justification.' In August and early September he finished several chapters, but with the news of the first war casualties he complains of 'tormenting' thoughts that remind him of his worries about Felice. At the beginning of October he took a week's leave from the office, resolved to 'drive the novel forwards'. This plan failed and he decided to take another week's leave, abandoning the novel for a new story, 'In the Penal Colony', and an additional chapter of his novel *Amerika*, both of which he finished.[22] Let us speculate for a moment. Motivated by the outbreak of the war and the legal framework of the novel he was then working on, Kafka conceived the idea of a military judicial process that takes place on a distant island. But the hidden subject of the story is his own isolated situation as a writer. He remembers his writing of 'The Judgment' two years earlier (at the beginning of his relationship with Felice), juxtaposing against it his recent failures in writing *The Trial* and several other longer narratives. The grotesque image of the not-yet-dead officer, suspended in the grip of the writing machine, serves as a self-portrait in his then stalled work on the novel, that is, in his ardently desired but failed attempt to achieve redemption through writing.[23]

[22] See Kafka's diary entry for 31 Dec. 1914.

[23] Again a variant to the story seems to contain a tongue-in-cheek reflection on Kafka's loss of his literary powers since 'The Judgment': 'Damned, miasmal tropical

Kafka frequently used the image of a machine to describe his writing. As he had noted to Felice on 1 November 1912 in an uncanny prefiguration of the officer's plight: 'My life consists, and basically always has consisted, of attempts at writing, mostly unsuccessful. . . . If there is a higher power that wishes to use me, or does use me, then I am at its mercy, if no more than as a well-prepared instrument. If not, I am nothing, and will suddenly be left hanging in a dreadful void.' Here we find the same conception of a passive waiting for a 'higher power' to 'write itself' out; the writer's body is no more than the vehicle, the 'instrument' for this process.

In early August 1914, just after the break with Felice and while waiting for the 'machine' to start functioning, Kafka commented on a similar death-like suspension between bourgeois life and literary inspiration:

> My talent for portraying my dreamlike inner life has thrust all other matters into the background; my life has dwindled dreadfully, nor will it cease to dwindle. . . . But the strength I can muster for that portrayal is not to be counted upon: perhaps it has already vanished forever . . . Thus I waver, continually fly to the summit of the mountain, but then fall back in a moment . . . it is not death, alas, but the eternal torments of dying.

Here the 'Spitze des Berges' or mountain 'summit' prefigures the 'spike' (also *Spitze*) of the apparatus that impales the officer in midair. Ideally the writing apparatus works, a text like 'The Judgment' is written, a fictional double of the author's self is executed and replaced by another protagonist. But when the machine malfunctions or a 'higher power' refuses to work, as it did in October 1914, Kafka's 'mad bachelor's life' becomes an infinitely suspended death-in-life without artistic or human justification.

'In the Penal Colony' thus represents a decisive turn in Kafka's conception of his own work. After two years of literary inactivity and at least three 'failed' narratives in the period after his break with Felice Bauer, his belief in his creative powers (what he punningly refers to as his 'Urteilskraft' in a later variant to the

air, what are you doing to me? I don't know what is happening. My power of judgment [*meine Urteilskraft*] has been left back at home in the North' (diary 8 Aug. 1917).

story) gives way to a pessimism and melancholy that recur repeatedly in his subsequent writings in the form of a protagonist's inability to die or an 'endless voyage'. Odradek, the strange creature in 'The Cares of a Family Man' is said to have 'no purpose' in life and hence cannot die. The protagonist in 'A Country Doctor' has answered a 'false alarm on the night bell' and is forced to wander eternally in the 'frost of this most unhappy of ages'. The Hunter Gracchus, after a fatal accident in the Black Forest, is also still alive: his 'death ship' has lost its way and ever since he sails 'through all the lands of the earth', at once Flying Dutchman and Wandering Jew.[24]

The non-transfigured death of the officer in 'In the Penal Colony' thus initiates what Kafka pessimistically considered the social and ethical sterility of a life dedicated to, dependent on, and ultimately usurped by literary ambition. Despite his ascetic commitment to art, despite the radical will with which he pursued his calling, in the final analysis Kafka judged himself to be a 'narcissist' who had spurned the 'gift of life' and was hence condemned to endure the spectacle of his own sham death. In an important letter to Max Brod of 5 July 1922, he defined his writing as 'devil's work' which took the form of 'vanity and narcissism' (*Genußsucht*). Such a writer, he claims, 'has a terrible fear of dying because he has not yet lived. By this I do not mean that wife and child, fields and cattle are essential to living. What is essential to life is only to forgo one's narcissism, to move into the house of life instead of admiring it and hanging garlands around it.' Summing up his existence as a writer, he concludes: 'I cannot go on living because I have not lived, I have remained clay, I have not blown the spark into fire, but only used it to illuminate my corpse.'

IV

The self-referential aspect of 'In the Penal Colony' described above does not rule out the political significance of a story written at the beginning of World War I which the author himself characterized in a letter to Kurt Wolff as arising from the 'painful-

[24] See the chapter dedicated to 'Hunter Gracchus' in Manfred Frank's *Die endlose Fahrt* (Frankfurt: Suhrkamp, 1979).

ness' of 'our times in general' (11 October 1916). Kafka was unmistakably attracted by Mirbeau's depiction of an arbitrary, dehumanizing judicial process, and used it as the basis for his own narrative. In the *Torture Garden*, to cite just one example, a 'miserable harbor worker' whose only crime is to have stolen a sack of rice has his skin removed and turned into an overcoat. 'He seemed to be wearing . . . an inverness', remarks the executioner gleefully. 'Never had the dog been better dressed, nor by a better tailor' (186). Guilt is irrelevant on this torture island, as the executioner also notes in a passage that caught Kafka's attention:

> 'You take . . . a condemned man, *or anybody else—for it isn't necessary for the success of my torture that the victim be condemned to anything at all.* You undress him . . . you make him kneel, his back bent, on the earth, where you fasten him with chains riveted to iron collars which bind his neck, his wrists, his calves and ankles. (191–2, my emphasis)

On Kafka's penal island, too, 'guilt is never to be doubted'. But the only instance of a crime the text presents is a soldier's failure to execute a senseless order—to salute his superior's door every hour through the night. For his 'crime' of falling asleep he is whipped—not on his back or his hands, but across his face, like a dog. Punished 'like' a dog, the soldier responds in kind, with the language of an animal asking for more human treatment: 'Throw that whip away or I'll eat you alive' (*ich fresse dich*), the verb *fressen* normally being reserved for animals.[25] For his execution this 'criminal' is chained not just at his arms and legs but, like Mirbeau's prisoner and like a dog, at the neck: '[T]he condemned man [was bound by] a heavy chain controlling the small chains locked on the prisoner's ankles, wrists, and neck' (*CS* 140). What is worse, the prisoner has internalized this animal treatment: 'In any case, the condemned man looked so like a submissive dog that one might have thought he could be left to run free on the surrounding hills and would only need to be whistled for when the execution was due to begin.'

[25] In a variant the 'civilized' European explorer calls himself a 'Hundsfott' (cur) for not denouncing the execution procedure: 'but then he took it literally and began running around on all fours' (diary 7 Aug. 1917). As noted in Ch. 5, Kafka's protagonists are repeatedly shown to literalize figures of speech.

Cesare Lombroso and Hanns Gross maintained that tattoos and other corporeal marks were the 'symptoms' of an internal criminal nature. Kafka's story takes this idea and reverses it: an uneducated, unsuspecting, essentially innocent native is seized by the military authorities of a European colonial power and has the marks of guilt written into his skin until he himself accepts this judgement in a moment of 'enlightened' but unfortunately fatal vision: 'Enlightenment comes to the most dull-witted', comments the officer. 'You have seen how difficult it is to decipher the script with one's eyes; but our man deciphers it with his wounds' (*CS* 150). As in *The Trial*, whose metaphorical and conceptual structures are internally linked with those of 'In the Penal Colony', guilt is *produced* by the legal apparatus, which also kills a man who has not done anything wrong, 'like a dog'.

Within this circle of arbitrary judicial process, however, Kafka uses the contemporary stereotype linking 'marked' criminals with 'decadent' artists as the occasion for his own self-judgement and condemnation. By 1914 he shared Loos's anti-ornamental views, which implied a critique of his own beginnings as a *Jugendstil* aesthete. For years he had attempted to purge ornament from his personal life as well as his writing, 'dieting in all directions' for the sake of his functional writing machine. But this Loosian ascesis involved not so much a break with aestheticism as a radicalization of its basic tenet: the fusion (and confusion) of life with art. This is what he attempted to explain to Felice Bauer in response to a graphologist's claim that his handwriting showed traces of 'literary interests' and an 'extremely sensual' nature: 'I am by no means "extremely sensual", but have a magnificent, inborn capacity for asceticism . . . I have no literary interests, but am made of literature. I am nothing else, and cannot be anything else' (14 August 1913). A year later, however, this proud claim of 'being' literature would be denounced as unredeemed narcissism and, when the 'higher power' failed to write, as the 'eternal torments of dying'.

The denunciation of a colonial power's arbitrary legal system is thus also a brutal self-criticism of the writer who has turned himself into 'mere ornament'. This complex merging accounts for the ambiguity of a text which, from the beginning, has frustrated the critical search for a single interpretation of its meaning. 'Where does Kafka stand?' more than one reader has been at pains to ask. 'If he condemns the torture apparatus (as he must), how are we to interpret the officer's undeniably seductive, nostalgic account of its effects?' But Kafka is everywhere in his text at once—the machine, the officer, the European explorer, the Former Commandant, even the 'stupid-looking, wide-mouthed' prisoner who lives on 'stinking' fish. 'In the Penal Colony' depicts the ironic split of the writing self, which at once tortures and is tortured, executes and is itself destroyed. As Baudelaire had written of his own mordant poetic irony half a century earlier in 'L'Héautontimorouménos' ('The Self-executioner'): 'I am the wound and the knife! | I am the slap and the cheek! | I am the limbs and the rack, | The victim and the hangman!'

Literary history has not seconded Kafka's sombre assessment of his own achievements, in part because his 'failures'—the unfinished novels, the fragmentary, hermetic, self-referential character of his writing generally—have become symbolic of an age which has given up its belief in literary or religious transcendence. Kafka's work, and particularly the self-reflexive 'In the Penal Colony', stands as an icon of modernism's negative achievements: its break with tradition, the loss of aesthetic transcendence, the withdrawal of art and its human subject from the light of truth. 'Our art', he wrote in an aphorism of December 1917, 'is a being blinded by truth. Only the light on the receding grimace is true, nothing else'. This is the harsh light obscuring, not illuminating, the 'tropical' landscape of Kafka's text.

8

'Jewish' Music? Otto Weininger and 'Josephine the Singer'

The Jew doesn't sing.
(Otto Weininger, *Sex and Character*)

I

IN 'Josephine the Singer, or the Mouse Folk', his last story, Kafka took up a subject which he had explicitly sought to eliminate from his writing 'organism' as early as 1912: 'When it became clear in my organism that writing was the most productive direction for my being to take, everything rushed in that direction and left empty all those abilities which were directed toward the joys of sex, eating, drinking, philosophical reflection and above all music' (diary entry for 3 January 1912). Here music represents an organic, superfluous 'ornament' which the ascetic modernist must purge in order to write. Throughout his life Kafka aspired toward a non-musical, architectural purity in his writing, rather proudly characterizing his unmusical nature in a letter to Milena Jesenská as a source of strength: 'I have a certain strength, and if one wanted to designate it briefly and vaguely, it is my being unmusical.' None the less, in March 1924, gravely debilitated by the illness that would lead to his death a few months later, Kafka wrote his moving if enigmatic story about a singing mouse named Josephine.

Kafka's early conception of music is clearly indebted to the *fin de siècle* debate about Wagnerian 'decadence', initiated by Nietzsche in his polemical essay 'The Case of Wagner'. His antagonism to Wagner surfaces in his satirical depiction of Brunelda, the Wagnerian *Ur-weib* in *Amerika* who represents a repulsive, degraded Dionysianism: music as unfettered corporeal indulgence, sexuality, and violence; music as a monstrous *body* endowed with only the most primitive cognitive and moral faculties.[1] No figure could be more different from Brunelda than the mouse heroine of Kafka's last text. A delicate, slender creature, Josephine has all the human, higher qualities that Brunelda lacks: discretion, sensitivity, a deep respect for and dedication to her art. In a passage that recalls the 1912 diary entry quoted above, Josephine's delicate body is depicted as being wholly sacrificed to the art of song:

> So there she stands, the delicate creature, shaken by vibrations especially below the breastbone, so that one feels anxious for her, it is as if she has concentrated all her strength on her song, as if from everything in her that does not directly subserve her singing all strength has been withdrawn, almost all power of life, as if she were laid bare, abandoned, committed merely to the care of good angels, as if while she is so wholly withdrawn and living only in her song a cold breath blowing upon her might kill her. (*CS* 363)

Compared to the 1912 diary entry cited above, music in the mouse's body occupies the place of writing in Kafka's 'organism', the activity to which all other life energies have been sacrificed. Josephine's song implies a minimal purity that in his other stories is accessible only to animals—to Gregor Samsa in *The Metamorphosis* who 'hungers' for his sister's violin playing, or to the 'floating' musical dogs in 'Investigations of a Dog'.

The precise nature of Josephine's music is far from evident, however. The unnamed narrator's opening affirmation about 'the power of song' quickly gives way to a series of ambiguous statements that leave the reader wondering if Josephine's song is more than a thoroughly mouse-like whistling, indeed more than mere silence. 'Was her actual whistling notably louder and more alive than the memory of it will be?' the narrator asks at the end of the story. 'Was it even in her lifetime more than a simple memory?' (*CS* 376)[2] In general, commentators have tended to interpret such ambiguities ironically, taking the narrator's persistent

[1] See Reiner Stach's discussion of Brunelda in *Kafkas erotischer Mythos: Eine ästhetische Konstruktion des Weiblichen* (Frankfurt: Fischer Taschenbuch, 1987), 68–71. In Kafka's repeated linking of corporeal girth and music, one should not forget the example of Kafka's corpulent friend Franz Werfel, whom he saw as the embodiment of the musical poet. Werfel gave Kafka a copy of his novel about Verdi in 1924, when the author of 'Josephine' was correcting proofs of his story on his deathbed.

[2] Here and in the following citations I have changed the English translation from 'piping' to 'whistling', which is closer to the everyday, human connotations of *pfeifen*.

qualifications, misstatements, and retractions as the sign of an unreliable narrative where nothing is to be trusted. In these readings Josephine's music is reduced to mere showmanship and corporeal rhetoric—her song is literally nothing, and in no way distinguishes her from the other mice. Other aspects of the narrative—Josephine's female gender, her animal nature, the ethnic or historical reality of the mouse *Volk*—have similarly been denied by critics stressing the formally closed, self-referential, 'empty' character of the text. From a deconstructive perspective, Margot Norris has thus argued that 'Josephine's song is the trace, the presence of an absence', comparable to Lacan's *parole vide*. The allusions to the protagonist's female or animal identity, Norris maintains, are progressively 'emptied of their cultural content' or 'reduced to their biological and insignificant difference'.[3]

Such anti-mimetic interpretations have an undeniable persuasiveness for Kafka's text, which slyly avoids all overt historical or biographical reference. But they fail to address specific questions raised by the story: Why music? Why mice? Why a female protagonist? Why the nationalist discourse of a *Volk*? Even if one allows that the text tends toward a reduction of Josephine's song to 'a mere nothing in voice, a mere nothing in execution' (*CS* 367), one still needs to account for the specific parameters within which this reduction takes place. Finally, if Josephine's song is literally 'nothing', how are we to account for the 'enormous influence' which she undeniably exerts on the other mice? As even the suspicious narrator admits, this is the 'real riddle which needs solving'.

To answer these questions I will first sketch several ideological assumptions about music in German and Austrian culture at the turn of the century when Kafka first began writing. My thesis is that these assumptions implied a discourse of race and gender that pertains directly to his figuration of music in 'Josephine the Singer' as well as his understanding of his own 'unmusical' nature. Specifically, Otto Weininger's theses about women and Jews in *Sex and Character* (1903) will be shown to bear directly on Kafka's last story. Only when the historical connections between

[3] M. Norris, *Beasts of the Modern Imagination* (Baltimore: Johns Hopkins University Press, 1985), 130–1.

these issues have become clear can one begin to interpret its central figures: the 'theatrical' female singer and the 'unmusical' mouse *Volk*.

II

One of the most pernicious and fallacious stereotypes about Jews in Europe at the end of the nineteenth century is that they were unmusical. An early, influential formulation of this view is Richard Wagner's essay 'Judaism in Music' (1850). There, working from a Romantic conception of an originary 'folk' spirit, Wagner denied Jews an authentic relation to music and musical genius on the basis of their acquired, 'guest' relationship to the national cultures and languages in which they reside: 'The Jew speaks the language of the country in which he has lived from generation to generation, but he speaks it as a foreigner.'[4] Deprived of an organic relation to the *Volk*, Jews are deemed incapable of creating true poetry within this national culture: 'In this language, in this art, the Jew can only imitate, he can create neither poem nor work of art' (28). By the same logic Wagner denied Jews access to the realm of German song and music, which supposedly arise spontaneously from the genius of the *Volk*. 'Works of Jewish music', Wagner claims, 'often produce in us the kind of effect we would derive from hearing a poem by Goethe, for example, translated into that jargon we know as Yiddish' (33).

This last claim was particularly damning, for it fed on the street-level perception of recently 'emancipated' Jews as being incapable of speaking High German without a peculiar 'Yiddish' intonation, a 'hissing', abrasive sound accompanied by aggressive gesticulation. 'Contact with our culture has not, even after two thousand years, weaned the Jew away from the peculiarities of Semitic pronunciation. The shrill, sibilant buzzing of his voice falls strangely and unpleasantly on our ears' (28). Wagner is describing what in German was commonly referred to as *mauscheln*, literally, 'to speak (German) like Moses' and which was interpreted as a sign of the Jew's 'inhuman', 'deceptive' nature: 'When we

[4] Reprinted in *Richard Wagner: Stories and Essays*, ed. C. Osborne (London: Peter Owen, 1973), 27.

listen to a Jew talking we are unconsciously upset by the complete lack of purely human expression in his speech. The cold indifference of its peculiar "blabber" can never rise to the excitement of real passion. . . . [The] Jew . . . will always be evasive, because he is incapable of really deep feeling' (29).

Wagner's main examples of Jews as foreigners in music were Felix Mendelssohn and Giacomo Meyerbeer, 'superficial' composers, who in his view were incapable of penetrating the depths of the 'German soul'. Yet although Wagner deems the Jew 'completely incapable of communicating artistically with us either by his appearance or his speech, and least of all by his singing' (29), he also claims that superficial 'Jewish' music has 'succeeded in completely taking over public taste' in the modern period. Wagner resolves this contradiction with the claim that music is the easiest art to imitate, and that Jews are particularly adept at mimicking the sounds of others. The result is not truly human music in the tradition of Bach and Beethoven, but a modern 'gabble whose painful accuracy and deceptive similarity [is] like that of parrots who repeat human speech, and [is] just as lacking in feeling and real expression as these foolish birds' (31). Wagner also explains away Heine, arguably the most musical of contemporary German poets and one who had furnished him with material for his own operas, with a similar specious and self-serving logic. For Wagner Heine is the symbol of the 'Verjudung' of modern art where 'poetry has become a lie.' He is the 'conscience of Judaism', Wagner claims, 'just as Judaism is the defaming conscience of our modern civilization' (39).

Wagner's views, though controversial, had become widely accepted commonplaces in the anti-Semitic atmosphere of the Austro-Hungarian *fin de siècle*, even among Jews. We find them in an academic variation in Otto Weininger's doctoral dissertation, which, published under the title *Geschlecht und Charakter* (*Sex and Character*) in 1903, made the 23-year-old Viennese author a European celebrity during the first decades of the century, admired by Kraus, Wittgenstein, Strindberg, and eventually Mussolini. Weininger, a Jew who converted to Christianity after receiving his doctorate, accepted the racial notion of a 'German' and a 'Jewish' music, arguing that the latter was 'loud', 'ostentatious', 'plebeian'.[5] Beethoven, with the strength of his 'masculine' melodic line, represented for Weininger the paradigm of German musical genius. In strict musicological terms Weininger should have been opposed to Wagner's music for its subordination of melody to harmonic colour, for its 'loud' and 'theatrical' effects, for its appeal to the same boulevard public that Meyerbeer and Halévy had conquered in Paris with their grand-opera productions. Indeed, he declares that Wagner's early operas 'are not exempt from a certain Jewish component' (408). But Wagner supposedly 'overcame' this Jewishness and Weininger praises later works like *Siegfried* and *Parsifal* as the most 'un-Jewish', most German music imaginable, the latter opera remaining 'eternally inaccessible to the fully authentic Jew' (408).

Weininger adds to Wagner's racial stereotypes the dimension of gender. In his system of categorization, Jews share a fundamental similarity with women, who are also denied a deep, innate relationship to music: 'The absolute insignificance of women in the history of music can undoubtedly be explained by much deeper reasons; but it proves first of all their lack of artistic imagination. For musical creativity requires infinitely more imagination than even the most manly woman possesses' (151). Of all the arts, music not only demands the most creativity, the most powerful (male) *Drang zur Form*, it is also the most abstract art, with no corresponding term in empirical reality. Since Weininger defines women (like Jews) as 'materialists', prisoners of their bodies and the material world, of commerce, sexuality, and fashion, they are deemed incapable of attaining an adequate level of metaphysical speculation and can thus never be truly musical.

At the center of Weininger's wildly dualistic, reductive *Weltanschauung* is his genius cult: the 'male principle' (M) is represented ideally by those individual artistic and scientific geniuses whose *memory* encompasses a radically larger section of the past than common mortals, and whose exceptional achievements stem directly from a powerfully coherent, individual, male character: 'A universal memory for all one's past experiences is therefore the most secure, general, identifiable sign of genius' (146), Weininger

[5] *Geschlecht und Charakter* (Vienna, Braunmüller, 1903). 408. All translations from the German text are my own.

writes, thus contesting the opinion among 'café literati' (read: Jewish intellectuals and artists) that 'productive individuals' have 'no memory'. Further: 'genius reveals itself in this regard as a kind of higher manliness; and therefore W cannot be a genius' (141).

Such speculation leads Weininger to a variation of Ernst Mach's 'egoless personality'. Jews and women, lacking the form-giving, creative M principle, have no true individual self: 'The authentic Jew has no self and therefore no self-worth [*Eigenwert*]' (412). Just as women and Jews have no desire for *Eigentum*, for stable property or land, and prefer the 'circulating commodities' of commerce and fashion, so too are they without an *Eigenart*, a strong, individual personality. Neither has an innate, deep relation to the state: creatures of the crowd, the 'horde', the masses, they willingly associate themselves with the two forms of political opposition that threaten the stability of the late nineteenth-century state: communism and the women's movement.

> That the Jew has been opposed to the State [*staatfremd*] not only recently but more or less from the beginning of history, points to the fact that he, like woman, lacks a true personality. . . . For one can understand female as well as Jewish unsociability only through this lack of a distinct self. Jews flock together like women; they do not interact with one another as independent, distinct beings, under the aegis of a supraindividual idea. (412)

The metaphorical register of Weininger's terms reveals his implicit agreement with the cultural prejudice of his period that labelled Jews and women as overly sensual, prone to 'animal' instincts and passion. A year after his death, a selection of his unpublished writings was printed which included notes on the 'Psychology of Animals'.[6] Weininger's chief idea here is that every aspect of the physical world—animals, plants, geological formations, etc.—finds its corresponding psychological term in the human soul. Particularly dogs, who have a 'remarkably profound relationship to *death*', catch his attention: 'The eyes of a dog inevitably give the impression that he has *lost* something: a certain mysterious relationship to his *past* . . . emanates from him. What he has lost is his self, his self-worth, his freedom' (131). With this lack of a self, of an *Eigenwert*, the dog is allied in

[6] Reprinted in 1912 in *Der Sturm*, the Expressionist journal to which Max Brod contributed, this particular essay had a strong impact on Kafka's circle.

Weininger's universe with the 'soulless' woman and Jew, both without the spiritual nature of the 'male principle'.[7]

No matter how offensive these ideas seem today, one should keep in mind their extraordinary reception in German and Austrian society around 1900. Weininger's 600-page doctoral thesis, burdened with tedious medical and academic terminology, none the less became an overnight best-seller and went through numerous reprintings in the first decade of the century, including a 'salon' version of quotable excerpts. Kafka was undoubtedly part of this reception, as recent studies have indicated.[8] However, before addressing myself to the question of Weininger's importance for 'Josephine the Singer', I would like to discuss briefly one other Viennese figure who was also influenced by Weininger and whom Kafka regarded as the spiritual leader of his Jewish–German literary world—Karl Kraus.

Kraus's essay 'Heine and the Consequences', published in his satirical weekly *Die Fackel* in August 1911 and delivered as a public lecture in Prague several months earlier (with Kafka in attendance), takes up many of the racial and sexual arguments developed by Wagner and Weininger before him. Like the author of *Sex and Character*, Kraus operates with stark oppositional pairs—form versus content, female language versus male creator, Romance versus Germanic cultures, life versus art, instrument versus ornament—in order to denounce the 'decadent' ornamentalism and 'feuilletonism' of contemporary German literature. Alluding to Heine's supposed syphilis, Kraus makes the author of the *Buch der Lieder* responsible for this journalistic tendency, a 'disease' which is supposedly of French origin: 'Without Heine no

[7] How not to be reminded here, for instance, of Kafka's depiction of the criminal in 'In the Penal Colony', the 'stupid-looking, wide-mouthed' creature who is so like 'a submissive dog' that one can let him run free on the surrounding hills and need only whistle to call him back to his own execution (*CS* 140)? One thinks also of Joseph K. in *The Trial* who is executed 'like a dog'.

[8] Reiner Stach claims that Kafka learned of Weininger early on, making use of his ideas in the characterization of women in his novels and discussing them with his friends through the 1920s. See his *Kafka erotischer Mythos*. Stach makes no mention of 'Josephine the Singer' in his study, and as far as I know the connection between Weininger and Kafka's conception of Judaism and music has not been dealt with previously. See also Hartmut Binder's early discussion of Weininger and Karl Kraus in *Motiv und Gestaltung bei Franz Kafka* (Bonn: Bouvier, 1966).

feuilleton. That is the French disease he has brought back to us' (7). But a careful reading of Kraus's text reveals that the French are merely a foil for the Jews, Heine's proximity to French culture serving as a cipher for his position as a pernicious outsider and foreigner *as a Jew* within the German language. Kraus's real targets are the Jewish journalists of the *Neue freie Presse*, the Jewish *Kaffeehausliteraten*, the largely Jewish members and clients of aestheticist movements and institutions in Vienna like the Wiener Werkstätte. Thus Kraus lumps together Jews and *fin-de-siècle* aesthetes, Heine's modern descendants: 'Today [Heine] can probably be bettered by every Itzig Witzig in the quickness with which he rhymes "ästhetisch" [aesthetic] with "Teetisch" [tea table].'

In attacking Heine's poetry, Kraus was going against popular opinion. Heine's *Buch der Lieder* had made him into one of the most-read poets of German, his Loreley poem, set to music and sung by Austrians and Germans throughout the Habsburg Empire and the Reich, achieving precisely the status of a German *Volkslied* denied by Wagner. But Kraus finds that Heine's verse is a cheap music which relies on 'atmosphere' (*Stimmung*), verbal tricks, and Gallic neologisms for its effect. He himself is against music:

> Whoever experiences literature deeply does not need to have a sense for music. . . . I am not musical; Wagner would disturb me [while writing]. And if I sought the same kitschy charm of melody in literature, I could not create literature in my nighttime hours. [*ich könnte in solcher Nacht keine Literatur schaffen*] (8)

Kraus's position here is worth noting, for his opposition to Heine's 'superficial' melody could easily have led him, like Weininger, to defend Wagner's German myths and 'infinite' melody. But Kraus, conscious of Wagner's importance for the very Jewish aesthetes and *Bildungsbürgertum* he was attacking, sides with Nietzsche in seeing Wagner as a decadent. His model is rather the High German classicism of Goethe, the simple word 'Farewell' at the end of *Iphigenia on Tauris* outweighing, so he says, all the poems in Heine's *Buch der Lieder*. Kraus opposes here music and literature, the outsider Heine to the classicist Goethe, cheap *Stimmung* to authentic *Schöpfung*. Or rather, he posits the existence of a higher, purer kind of music which Heine, as a talented but ungenial, 'characterless' poet, is incapable of achieving.

But is it really music that Kraus objects to? His hatred of the so-called *Jargon* (Yiddish) is well known; many of his stylistic and moral criticisms were directed against the 'contamination' of High German with 'foreign' linguistic idioms like Yiddish. However, this language of merchants and traders is recognizable, according to Kraus himself in his 1913 essay 'Er ist doch ä Jud' ('But He's a Jew'), precisely by its singsong character—a residue, he claims, of ancient Hebrew chants. Seeking to define the 'specifically Jewish' characteristics of contemporary German-speaking Jewry, he singles out the degraded 'musical' intonation of their speech, 'the chant-like intonation with which they conclude their business deals [and] which obligingly accompanies the sound of rolling coins'.[9] What Kraus objects to in Heine's 'music', his 'feuilletonism' and 'French' wordplays, is precisely this singsong language of the Jewish merchant, the '*mauschel* German' that supposedly sets apart the Jewish poetaster and journalist from the High German classical author. The implication of his argument is that this *mauschel* language is present even in the polished High German verse of the converted Heine. For Kraus (himself a converted Jew), the Jew remains a Jew and can always be identified through his language. Echoing Weininger, he thus sums up Heine's failure as a lack of character: 'This was [Heine]—a talent because without character. He simply confused poets with journalists.'[10]

There is little doubt about Kafka's proximity to both Weininger and Kraus. All three writers are of the same generation of assimilated German Jews, the sons of successful central European businessmen who sought entry into Austrian society by way of German culture. Weininger served the ideal of scholarly *Wissenschaft*, Kraus and Kafka that of Weimar literary classicism. Kafka knew Weininger's work at an early date and incorporated it into his own, and he remained an avid reader of Karl Kraus's satirical

[9] *Die Fackel*, 386 (Oct. 1913), p. 3.

[10] 'So war er: ein Talent, weil kein Charakter; bloß daß er die Artisten mit den Journalisten verwechselt hat' (32).

weekly *Die Fackel* all his life.[11] Yet although he initially identified with the 'national German' ideal of *Bildung* at the expense of his own Judaism, he did not follow his Viennese contemporaries down the path of religious conversion and public Jewish self-hatred. His early contact with the Yiddish theatre in 1911–12 resulted in an authentic awakening of his religious identity that left him forever divided between his origins as a Jew and his professional, literary ambitions in the (Christian) world of German literature. Kafka's characteristic response was to internalize the conflict of this division, 'absorbing' the same anti-Semitic and misogynist stereotypes that shaped the work of Weininger and Kraus, but without giving in to them as normative prescriptions. 'I have vigorously absorbed the negative element of the age in which I live', Kafka wrote in 1919 in an oft-cited passage, 'an age that is, of course, very close to me, which I have no right ever to fight against, but as it were a right to represent' (*DF* 99).

Nevertheless, Kafka was not immune to the phenomenon of Jewish self-hatred,[12] and his tendency to use animal and insect metaphors when talking about Jews has led critics to interpret the animal figures in his literary texts as the fictional literalizations of contemporary slurs.[13] Anti-Semites treat Jews like animals or

[11] See his letter to Robert Klopstock of 29 Feb. 1924 thanking the latter for his gift of *Die Fackel*, 'with which I indulged in those enervating evening orgies with which you are familiar'.

[12] This fact was obscured by Kafka's first editors, who excised openly anti-Semitic passages from his letters. The recent publication of the expanded edition of the letters to Milena Jesenská reveals many such remarks, including an extensive dialogue between an angel and Jewry, the latter characterized as deceitful by nature: 'It's inevitable that Jewry will twist the words of the angel whenever possible. . . . Jewry: What lies deep down is deceiving, but you can know a person by the surface . . . At this point at last, at last, good heavens, the angel pushes the Jews back down and frees himself' (*M* 230–1).

[13] Günther Anders was the first to focus on Kafka's literalizations of ordinary figures of speech, although not in this ethnic sense. On the question of anti-Semitism see also C. Stölzl, *Kafkas böses Böhmen: Zur Sozialgeschichte eines Prager Juden* (rev. edn. Frankfurt: Ullstein, 1989); S. Gilman, *Jewish Self-Hatred: Anti-Semitism and the Hidden Language of the Jews* (Baltimore: Johns Hopkins University Press, 1985), and Walter Müller-Seidel's recent *Die deportation des Menschen* (Stuttgart: Metzler, 1986). Kafka's equation of Jews and animals runs throughout his work and is not necessarily pejorative, as is evident in his tongue-in-cheek letter to Elsa and Max Brod of October 1917; while working on a farm, he found that goats 'look like thoroughly Jewish types, mostly doctors, though there are a few approximations of lawyers, Polish Jews, and a scattering of pretty girls in the flock. Dr. W., the doctor who treats me, is

disgusting vermin; Kafka takes the street metaphor literally, turning it into a fictional image or event: the monstrous bug Gregor Samsa, the 'assimilated' ape Red Peter, the floating dogs in 'Investigations of a Dog', the mole-like creature in 'The Burrow', the jackals in 'Jackals and Arabs' (first printed in Martin Buber's journal *Der Jude*), and finally Joseph K. in *The Trial*, who is killed 'like a dog'.[14]

The choice of the mouse figure in 'Josephine the Singer' may well obey a similar strategy, for at the turn of the century the vocabulary of anti-Semitic discourse included mice, rats, and other vermin suspected of bearing disease through invisible, subterranean channels.[15] But Kafka had another reason for employing the mouse image. Although etymologically related to the names Mauschel, Moishele, and Moses, the verb *mauscheln*—to speak German 'like a Jew'— recalls the German word for mouse, *Maus*. In this sense the language spoken by the mice in 'Josephine'—what one might term their '*Mäusedeutsch*'—can be interpreted as Kafka's fictional version of *Mauscheldeutsch* and, perhaps, as a figure for his own Jewish–German language. If so, the *Volk* referred to in the story would not be the Jewish people generally, as commentators have often assumed, but the German–Jewish people at a particular moment in history, that is, the generation of

heavily represented among them. The conference of three Jewish doctors whom I fed today were so pleased with me that they would hardly let themselves be driven home in the evening for milking' (*L* 150–1).

[14] Weininger writes for instance that the Jew is 'like a parasite who changes in each host, taking on such a fully different appearance that one is led to think that he has become a different animal each time, whereas he always remains the same' (*Geschlecht und Charakter*, 430). consider also the recently restored passage from a letter to Milena Jesenská of mid-November 1920: 'I've been spending every afternoon outside on the streets, wallowing in anti-Semitic hate. The other day I heard someone call the Jews a "mangy race". Isn't it natural to leave a place where one is so hated? (Zionism or national feeling isn't needed for this at all.) The heroism of staying on is none the less merely the heroism of cockroaches which cannot be exterminated, even from the bathroom' (*M* 212–13). Kafka reacts against the animal metaphor of 'mangy race', but reproduces it in the implicit analogy between himself as a Jew (and author of *The Metamorphosis*) and cockroaches.

[15] See Christoph Cobet, *Der Wortschatz des Antisemitismus in der Bismarckzeit* (Munich: Fink, 1973). The use of the mice image is not limited to Kafka's period. Art Spiegelman, in a literalization not unlike Kafka's, uses the cat and mouse figures in his comic book retelling of the Holocaust, *Maus*. See also Johannes Bobrowski's use of the same notion in his short prose text 'Mäusefest'.

'Western Jews' between emancipation and Zionism to which Kafka felt he belonged.[16]

This hypothesis is supported by Kafka's view of *mauscheln* as the language that his generation of German-Jewish writers was destined to speak. In 1921 Kafka's friend Franz Werfel, a Prague Jew who would later convert to Catholicism, had subjected Kraus to a crude attack in his play *Spiegelmensch*. Kraus replied with an equally crass satire reproaching Werfel, who was then the most successful young writer in Austria and Germany, with a faulty command of High German, that is, with his Prague *Mauscheldeutsch*, the sign of his 'Yiddish' and 'Eastern' origins.[17] Conscious of the hypocrisy of this attack, Kafka points out in a now celebrated letter to Max Brod of June 1921 that Kraus's satire is itself an example of *Mauscheldeutsch*: '[His] wit principally consists of Yiddish-German—*mauscheln*—no one can *mauscheln* like Kraus, although in this German-Jewish world hardly anyone can do anything else.' Significantly, Kafka does not lay the blame for this 'frightful inner predicament' on an anti-Semitic German culture, but on the 'Jewishness' of the fathers, again using an insect metaphor:

> Most young Jews who began to write German wanted to leave Jewishness behind them, and their fathers approved of this, but vaguely (this vagueness was what was outrageous to them). But with their posterior legs they were still glued to their father's Jewishness and with their waving anterior legs they found no new ground. The ensuing despair became their inspiration.

III

Let us now read 'Josephine the Singer' as a text about 'mice' written in the language of *Mäusedeutsch*, or rather *Mauscheldeutsch*,

[16] 'I have vigorously absorbed the negative element of the age in which I live . . . I have not been guided into life by the hand of Christianity—admittedly now slack and failing—as Kierkegaard was, and have not caught the hem of the Jewish prayer shawl—now flying away from us—as the Zionists have. I am an end or a beginning' (25 Feb. 1917, *DF* 99–100).

[17] Kraus's celebrated (and untranslatable) witticism about the Prague circle of Jewish–German poets—'Es werfelt und brodet und kafkat und kischt'—rests on a similar prejudice that their 'Eastern' idiom was besmirching the purity of High German.

the supposedly deceitful 'secret language' of the Jews.[18] Kafka's narrator begins his story by referring to a 'certain practical cunning' which is the mouse people's 'greatest distinction'. Who is the narrator? Is he male (as most commentators assume) or, like Josephine, female? And in what form are we to understand 'his' narration as taking place? We read a written text, but the mouse folk are explicitly described as without a historical tradition. Unlike, say, Kafka's earlier story 'A Report to an Academy' in which a talking ape addresses a group of scholars, 'Josephine' rigorously refuses to identify the setting or protagonist of its own utterance. We have no way of knowing who is speaking to whom or in what form, no way of knowing how the written text we are reading has emerged from the mouse culture. This is one example of the text's slippery 'mouse' language, the *mauscheln* of a people 'who love slyness beyond everything' (*CS* 365).

Part of the deceptiveness of Kafka's text involves the use of anti-Semitic, misogynist stereotypes to characterize both Josephine and the mouse people—stereotypes which coincide to a remarkable degree with Weininger's formulations.[19] The chief coincidence concerns music: 'The Jew doesn't sing', Weininger claims categorically; Jews have a 'curious aversion to song' (*Geschlecht und Charakter* 436). The mice in 'Josephine' are repeatedly characterized as an 'unmusical people', caught up in the material cares of daily life, too 'heavy' and 'old' to rise up to the 'abstract' heights of music: 'we are not in general a music-loving race. Tranquil peace is the music we love best; our life is hard, we are no longer able, even on occasions when we have tried to shake off the cares of daily life, to rise to anything so high and remote from our usual routines as music' (*CS* 360).

[18] As Sander Gilman has noted, *Mauscheldeutsch* was commonly viewed as the 'secret language' of the Jews, the 'incomprehensible' and 'deceitful' dialect they were accused of using with each other to take advantage of non-Jews. Here and in the following pages I am indebted to his remarkable study *Jewish Self-Hatred*, although Gilman does not discuss Kafka's text or the question of 'Jewish music'.

[19] Weininger's 'influence' on Kafka is not the point of my argument, which is about cultural stereotypes shared by large segments of society. What is important is that Weininger's ideas were part of Kafka's Jewish–German circle in Prague. His friend Oskar Baum delivered a lecture on 'Sex and Character' in February 1921, which another friend, Johannes Urzidil, reviewed for the Prague Zionist newspaper *Selbstwehr*. Kafka asked Baum for a copy of his lecture in a letter of April 1921.

As noted above, Weininger likens Jews to women in their supposed lack of an 'identity principle', which leads them to prefer the group, the 'masses', or the animal horde. 'Jews flock together like women', he claims; even when they are alone, they live in a state of 'Verschmolzenheit', a physical merging with others (*Geschlecht und Charakter*, 255). Precisely this state of corporeal merging characterizes the way of life of Kafka's animal *Volk*: 'we like to come together, we like to huddle close to each other . . . warmly pressed body to body . . . in the great, warm bed of the community' (*CS* 366, 364). Weininger repeats the stereotype of Jews as a 'rootless' people that have developed a 'facile agility' (*Beweglichkeit*) in adapting to other cultures (*Geschlecht und Charakter*, 429). Kafka's mice are 'always on the run' (*immer in Bewegung*), scurrying about without 'a clear purpose'. Weininger's sexually obsessed women and Jews want only the physical merging of 'Kuppelei,' coitus or animal mating. Kafka's choice of protagonist leads to the inevitable observation about the mice's fertility: 'One generation—and each is numerous—treads on the heels of another . . . from our race come pouring at the briefest intervals the innumerable swarms of our children' (*CS* 368).

For Weininger, the 'animal' behaviour of Jews and women is proof of their lack of a 'self', which he also calls 'personality', 'character', and 'soul'. Both are by nature 'duplicitous'; they lack an 'inner simplicity' and cannot help but lie, cheat, and deceive. This is the reason for the alleged deceitfulness of *Mauscheldeutsch*, which he also subcribes to: 'The Jew's psychic makeup is characterized by a certain duplicity. . . . He never gets beyond this ambiguity, this duplicity, indeed this multiplicity' (*Geschlecht und Charakter*, 434). Similarly, Weininger appeals to popular sayings as proof of women's 'inherent' tendency to deceive; they 'lie, even without knowing it' (194). In Kafka's text, the sly mouse people are given to 'superficial' chatter and are incapable of 'unconditional devotion' to a single idea: 'unconditional devotion is hardly known among us; ours are people who love slyness beyond everything' (*CS* 365). While listening to Josephine with ostensibly respectful attention, the mice are in fact not far from laughter (*CS* 365).

Presumably, Josephine believes in the exceptional nature of her song and the justification for her artistic fame. She is not like the other mice: she has a name, is musical, insists on the Weiningerian 'identity principle' that raises her above the 'masses' of the mouse folk, although she is not a composer, only a performer of music.[20] But the narrator clearly does not believe in her difference and proceeds to dismantle it with Weiningerian arguments. For the author of *Sex and Character*, women are 'without a soul', without individual character; metaphysically speaking, they are 'nothing': 'Women have no existence and no essence; they *are* nothing, they are *nothing* . . . women have no part of ontological reality' (383). Similarly, the narrator undermines the ontological reality of Josephine's song, her soul or essence, by ironic qualifications and wordplays suggesting its non-existence. She is described as 'a mere nothing in voice, a mere nothing in execution' (*CS* 367); her song is 'nothing out of the ordinary', what little there is being reduced by the mouse folk to 'the least possible trace' (*die möglichste Nichtigkeit*).

In Weininger's system, women attempt to cover up their metaphysical 'lack' or 'nothingness' with an artificial, seductive, 'theatrical' appearance. Their true self is their body, whose language they artfully manipulate in order to deceive men. Similarly, Josephine's musical performances are primarily corporeal, visual: 'to comprehend her art it is necessary not only to hear but to see her' (*CS* 361). To gather an audience, she merely assumes a theatrical stance, 'head thrown back, mouth half-open, eyes turned upwards, in the position that indicates her intention to sing' (*CS* 364). Whether or how she actually sings is left in doubt, the narrator suggesting that she has only corporeal rhetoric and trick effects with which to subjugate her audience. Gradually Josephine appears as an impostor who is trying to pass off her ordinary whistling as something special, as art. According to the narrator, her singing is really only like nut-cracking, which the

[20] Much of the anti-Semitic discourse denying Jews a musical nature focused on the lack of Jewish composers. Jewish performers were plentiful and could be explained by the Jews' supposed talent for mimicry. In 'Josephine' there is never any mention of musical composition, only performance. Kafka's 'artist figures' (the Hunger Artist, Red Peter, the circus rider in 'Up in the Gallery') are always only performers, which is perhaps a sign of his internalization of the stereotype that Jews were incapable of true originality. My thanks to Andreas Huyssen for clarifying this point.

mice can do *better* than Josephine; she merely dares 'to collect an audience in order to entertain it with nut-cracking' (*CS* 361).

Josephine's 'delicate' feminine appearance is also described as a façade which repeatedly breaks down to reveal her 'true' animal self. When challenged, she becomes 'arrogant', 'sarcastic', and 'vulgar' (*gemein*, *CS* 362). Denied a sufficient audience, 'she turns furious, then she stamps her feet, swearing in most unmaidenly fashion; she actually bites' (*CS* 364). Like Weininger's coquettish, narcissistic, hysterical female, dependent on male compliments for a sense of her own worth and always ready to 'break into tears' to awaken male pity (*Geschlecht und Charakter*, 254), Josephine is blinded by 'self-conceit', easily seduced by her flatterers, and subject to temper tantrums and crying.

Weininger infantilizes women by declaring them not so much immoral as amoral, lacking even the (male) cognitive faculties to recognize their own transgressions: 'I claim therefore not that woman is evil or immoral but that she can never be evil, only amoral, vulgar [*gemein*]' (254). Josephine also considers herself 'beyond the law', behaving in an unwittingly amoral fashion that endangers the other mice (*CS* 371). She expects to profit from her situation as woman and artist, claiming an exemption from daily labour. When forced to do manual labour, she characteristically resorts to deception, feigning an injury to her foot. But although she 'limps and leans on her supporters', the narrator claims, 'no one believes she is hurt'. She is also vengeful, waging a secret campaign against her opponents, spreading rumours about measures she might take to punish them, and finally depriving them of her song altogether.

In the end, one senses in the narrator's guileful portrayal an element of Weiningerian suspicion of Josephine as both Jew and woman: theatrical, deceitful, alternately hysterical and coldly calculating, without a true musical personality and therefore all the more dangerously seductive:

> Since she cannot very well go on limping forever, she thinks of something else, she pleads that she is tired, not in the mood for singing, feeling faint. And so we get a theatrical performance as well as a concert. We see Josephine's supporters in the background begging and imploring her to sing. She would be glad to oblige, but she cannot. They comfort and caress

> her with flatteries, they almost carry her to the selected spot where she is supposed to sing. At last, bursting inexplicably into tears, she gives way, but when she stands up to sing . . . she cannot do it after all, an unwilling shake of the head tells us so and she breaks down before our eyes. . . . And in the end . . . she moves off, refusing all help from her supporters and measuring with cold eyes the crowd which respectfully makes way for her. (*CS* 375)

IV

The above portrait of Josephine is distorted, for I have deliberately emphasized the disparaging tenor of the narrator's remarks. The distortion is primarily one of tone: although the narrator often seems to side against Josephine, his tone of voice makes clear that he is speaking from within the group that includes her, as an insider for whom certain critical remarks are permissible. For all his veiled disparagement and suspicion, his attitude is primarily one of affection and concern for Josephine. If his voice is paternalistic, as some critics have claimed, it is not the voice of patriarchy, power, or domination. Oppression of any direct, violent sort is not part of the mouse folk's existence; aggression comes from the outside.

This is the crucial difference separating Kafka from Weininger. Although the author of 'Josephine' has absorbed contemporary stereotypes of Jews and women, he transforms them into something different by depicting them from within the group, as an insider. Precisely because narration proceeds from a mouse, the animals are given the human status denied them by the racial stereotype; indeed, the mice are depicted as a delicate, art-loving people whose existence is threatened by external (human? feline?) aggressors. Weininger's discourse is 'schizophrenic'—he speaks of Jews as if from the outside, as if he were himself not Jewish. His analyses display an utter lack of humour, which, coupled with his dogmatic, fanatical insistence on the validity of his reductive terms, gives his 'scholarly' work an intolerably scornful, accusatory tone, certain passages reading like the worst fascist political propaganda. The voice in Kafka's text on the other hand is remarkable for its sense of irony, nuance, understatement, comedy. The narrator's *Mauscheldeutsch* is a 'sly' language but one that is basically innocent, childlike, 'without any malice'.

If one listens for this note of understatement and does not try to reduce the ambiguities and paradoxes of the narrator's language to empty nonsense, one can detect in Kafka's text a subtle reversal of Weininger's thesis about a 'Jewish' or 'female' lack of self. The key passage comes midway through the story, just after the narrator has explained that the mouse people, 'too old for music', content themselves with 'a little whistling' here and there. 'Who knows', he asks, 'there may be talents for music [*Musiktalente*] among us, but if there were, the character of our people would suppress them before they could unfold' (*CS* 369). Echoing Weininger's opposition of 'superficial' (Jewish) talent and 'deep' (Germanic) character, the narrator asserts that the 'character' of the people, of the 'comrades' (*Volksgenossen*), suppresses individual 'talents.' Weininger's notion of individual *Charakter* is displaced on to its opposite, becoming in Kafka's text the vital attribute of the mice 'Volk'.

This suppression does not fully eradicate Josephine's individual voice. She can whistle or sing or 'whatever she likes to call it', says the narrator, for 'any music there may be in it is reduced to the least possible trace [*die möglichste Nichtigkeit*]; a certain tradition of music is preserved, yet without weighing us down in the slightest' (*CS* 369–70). Precisely the 'minimal' quality of Josephine's song suits the delicate, light-weight mice. A musical character in Weininger's sense of male genius would overwhelm them, whereas Josephine's almost non-existent 'talent' allows for the preservation of the mouse folk's musical tradition, which has survived through history 'in legends and some songs'. The mice reduce her song not to Weininger's absolute category of *Nichtigkeit*, but to the understated 'almost nothingness' that allows this tiny people, 'almost' without memory or a musical tradition, to maintain itself in history.

This 'trace' of Josephine's song, understood not as Lacan's *parole vide* or Derrida's *différance*, but as an actual if minimal quantity, paradoxically obtains the greatest result. Admittedly, her claims to be the 'saviour' of her people are dismissed by the narrator as theatrical show: 'it is easy, I say, to stage oneself after the event as the savior of our people, who have always somehow managed to save themselves' (*CS* 366). Yet something like collective redemption occurs through Josephine's almost silent whistling, which is described in the following, unusually lyrical passage as a momentary freedom from daily cares:

> At her concerts . . . in the brief intervals between their struggles, our people dream, it is as if the limbs of each were loosened, as if the harried individual once in a while could relax and stretch himself at ease in the great, warm bed of the community. . . . Something of our poor brief childhood is in [her whistling], something of lost happiness that can never be found again, but also something of active daily life, of its small gaieties, unaccountable and yet springing up and not to be obliterated. . . . Of course it is a kind of whistling. Why not? Whistling is our people's daily speech, only many a one whistles his whole life long and does not know it, where here whistling is set free from the fetters of daily life and it sets us free too for a little while. (*CS* 370)

Here is the secret to the riddle posed by the narrator at the beginning of the text, the riddle of Josephine's 'enormous influence'. The 'least possible trace' of music, the 'almost nothingness' of her song, its resemblance to the everyday language of the mice—this makes possible the collective dreaming in which their past is recovered. Josephine's song redeems the mouse *Volk*, at least 'for a little while'.

It would be wrong however to insist on a messianic resolution of 'Josephine the Singer'—wrong because the *Mauscheldeutsch* in which it is composed keeps the story open, suspended between meanings, resistant to any single conclusive interpretation. Perhaps the 'saviour' of her people, Josephine still behaves egotistically, shortening her 'coloraturas', refusing to perform, and eventually disappearing into the folk rather than leading it into a Promised Land:

> Josephine, redeemed from the earthly sorrows which to her thinking lay in wait for all chosen spirits, will happily lose herself in the numberless throng of the heroes of our people, and soon, since we are no historians, will rise to the heights of redemption and be forgotten like all her brothers. (*CS* 376)

Josephine's disappearance into the unwritten chronicles of her people has proved a particularly vexing problem, leading some critics to argue that the mice cannot be equated with the Jews, who traditionally have been a historically conscious people. But at the turn of the century a widespread view held that Jews in the

Diaspora were without a historical tradition, 'history' having ended for them with the destruction of the Temple.[21] This view is a corollary of the belief that assimilated 'Western' Jews, cut off from the tradition and language of their forefathers, were without cultural 'memory', without a past. Hence Weininger's opposition between the Germanic genius endowed with 'universal memory', and Jews without either individual or collective memory. Kafka saw himself as a 'Western Jew' without memory or a stable, inherent relation to tradition.[22] Calling himself 'the most typical Western Jew' among his acquaintances, he explained to Milena Jesenská that 'not one second of calm has been granted me, nothing has been granted me, everything must be earned, not only the present and future, but the past as well—something which is, perhaps, given every human being—this too must be earned'.[23]

The misogynist, anti-Semitic discourse of Kafka's period denies women and Jews the capacity for memory and therefore for redemption. Without a true, individual self, ensconced in their material existence, they can neither remember the past nor project themselves into the future.[24] Kafka absorbs these claims into his text, but again reverses them into a series of 'Mauschel' paradoxes. His mice are 'no historians', their memory of Josephine's song will weaken and fade away, she will be forgotten, her talent effaced by the character of the anonymous folk. But precisely this quality of being forgotten, absorbed by the *Volk*-body, guarantees her redemption and immortality. Josephine's disappearance into the unhistorical *Volk* leads to the 'heights of redemption'; her loss

[21] See Ritchie Robertson's illuminating discussion of this question in *Kafka: Judaism, Literature and Politics* (Oxford: Oxford University Press, 1985).

[22] See Giuliano Baioni's discussion in the first chapter of his *Kafka: Letteratura ed ebraismo* (Turin: Einaudi, 1984).

[23] (*M* 217). By 'Western Jew' Kafka means the assimilated European Jew of the late 19th and early 20th centuries—a concept that may be related to the narrator's remark that Josephine is 'a small episode in the eternal history of our people' (*CS* 376).

[24] Like Nietzsche's cow at the beginning of his essay 'Use and Abuse of History', Weininger's 'absolute' woman cannot even remember to remember—hence her 'inherently' criminal, deceptive nature. But because woman cannot remember, she is also incapable of experiencing guilt and therefore cannot be 'redeemed' (*Geschlecht und Charakter*, 329). she lives without a sense of the past and with no thought for the future; she has no need for 'immortality', no *Unsterblichkeitsbedürfnis* and no *Erlösungsbedürfnis*.

of artistic individuality to a place among the people's heroes; her non-existent song to the eternal memory constituted by the narrator's story. And the only way to make sense of these contradictions is to allow them not to make sense, to read them as the 'slippery' language of a people that 'loves slyness beyond everything'.

V

This reading may seem like a somewhat devious way to arrive at a familiar conclusion—that Josephine's song serves Kafka as a figure for his own literary language. But the detour seems warranted because of the political register to the language in 'Josephine', which in this regard is quite unlike his other writings and has generally been overlooked in the critical literature. Words like 'Volksgenossen' (comrades) and 'Volkversammlungen' (folk rallies), the repeated references to an 'enemy' lying in wait, the dangers of external aggressors, indicate a particular concern with the politics and political language of the 1920s. In that period the relations between Germans and Jews were becoming increasingly violent. To cite only one telling example: in 1922 Hans Blüher published his *Secessio Judaica*, a proto-Nazi call for the definitive separation of Jews and Germans as 'racially incompatible' peoples; Kafka, who had admired Blüher's earlier work on male eroticism, was deeply disturbed by the book and asked his friend Robert Klopstock to write the response that he himself felt incapable of writing.[25] Late in 1923, a few months before writing 'Josephine', he witnessed the anti-Jewish pogroms that swept through the streets of Berlin, pointing to events to come. His friend Robert Weltsch described them in the *Berliner Rundschau* thus: 'The hate-filled [German] faces which stare at Jewish phantoms, the undiluted animosity for Jews, the approval of the broadest circles of the population for the most dreadful crimes against Jews, show us

[25] Even here Kafka uses the language of animals for his Jewish perspective: 'It does not have to be a refutation, only an answer to [the book's] appeal. . . . It is tempting to let one's animals graze on this German and yet not entirely alien pasture, after the fashion of the Jews [*nach Judenart*]' (Letter of 30 June 1922).

that as Jews we can be shot down like animals.[26] It was in this political climate that Kafka began 'The Burrow', a story about a mole-like animal that lives underground, anxiously awaiting the attack of an unseen enemy; that he wrote or contemplated writing a play and a story about a Jew tried for ritual murder;[27] and that he conceived 'Josephine the Singer, or the Mouse Folk'.

Kafka was always convinced that his German prose had a 'Jewish' accent to it. To his Czech translator Milena Jesenská he once pointed out that the tiny word *nur* (only) in his early story 'The Tradesman' was a 'Prague-Jewish *nur*'.[28] For much of his life he sought to reduce this ethnic accent to a minimum, fashioning one of the most neutral, limpid prose idioms of twentieth-century German literature. In 'Josephine the Singer', however, he makes this ethnic sign of difference the subject of the narrator's musings, attempting to explain how an almost inaudible voice can have such an 'enormous influence' on his audience. As such the story represents a coming to terms with his role as a writer in and for the 'Volk' of assimilated Jewish Germans, a role that he felt Karl Kraus and his friend Franz Werfel had failed to assume.[29] In a time of inflated political rhetoric as well as extreme political events, Kafka responds with a literary text that makes use of the least likely political weapon: understatement, the voice of the animal, the woman, the Jew. It is the music of 'Mäusedeutsch', his own peculiar variation of the *Mauscheldeutsch* castigated by anti-Semites as the mark of Jewish difference. And the only ornament he let stand.

[26] The last phrase reads: '. . . daß wir Juden heute fast vogelfrei geworden sind.' *Jüdische Rundschau*, as quoted by Stölzl, *Kafka böses Böhmen*, 106.

[27] Reference here is to the ritual murder trial of Mendel Beilis of 1911–13, and which Kafka followed in the *Selbstwehr*. See Robertson, *Kafka: Judaism, Literature and Politics*, 12 and 274; and A. J. Band, 'Kafka and the Beiliss [*sic*] Affair', *Comparative Literature*, 32 (1980), 168–83.

[28] The full quote reads: 'this "*nur*" is a Prague–Jewish *nur*, signifying a challenge, like "go ahead and do it."' (*M* 207).

[29] Kafka was severely disappointed by Werfel's play *Schweiger* (1922), which had satirized Otto Gross, the anarchist disciple of Freud who died of starvation in 1920. In a letter to Werfel of December 1922, apparently never posted, Kafka criticized the play as representing a 'retreat from leadership . . . a betrayal of the generation, a glossing over, a trivializing, and therefore a cheapening of their sufferings'.

Epilogue: The Invisible Dandy

BARBEY d'Aurevilly relates that Beau Brummell's cardinal rule in dressing as a dandy was never to be noticed: 'Pour être bien mis, il ne faut pas être remarqué.'[1] But then again, Barbey admits, the dandy is one of those spirits, like the orator or the great actor, 'who speak to the body with his body'. Not to stand out and yet to speak with one's material self; to disappear into an ever more refined elegance and yet preserve the ability to speak, to convince, even to surprise and shock—within these contradictory parameters moves a phenomenon that has sometimes been interpreted as the last glimmer of aristocratic Europe, sometimes as the beginning of modernity. In any case, as Barbey notes, dandyism is a manner of being in the world, *une façon d'être*, one that does not depend merely on its worldly, visible manifestation.

One of Kafka's earliest and deepest wishes was to disappear. We see it in his relations with his parents, his friends, his editors, to whom he always said he would be more grateful to them for not publishing than for publishing his writings. We see it in his relation to language, in the desire to make himself smaller and smaller, to disappear into the dot over an 'i' or the initial 'K.' or a scrupulously correct use of High German. Virtually all of his literary protagonists disappear. And yet Kafka wanted to be seen, to be heard, to be read. He wanted to shock, to write books that would work like a fist or an axe on bored, self-satisfied readers. He chose his clothing with care, adopted a reserved but refined manner, worked his body into athletic form, and above all fashioned a literary style so polished and correct that initially it seemed not to be a style at all: a dramatically transparent style that could make its author heard without calling attention to him,

[1] From his essay *Du dandysme et de G. Brummell* (Paris: Éditions d'Aujourd'hui, 1977), 51.

without contradicting his wish to be in the world and, simultaneously, to disappear.

For Baudelaire the dandy represented the will toward distinction and originality in a democratic age that 'invades and flattens everything' into a dull, sordid equality.[2] For the young German–Jewish aesthetes and writers at the turn of the century who followed French and English examples, the dialectic of distinguishing oneself without being noticed inevitably had a different political meaning. Their parents and relatives, often enough professionals in the clothing business, stood out as Jews, looked and dressed 'like Jews' in the eyes of an anti-Semitic public; at the same time, however, they were in the process of giving up their religious beliefs and trying to assimilate into German society. The sons (for the question of female clothing is entirely different for social and historical reasons) fled from this unhappy combination into a more refined, aristocratic, less visibly 'Jewish' elegance. For Kafka, the embrace of German art, literature, and sartorial elegance went hand in hand with the attempt to cover over his Jewish origins, as in the letter to Oskar Pollak of 1903 in which he mentions a demonstration of 'noisy' Jewish shop clerks on the Graben in Prague, with 'their red carnations and their stupid and Jewish faces' (*L* 10). Aestheticism offered him the chance to escape the father's narrow, 'dirty' shop for the broad vistas of European culture. As he claimed in a stanza of French verse, penned during his 1910 trip to Paris:

> moi je flâne
> qu'on m'approuve ou me condamne
> je vois tout
> je suis partout[3]

In the above pages I have traced Kafka's itinerary from these aesthete and 'deutschtümelei' beginnings to his tentative acceptance of his role as 'singer', however 'unmusical', for a German–Jewish

[2] From the chapter on the dandy in his essay 'The Painter of Modern Life', in *The Painter of Modern Life and Other Essays*, trans. and ed. J. Mayne (London: Phaidon Press, 1964), pp. 26–9.

[3] 'I'm a *flâneur* / And whether one approves of me or condemns me / I see everything / I'm everywhere.' From *Max Brod: Franz Kafka: Eine Freundschaft: Reiseaufzeichnungen*, ed. M. Pasley (Frankfurt: Fischer, 1987), 50.

people—an itinerary that sets itself off from the *Verkehr* of his father's fancy goods, from the 'clothing' of an unessential social and temporal reality. At one level we encounter his wish to do away with clothes altogether, to undress body and soul until the self has merged with a sacred, imperishable flame: 'you must take off your shoes, yet not only your shoes, but everything; you must take off your traveling garment and lay down your luggage; and under that you must shed your nakedness and everything that is under the nakedness.' But in the increasingly nationalist, anti-Semitic climate in Prague following the dissolution of the Habsburg monarchy, a German Jew had more material fears. 'It's a little as if instead of just having to wash up and comb one's hair before taking a walk, a person is constantly missing everything he needs to take with him', Kafka noted to Milena Jesenská in 1920.

> And so each time he has to sew his clothes, make his boots, manufacture his hat, cut his walking stick, etc. Of course it's impossible to do all of that well; it may hold up for a few blocks, but then suddenly, at the Graben, for example, everything falls apart and he's left standing there naked with rags and pieces. And now the torture of running back into the Altstädter Ring! And in the end he runs into an angry mob on the Eisengasse, hot in pursuit of Jews. (*M* 218).

Things were scarcely better in Berlin, where a wave of anti-Semitic violence swept through the streets in early November 1923, shortly after Kafka had moved there from Prague. His companion Dora Dymant relates several anecdotes that bear interestingly on their tenuous existence there. Although they had hardly enough money to buy butter or a newspaper, Kafka insisted on being well dressed and had his suits made by a first-class tailor. Before going out he would observe himself critically for a long time in the mirror—not out of vanity but from a desire to be 'correct'—so correct he would not stand out. The two of them also dreamed of starting a small restaurant in which Kafka would have worked as the waiter. Dora recalls: 'In this way he would have been able to observe everything, be in the midst of everyday life, without being seen himself. Basically that's what he did, although in his own way.'[4] For Baudelaire the perfection

[4] From J. P. Hodin's 'Erinnerungen an Franz Kafka', *Der Monat*, 8/9 (June 1949), 93.

of a dandy's *toilette* consisted in 'absolute simplicity', which in fact is 'the best way to distinguish oneself'. For Kafka the 'perfection' of his clothing and physical appearance was animated by the fear of standing out, the fear that everything might suddenly 'fall apart' and leave one standing 'naked with rags and pieces'. And that as a Jew he would be especially recognizable when naked.

In a letter to Max Brod of August 1920, Milena Jesenská, perhaps with this fear of Kafka's in mind, sought to explain why she thought he would never recover from his tuberculosis:

> [W]e are all capable of living, because at one time or another we have all taken refuge in a lie, in blindness, enthusiasm, optimism, a conviction, pessimism, or something else. But he has never fled to any refuge, not one. He is absolutely incapable of lying, just as he is incapable of getting drunk. . . . That is why he is exposed to everything we are protected from. He is like a naked man among the clothed. (*M* 245)

Bibliography

Because of the voluminous extent of the Kafka secondary literature, the following bibliography lists only the works cited in this study. Primary literature by Kafka's contemporaries is listed according to the same principle.

1 Contemporary Sources

Avenarius, Ferdinand (ed.), *Der Kunstwart*, (1887–1937).

Bie, Oskar, *Der gesellschaftliche Verkehr* (Berlin: Gurlitt, 1905).

Bourget, Paul, *Essais de psychologie contemporaine* (Paris: Lemerre, 1883).

Brod, Max, *Experimente* (Berlin: Axel Juncker, 1907).

Gross, Hanns, *Criminalpsychologie* (Graz: Leuschner & Lubensky's, 1898); English version, published as *Criminal Psychology: A Manual for Judges, Practitioners, and Students*, trans. H. M. Kallen (Boston: Little, Brown & Co., 1911).

——*Handbuch für Untersuchungsrichter als System der Kriminalistik* (Graz: Leuschner and Lubensky's, 1893). English version published as *Criminal Investigation. A Practical Textbook for Magistrates, Police Officers and Lawyers*, adapted by J. Collyer Adam (London: Sweet & Maxwell, 1924).

Haeckel, Ernst, *Kunstformen der Natur* (Leipzig: Bibliographisches Institut, 1899–1903).

——*Die Natur als Künstlerin* (Berlin: Vita, 1913).

Holitscher, Arthur, *Amerika Heute und morgen* (Berlin: Fischer, 1912; 2nd edn. 1913).

Janouch, Gustav, *Conversations with Kafka*, 2nd edn., trans. Goronwy Rees (New York: New Directions Books, 1971).

Just, Adolf, *Kehrt zur Natur zurück!* (Blankenburg im Harz: Verlag der Heilerdegesellschaft Luvos, 1896; 12th edn., 1930).

Lombroso, Cesare, *L'uomo delinquente* (Turin: Fratelli Bocca, 1875; 4th edn., 1889).

Loos, Adolf, *Ins Leere gesprochen: 1897–1900*, ed. A. Opel (Vienna: G. Prachner, 1981; repr. of original 1921 edn.); English edn., *Spoken into the Void* (Cambridge: MIT Press, 1982).

Trotzdem: 1900–1930, ed. A. Opel, (Vienna: G. Prachner, 1982; reprint of original 1931 edn.).

——*Die Potemkinsche Stadt*, ed. A. Opel (Vienna: G. Prachner, 1983).

——*Konfrontationen: Schriften von und über Adolf Loos*, ed. A. Opel (Vienna: G. Prachner, 1988).

Mirbeau, Octave, *Torture Garden* (New York: Citadel Press, 1948).

MÜLLER, JENS PETER, *Mein System* (Cophenhagen: Holger Tillge, 1905; distributed in Germany by K. F. Koehler, 3rd edn.).

NORDAU, MAX, *Entartung* 1892; 2nd edn. trans. as *Degeneration* (New York: Howard Fertig, 1968).

SCHULTZE-NAUMBURG, PAUL, *Kunst und Kunstpflege* (Leipzig: Eugen Diederich, 1901).

——*Häusliche Kunstpflege* (Jena: Eugen Diederich, 1905).

——*Die Kultur des weiblichen Körpers als Grundlage der Frauenkleidung*, illustrations by J. V. Cissarz (Leipzig: Eugen Diederich, 1903).

STRINDBERG, AUGUST, 'Einsam', in *Neue Rundschau* (Berlin: Fischer, 1904).

WEININGER, OTTO, *Geschlecht und Charakter* (Vienna: Braunmüller, 1903; repr. Munich: Matthes & Seitz, 1980).

——*Über die letzten Dinge* (Munich: Matthes & Seitz, 1980).

2. SECONDARY KAFKA LITERATURE

ADORNO, THEODOR W., 'Notes on Kafka', in *Prisms*, trans. Samuel and Shierry Weber (Cambridge, Mass.: MIT Press, 1983).

ANDERS, GÜNTER, *Franz Kafka*, trans. A. Steter and A. K. Thorlby, (London: Bowes & Bowes, 1960).

ANDERSON, MARK, (ed.), *Reading Kafka: Prague, Politics, and the Fin de Siècle* (New York: Schocken Books, 1989).

BAIONI, GIULIANO, *Kafka: Letteratura ed ebraismo* (Turin: Einaudi, 1984).

BECK, EVELYN TORTON, *Kafka & the Yiddish Theater: Its Impact on His Work* (Madison, Wis.: University of Wisconsin Press, 1971).

BEICKEN, PETER, *Franz Kafka: Eine kritische Einführung in die Forschung* (Frankfurt: Fischer Taschenbuch, 1974).

BENJAMIN, WALTER, 'Franz Kafka' and 'Some Reflections on Kafka', in *Illuminations*, ed. H. Arendt, (New York: Schocken Books, 1st paperback edn. 1969).

BINDER, H. (ed.), *Kafka-Handbuch*, vols. i and ii (Stuttgart: Alfred Kröner, 1979).

——*Kafka-Kommentar*, vol. i: stories (Munich: Winkler, 1975); vol. ii: novels and aphorisms, (1976).

BORN, J. (ed.), *Kafka-Symposion* (Berlin: Wagenbach, 1965).

BROD, MAX, *Franz Kafka: A Biography* (New York: Schocken Books, 1947; 2nd enlarged edn. 1960).

CANETTI, ELIAS, *Kafka's Other Trial* (New York: Schocken Books, 1974).

CERSOWSKY, PETER, *'Mein ganzes Wesen ist auf Literatur gerichtet': Franz Kafka im Kontext der literarischen Dekadenz* (Würzburg: Königshausen & Neumann, 1983).

CORNGOLD, STANLEY, *The Commentators' Despair: The Interpretation of Kafka's 'Metamorphosis'* (Port Washington: Kennikat Press, 1973).

——*Franz Kafka: The Necessity of Form* (Ithaca, NY: Cornell University Press, 1988).

David Claude, (ed.), *Franz Kafka: Themen und Probleme* (Göttingen: Vandenhoeck, 1980).

Frank, Manfred, *Die endlose Fahrt* (Frankfurt: Suhrkamp, 1979).

Jahn, Wolfgang, *Kafkas Roman 'Der Verschollene' ('Amerika')* (Stuttgart: Metzler, 1965).

——'Kafka und die Anfänge des Kinos', *Schiller Jahrbuch*, 6 (1962), 353–68.

Loose, Gerhard, *Franz Kafka und Amerika* (Frankfurt: Klostermann, 1968).

Löwy, Michel, 'Theologia negativa et utopia negativa: Franz Kafka', in *Rédemption et Utopie: Le Judaïsme libertaire en Europe Centrale* (Paris: Presses Universitaires de France, 1988); repr; in English as 'Libertarian Anarchism in *Amerika*', in M. Anderson (ed.), *Reading Kafka: Prague, Politics, and the Fin de Siècle* (New York: Schocken Books, 1989).

Müller-Seidel, Walter, *Die Deportation des Menschen* (Stuttgart: Metzler, 1986).

Norris, Margot, 'The Fate of the Human Animal in Kafka's Fiction', 'Sadism and Masochism in "In the Penal Colony" and "A Hunger Artist"' in *Beasts of the Modern Imagination* (Baltimore: Johns Hopkins University Press, 1985); repr. in M. Anderson (ed.), *Reading Kafka: Prague, Politics, and the Fin de Siècle* (New York: Schocken Books, 1989).

Pawel, Ernst, *The Nightmare of Reason: A Life of Franz Kafka* (New York: Farrar, Straus & Giroux, 1984).

Politzer, Heinz, *Franz Kafka: Parable and Paradox* (Ithaca, NY: Cornell University Press, 1962; revised and expanded paperback edn., 1966).

Robert, Marthe, *Seul, comme Franz Kafka* (Paris: Calmann-Lévy, 1979).

Robertson, Ritchie, *Kafka: Judaism, Literature and Politics* (Oxford: Oxford University Press, 1985).

Sokel, Walter, *Franz Kafka: Tragik und Ironie* (Frankfurt: Fischer Taschenbuch, 1976).

Stach, Reiner, *Kafkas erotischer Mythos: Eine ästhetische Konstruktion des Weiblichen* (Frankfurt: Fischer Taschenbuch, 1987).

Stölzl, Christoph, *Kafkas böses Böhmen: Zur Sozialgeschichte eines Prager Juden* (Munich: text und kritik, 1975; corrected paperback edn., Frankfurt: Ullstein, 1989).

Wagenbach, Klaus, *Franz Kafka: Eine Biographie seiner Jugend* (Berne: Francke, 1958).

3 General

Aschheim, Steven E., *Brothers and Strangers: The East European Jew in German and German Jewish Consciousness, 1800–1923* (Madison, Wis.: University of Wisconsin Press, 1982).

BAUDELAIRE, CHARLES, *The Painter of Modern Life and Other Essays*, trans. and ed. J. Mayne (London: Phaidon Press, 1964; repr. New York: Da Capo Press, 1986).

BROD, MAX, *Streitbares Leben* (Frankfurt: Insel, new edn., 1979).

BURGER, CHRISTA, BURGER, PETER, and SCHULTE-SASS, JOCHEN (eds.), *Naturalismus/Ästhetizismus* (Frankfurt: Suhrkamp, 1979).

COBET, CHRISTOPH, *Der Wortschatz des Antisemitismus in der Bismarckzeit* (Munich: Fink, 1973).

FISCHER, JENS MALTE, *Fin de siècle: Kommentar zu einer Epoche* (Munich: Winkler, 1978).

GILMAN, SANDER, *Jewish Self-Hatred: Anti-Semitism and the Hidden Language of the Jews* (Baltimore: Johns Hopkins University Press, 1985).

——'Strauss, the Pervert, and Avant-Garde Opera of the Fin de Siècle', *New German Critique*, 43 (1988), 35–68.

——*Difference and Pathology: Stereotypes of Sexuality, Race and Madness* (Ithaca, NY: Cornell University Press, 1985).

GINZBURG, CARLO, 'Clues: Morelli, Freud, and Sherlock Holmes' in U. Eco and T. Sebeok (eds.), *The Sign of Three: Dupin, Holmes, Peirce* (Bloomington, Ind.: Indiana University Press, 1984).

GREEN, MARTIN, *The von Richthofen Sisters. The Triumphant and the Tragic Modes of Love* (Albuquerque, NM: University of New Mexico Press, 1974).

——*Mountain of Truth: The Counterculture Begins, Ascona, 1900–1920* (London, University Press of New England, 1986).

HERMAND, JOST (ed.), *Jugendstil* (Darmstadt: Wissenschaftliche Buchgesellschaft, 1971).

HURWITZ, IMANUEL, *Otto Gross: Paradiessucher zwischen Freud und Jung* (Frankfurt: Suhrkamp, 1982).

JANIK, ALLAN and TOULMIN, STEPHEN, *Wittgenstein's Vienna* (New York: Simon & Schuster, 1973).

JOHNSTON, WILLIAM M., *The Austrian Mind: An Intellectual and Social History, 1848–1938* (Berkeley, Calif.: University of California Press, 1972).

KOHN, HANS, *The Mind of Germany: The Education of a Nation* (New York: Harper & Row, 1960).

LATRAVERSE, FRANÇOIS, and MOSER, WALTER (eds.), *Vienne au tournant du siècle* (Paris: Albin Michel, 1988).

LE RIDER, JACQUES, *Modernité viennoise et crises de l'identité* (Paris: Presses Universitaires de France, 1990).

——*Le Cas Otto Weininger: Racines de l'antiféminisme et de l'antisémitisme* (Paris: Presses Universitaires de France, 1982).

MATHES, JÜRG, (ed.), *Prosa des Jugendstils* (Stuttgart: Reclam, 1982).

——*Theorie des literarischen Jugendstils*, (Stuttgart: Reclam, 1984).

MATTENKLOTT, GERT, *Bilderdienst: Aesthetische Opposition bei Beardsley und George*, expanded edn. (Berlin: Syndikat, 1985).

MOSES, STÉPHANE, and SCHÖNE, ALBRECHT (eds.), *Juden in der deutschen Literatur* (Frankfurt: suhrkamp, 1986).

MOSSE, GEORGE, *Nationalism and Sexuality: Respectability and Abnormal Sexuality in Modern Europe* (New York: Howard Fertig, 1985).

SCHEIBLE, HARTMUT, *Literarischer Jugendstil in Wien* (Munich: Artemis, 1984).

SCHOLEM, GERSHOM, *Zur Kabbala und ihrer Symbolik* (Frankfurt: Suhrkamp Taschenbuch Verlag, 1981).

SCHORSKE, CARL, *Fin-de-siècle Vienna: Politics and Culture* (New York: Vintage Books, 1981).

STERN, FRITZ, *The Politics of Cultural Despair* (Berkeley, Calif.: The University of California Press, 1961; paperback edn. 1989).

TODOROV, TZVETAN, *Introduction à la littérature fantastique* (Paris: Editions du Seuil, 1970).

'Vienne: Début d'un siècle,' *Critique* 31, 339–40 (1975).

WOLFF, KURT *Briefwechsel eines Verlegers: 1911–1963* (Darmstadt: B. Zeller & E. Otten, 1966).

WUTHENOW, RALPH-RAINER, *Muse, Maske, Meduse: Europäischer Ästhetizismus* (Frankfurt: Suhrkamp, 1978).

Index